MERTON & BUDDHISM

MERTON & BUDDHISM

WISDOM, EMPTINESS, AND EVERYDAY MIND

Edited by Bonnie Bowman Thurston
Illustrated by Gray Henry

FONS VITAE

The Fons Vitae Thomas Merton Series

Merton & Sufism: The Untold Story, 1999
Merton & Hesychasm: The Prayer of the Heart, 2003
Merton & Judaism: Holiness in Words, 2003

Future Thomas Merton Series editions
Merton & Hinduism
Merton & Taoism

First published in 2007 by
Fons Vitae
49 Mockingbird Valley Drive
Louisville, KY 40207
http://www.fonsvitae.com

Copyright Fons Vitae 2007

Library of Congress Control Number: 2006940806

ISBN 1-887752-84-6

See page 261 for permissions.

Cover photograph of Chatral Rinpoche Dorje Senge taken
in 1991 by Gray Henry. Background: The Heart Sutra.

This book was typeset by Neville Blakemore, Jr.

Printed in Canada

CONTENTS

CONTENTS, continued

THE FONS VITAE
THOMAS MERTON SERIES

Professional theologians and lay readers, scholars and spiritual seekers in a broad spectrum of religious practice regard the Cistercian monk Thomas Merton (1915–1968) as one of the most important spiritual writers of the last half of the twentieth century. The writing impelled by his monastic life's interests in the world's religious traditions are recognized as a seminal and continuing catalyst for inter-religious dialogue in the twenty-first century.

Ewert Cousins, a distinguished Professor of Religion and the General Editor of both the World Spirituality Series and the Classics of Western Spirituality Series of Paulist Press, has called Merton an "axial figure" who bridges within his own experience and theological work the contemporary estrangements between religious and secular perspectives. Dr. Cousins has publicly shared his opinion that Thomas Merton means almost more today to many than he actually did in his lifetime. He is becoming an iconic figure who models inter-religious dialogue for those who are seeking a common ground of respect for the varied ways in which human beings realize the sacred in their lives. Merton's life and writing, especially when it focuses on the contemplative practices common to the world's major religions, have indeed become a forum, or a "bridge" in Cousins' term, upon which those engaged in inter-religious dialogue can meet and engage one another.

In his reaching out to living representatives of the world's various religious traditions by correspondence, and by his immersing himself in the study of religious traditions other than his own Roman Catholicism, Merton models the inclusivity of intellect and heart necessary for fruitful inter-religious dialogue. His personal journal for April 28, 1957, witnesses to his zeal for a unity of learning and living as a method of personal "inner work" for ensuring communication and respect among religious persons:

> If I can unite *in myself*, in my own spiritual life, the thought
> of the East and the West, of the Greek and Latin Fathers, I
> will create in myself a reunion of the divided Church, and

from that unity in myself can come the exterior and visible unity of the church. For, if we want to bring together East and West, we cannot do it by imposing one upon the other. We must contain both in ourselves and transcend them both in Christ.

The Fons Vitae publishing project for the study of world religions through the lens of Thomas Merton's life and writing brings Merton's timeless vision of all persons united in a "hidden ground of Love" to a contemporary audience. The first three volumes of the Fons Vitae Thomas Merton Series, *Merton & Sufism, Merton & Hesychasm* and *Merton & Judaism* featured essays by international scholars who gathered in three academic conferences in Louisville, Kentucky to assess the value of Merton's contributions to inter-religious dialogue. Each volume includes Merton's own writing across various genres—essays, poetry, transcriptions of his lectures to the novices at Gethsemani—that highlighted Merton's interest in contemplative traditions other than his own.

This fourth volume, *Merton & Buddhism*: *Wisdom, Emptiness and Everyday Mind*, in many ways is a summing up of not only Merton's interest in the various forms of Buddhism, but also of aspects of his life's work—photography, poetry and brushwork—where his spiritual transformation takes form. We find that Merton is "fleshed out." Through the scholarly contributions presented in this volume, we come to see which ideas in the various schools of Buddhism were of *living value* to one of the world's most cherished Christian monks, and how these seem to have led on to his own "satori."

Succeeding volumes in this series will include studies of *Merton & Hinduism*: *The Vedanta*, followed by *Merton & Taoism*. We hope that the Fons Vitae Thomas Merton Series will find a place in the libraries of those persons who promote the study and practice of contemplative religious traditions.

Jonathan Montaldo and Gray Henry
General Editors
for the Fons Vitae Thomas Merton Series

DEDICATION

This book is dedicated with love
to my mother, Christina Lee Brown,
who introduced me to the
profound path of faith and prayer
through the Roman Catholic church.
It was also she who introduced me
to the work of
Thomas Merton,
whose writing pointed out for me
the extraordinary Buddhist teachings.
It is through these teachings that
my relationship with the Divine
has deepened beyond measure
and for this gift I am eternally grateful.

Owsley Brown III
December 15, 2006
San Francisco

From the Dambulla Rock Temple, Sri Lanka,
visited by Thomas Merton in 1968.

DEDICATION OF MERIT

May all beings enjoy happiness and the roots of happiness.
May they be free from suffering and the roots of suffering.
May they not be separated from the great happiness devoid
    of suffering.
May they be free from passion, aggression, and prejudice.

"And what I say to you I say to all: Keep awake."
                                    Jesus of Nazareth
                                    St. Mark 13:37

"I am just beginning to awaken and to realize how much more
awakening is to come."
                                    Thomas Merton
                                    January 25, 1965

THOMAS MERTON'S PRAYER

The following prayer was offered by Thomas Merton at the First Spiritual Summit Conference in Calcutta. It appears as part of Appendix V in *The Asian Journal of Thomas Merton*. We offer it again here as the context from which this book arose and in which it has been prepared for publication.

> Oh God, we are one with You. You have made us one with You. You have taught us that if we are open to one another, You dwell in us. Help us to preserve this openness and to fight for it with all our hearts. Help us to realize that there can be no understanding where there is mutual rejection. Oh God, in accepting one another wholeheartedly, fully, completely, we accept You, and we thank You, and we adore You, and we love You with our whole being, because our being is in Your being, our spirit is rooted in Your spirit. Fill us then with love, and let us be bound together with love as we go our diverse ways, united in this one spirit which makes You present in the world, and which makes You witness to the ultimate reality that is love. Love has overcome. Love is victorious. Amen.

PREFACE

When Buddhism, and particularly Zen, moved into the mainstream of popular culture in America in the 1960s, Thomas Merton was already significantly ahead of the curve. He had been a serious student of Buddhist traditions in the 1950s and was thus positioned to be one of its pioneer interpreters to Christians. Merton's books *Mystics and Zen Masters* (1961/67) and *Zen and the Birds of Appetite* (1968) were readily available to Christian readers and from the pen of a trusted spiritual writer. When I took a graduate level Buddhist-Christian Dialogue course at Harvard in the early 1980s, *Zen and the Birds of Appetite* was one of the primary text books.

Since his death in 1968, a great many Christians have wondered about Merton's immersion in Buddhism, and many Merton scholars have written about it. (See the bibliography at the end of this volume.) Because it has traditionally been understood that Christianity makes exclusive claims on those of us who follow Jesus, when a great master in our tradition studies (and practices) another way, eyebrows are raised. A fellow monk, one of Merton's students at Gethsemani from 1952-1955, and former Abbot of the Abbey of the Genesee in New York, John Eudes Bamberger, O.C.S.O. in chapter 5 of his recent book, *Thomas Merton: Prophet of Renewal*, has placed Merton's interest in its proper context.[1] He writes:

> Merton's exploration of Eastern religious traditions influenced the evolutions of his views on contemplation. ... A careful examination of his extensive writings on this subject reveals that there is no basis for the opinion that Merton's faith in the Church or in his Cistercian vocation was ever modified, much less weakened by, his interest in the East. His contacts with these traditions both by study and dialogue with members of these traditions certainly had an impact on his views of monastic life and contemplation. This influence was a wholesome one in that it led him to emphasize the fundamental simplicity and other central elements of the contemplative life.[2]

Bamberger continues, "The appeal of these Asian thinkers for Merton was their emphasis on the fullness of meaning to be found in the concrete reality of ordinary life."[3] I think the reader will find that the essays in this volume, essays primarily by Buddhists and Buddhist scholars, concur with Dom John Eudes' assessment.

On February 19-23, 2005, the Thomas Merton Foundation of Louisville, Kentucky, (now renamed The Merton Institute for Contemplative Living) with the support of The Louisville Presbyterian Seminary, The Cathedral Heritage Foundation (now the Center for Interfaith Relations), and The Crane House sponsored a conference at Laws Lodge, Louisville Seminary, entitled "Merton and Buddhism: Wisdom, Emptiness and Everyday Mind." The conference participants had the opportunity to hear a lecture by distinguished Indo-Tibetan scholar, Robert Thurman, to hear papers on Merton by several well-respected Buddhist scholars, to engage them in dialogue, and to participate in a variety of devotional practices. That conference was the genesis of this book.

Let me orient readers to the material. This volume opens with a concise overview of Buddhism by Buddhist scholar, Roger Corless and my brief survey of Merton's acquaintance with Buddhism. The longest section of the book, "Merton and Buddhist Traditions," is comprised of the text of the papers given at the conference. Taken together, they look at Merton's work in Theravada, Tibetan and Zen traditions of Buddhism. The unique contribution of these essays is that, instead of Merton scholars writing on Merton and Buddhism, Buddhist scholars are evaluating Merton's knowledge and application of it. Now, a generation after Merton's death, it is refreshing to find his work rigorously evaluated by Buddhist scholars and specialists. Were his sources good ones? How widely had he read? How much did he really know? To what degree was his practice really Buddhist? Some of the material in this book challenges the "received wisdom" about Merton and Buddhism. To my mind that is a very good thing. (And those interested in Buddhism will find herein lively contributions to the evaluation of D.T. Suzuki's presentation of Zen to the West.)

Unlike previous volumes in this series by Fons Vitae Press, readers will not find a great deal of new "Merton on Buddhism" material. That is largely because most of Merton's writing on Buddhism was published during his lifetime or very shortly thereafter. If Merton's acquaintance with Islam was under-exposed, Merton's acquaintance with Buddhism was over-exposed. There is not, in my estimation, much of significance that Merton wrote about Buddhism that isn't widely available. What we have tried to do in this book is to demonstrate how Merton's studies in Buddhism affected his work in the arts (the section "Buddhist Traditions and Thomas Merton's Art"), to provide a bit more human information about his Asian travels ("Footnotes to the Asian Journey of Thomas Merton"), and to offer the serious student a complete bibliography of secondary materials on Merton and Buddhism.

Perhaps a note on the details of the editing is in order. Because we are dealing here with many languages and scholars trained in various traditions, the editing presented some challenges. Instead of trying to standardize the use of italics or punctuation, I have left each writer to italicize and punctuate as he or she felt appropriate. (This was a huge challenge for this gentle editor, who started her academic life as an English teacher; one is always in recovery from this, never cured.) Similarly, the citation style of each essay was left to its author. While this may give the book a slightly unusual appearance, it in no way diminishes the reader's access to the sources the scholars consulted, and that, after all, is the point of citation.

As editor, I must say that I cannot imagine working with more helpful and congenial scholars than those represented in this volume. Each is a recognized authority and highly regarded in his or her field. Each was extremely generous in time, attitude and patience. I am profoundly grateful to all who contributed to the volume. Special thanks to Roger Lipsey who made contact with James George and Lobsang Lhalungpa possible and to Paul Pearson of the Thomas Merton Studies Center at Bellarmine University in Louisville, Kentucky who has provided a most extraordinary bibliography and who cheerfully helped me check references and was my expert on all things Mertonian. Without the generosity of Fons Vitae Press the book would not have seen the light of day. Enormous gratitude is due Neville Blakemore, Jr. of the press for technical expertise and to Gray Henry, its moving spirit. Had there been no conference, there would have been no book, and so on behalf of those many of us who so benefitted from that weekend, to those who planned and executed it, and especially Robert Toth, Jonathan Montaldo, Helen Graffy, and Pat Reno, many, many thanks.

Some years before our meeting, down the road from Louisville in July, 1996 at the Abbey of Gethsemani in Trappist, Kentucky fifty Buddhist and Christian monks and nuns and other practitioners met in prayer and conversation. The results of their dialogue were edited by Donald W. Mitchell and James A. Wiseman, O.S.B. (who also contributed to this endeavor) and published as *The Gethsemani Encounter*.[4] The volume contains many references to and several tributes to Thomas Merton. The initial remarks of the tribute to Thomas Merton by His Holiness the Dalai Lama provides an apt ending to these remarks and a wonderful opening to this collection:

> From the point of view of a religious practitioner, and in particular as a monastic, Thomas Merton really is someone that we can look up to. ...he had the complete qualities of hearing—which means study, contemplating, thinking on the teachings—and of meditation. He also had the qualities of being learned, disciplined and having a good heart. He not only was able to practice himself, but his perspective was very, very broad. Thus it seems to me that ...we should seek to be following his example.... In this way, even though the chapter of his life is over, what he was hoping to do and seeking to do can remain forever. ...it seems to me that if all of us followed this model, it...would be of very great benefit to the world.[5]

Bonnie Bowman Thurston
Feast of the Conversion of St. Paul
January 25, 2005

NOTES

1. John Eudes Bamberger, O.C.S.O., *Thomas Merton, Prophet of Renewal* (Kalamazoo: Cistercian Publications, 2005).

2. Bamberger 63.

3. Bamberger 65.

4. Donald W. Mitchell & James A. Wiseman, O.S.B. (eds.), *The Gethsemani Encounter* (New York: Continuum, 1998).

5. H.H. the Dalai Lama quoted in *The Gethsemani Encounter* 260.

The upper photograph is of Thomas Merton and the Dalai Lama and was taken in 1968; it hangs in the library at the Gethsemani Monastery. The *kata* hanging over this photograph was the one placed by the Dalai Lama many years later on Merton's grave, as shown in the lower photograph.

Perfection and emptiness work together for they are the same: the co-incidence of momentary form and eternal nothingness. Form: the flash of nothingness. Forget form, and it suddenly appears, ringed and rever-berating with its own light, which is nothing. Well, then: stop seeking. Let it all happen. Let it come and go. What? Everything: i.e., nothing.

Thomas Merton, *Cables to the Ace*

PART I
INTRODUCTORY ESSAYS

The nature of the mind is Buddha from the beginning.
Mind has no birth or cessation: It is like the sky.
If the pure meaning of the equality of all phenomena is realized,
And if that understanding is maintained without any seeking,
That is the meditation.

Manjusritmitra

AN OVERVIEW OF BUDDHISM

Roger J. Corless

Basic Teachings

Buddhists generally hesitate to construct a creedal system, and some Buddhists reject all world views, including agnosticism, as deluded. Buddhism does not accept the existence of an *ultimate reality* or metaphysical absolute; rather, it seeks to explain the *ultimate nature of reality*—reality as it really is and not how it seems to ordinary, deluded consciousness. Instead of proclaiming a common doctrine, Buddhism adopts a therapeutic approach to the healing of the pain which is inescapable from the striving of beings for existence or for non-existence. The core therapy is encapsulated in the Fourfold Truth: *duhkha* (pain, difficulty, unsatisfactoriness), its cause, its cure, and the treatment.

The Fourfold Truth

(1) *Duhkha* refers to the whole spectrum of suffering from extreme pain, which, even if extended, is transitory, to an enduring sense of unsatisfactoriness pervading all existence. The word is not easy to translate and is best left in Sanskrit.[1]

(2) *Duhkha* arises from grasping at reality, which is essentially fluid.

(3) *Duhkha* ends when grasping stops.

(4) The way to the ending of the arising of *duhkha* is formalized in the Eightfold Path (right view, right attitude, right speech, right action, right livelihood, right effort, right mindfulness, right concentration) and summarized in the Threefold Practice (conduct, meditation, wisdom.)

The Threefold Practice

(1) Conduct (*shila*) is the practice of right actions of body, speech and mind in daily life. The five basic pre-

cepts are: not to harm sentient beings; not to take what has not been offered; not to engage in sexual misconduct (a broad precept which is variously interpreted); not to speak falsely or in a manner which causes harm; not to drink alcohol (which further confuses the already confused mind). At the beginning of the path these precepts act as negative restraints on unskillful conduct. As the person grows more skillful, they become the basis for positive acts. For example, non-harming becomes the foundation for active compassion. This is typified in the ideal of the Bodhisattva[2], although it is true for all Buddhist traditions. Self-cultivation and outreach to other beings are interdependent and both are essential in authentic practice.

(2) Meditation (*samadhi*) is the practice of training the mind. The simile is used of the domestication of a wild animal such as a horse. The animal is caught, restrained, and made pliant to the trainer's will, but its spirit is not broken. In the same way, Buddhist meditation is not an attempt to blank (or "kill") the mind but to train it so that its energy is not wasted or misdirected. It has two interdependent aspects: calming the mind (*shamatha),* and focusing the calmed mind *(vipashyana)* so that it sees clearly and sharply.

(3) Wisdom (*prajña*) is the practice of studying the teachings so as to grow in wisdom and understanding. It has three stages: hearing the teachings, reflecting on them to determine that they are true, and living in accordance with them.

The threefold practice is summed up in the following scriptural verse: "Do not do anything harmful; perfect whatever is wholesome; purify your own mind: this is the instruction of the Buddhas" (*Dhammapada* 183, my translation[3]). It is similar in many ways to the threefold division of Benedictine spirituality: work (*opus manuum*), prayer (*opus dei*), and spiritual reading (*lectio divina*).

The teaching about reality as it really is, is called the Dharma. The Dharma is, therefore, in its essence, universal and eternal, but in its manifestation it is subject to disappearance and rediscovery at rare intervals. The one who rediscovers the Dharma is called a Buddha or "Awakened One." There have been many Buddhas in the past and there will be many in the future. The most recent Buddha is called the "historical Buddha" because he is the Buddha whose existence can be established by historical-critical research. His personal name was Siddhartha ("Successful"), his family name was Gautama ("Of the clan of Gotama"), and his special title was Shakyamuni ("The ascetic of the Shakya tribe"). He lived in the northeast region of the Indian subcontinent in the regions now known as India and Nepal. All Buddhist traditions maintain that Shakyamuni lived for about eighty years, but his date of birth has been variously set between 1029 and 623 B.C.E. Modern scholarship sets his dates at 563–483 B.C.E.

He is said to have been born into the warrior or princely *(kshatriya)* caste in Lumbini, in what is now Nepal. He married and fathered a son, but then renounced the household life, retiring into the jungle to seek enlightenment. There he found some gurus but rejected their teachings as inadequate and went off on his own. After some time he proclaimed his liberation in the Sutra "Turning the Wheel of the Dharma," a short text which includes the fourfold truth and the eightfold path and establishes a middle way between luxury and asceticism. He entrusted his teaching (the Dharma) to his community of monastic and lay followers (the Sangha) before leaving the phenomenal world (entering nirvana). "Going for Refuge" in the Buddha, the Dharma and the Sangha, as the indivisible Triple Treasure or Triple Gem *(Triratna)* of the Teacher, the Teaching, and the Taught, is the foundation of the Buddhist life.

LINEAGES

Going for refuge in the Sangha means that one's sense of being a Buddhist is strongly connected with one's sense of belonging to a certain community. This community may be felt to be linked with one's country or to a certain lineage superficially similar to a Christian denomination, or to a particular living teacher. The root teacher is the Buddha, and all authentic Buddhist teachers have some form of authorization which is regarded as being in an unbroken line back to the Buddha. Therefore, a division within Buddhism is more a *lineage* than a sect or denomination.

As Buddhism spread into north, south, and east Asia, it produced a large number of lineages. Buddhists sometimes liken this spread to the growth of a banyan tree with limbs sending down roots to embed in soil and aerial roots eventually appearing as separate trunks. There are now, according to Buddhist self-understanding, two main groups or families of lineages: *Theravada* and *Mahayana*.

Theravada Buddhism is found in Sri Lanka, Myanmar, Kampuchea, Laos and Thailand. It is most simply viewed as a single main lineage with a number of sub-lineages which define themselves by their country of origin, by their manner of observance of the monastic Rule *(Vinaya)*, or by the relative importance they give to doctrine or meditation. The symbiosis between the monk, who renounces family, property, and even concern for his own food, and the layperson, who provides for the monk's physical necessities, is a prominent feature of Theravadin society.

A Theravadin monk wears a habit made up of three strips of cloth wound around his body somewhat after the fashion of an Indian woman's sari. The color is known as *kasaya*, literally "earthy," and varies between various shades of yellow, orange, or brown. There are no nuns, strictly speaking, for the transmission of their ordination lineage has been lost; but there are many women who, observing a modified Rule, live as if they were nuns and wear a habit similar to that of the monks. Buddhist monks of all traditions are clean shaven and monks and nuns shave their heads (or, at the least, have very close cropped hair). Some monks shave their eyebrows. There is no standard English form of address for Theravadin monks but the word *Bhante* (pronounced BAN-tay) is sometimes used, and Venerable is generally acceptable.

Mahayana Buddhism is divided broadly into two socio-cultural groups: the Inner Asian and the East Asian.

Inner Asian Mahayana is found in Tibet, Nepal, Sikkim, Bhutan, Mongolia, and regions culturally dependent upon those countries. Inner Asian Mahayana is the inheritor of the great Buddhist universities of the Indian subcontinent which flourished between approximately the first and the tenth centuries C.E. It often has, in consequence, a strong emphasis on scholarship and a distinctly academic appearance. It divides the Dharma into three units which, like university courses, are to be followed in sequence: Hinayana, the training in self-benefit and an ethic of non-harming; Mahayana, the training in benefitting others and an ethic of compassion; and Vajrayana (or Tantra), a means of cutting off ordinary

A Theravadin monk wears a habit made up of three strips of cloth wound around his body…

Theravadin Lineage.   Cambodia

Theravadin Lineage.   Thailand and Laos

Inner Asian Mahayanan Lineage.   Tibet

East Asian Mahayanan Lineage   Japan and China

Theravadin Lineage.   Colombo, Sri Lanka

Theravadin Lineage.   Pagan, Myanmar

perception and, acting from the pure perspective of a Buddha, embodying all the virtues. This sequence is called the graded path (Tibetan: *lamrim*).

There are two major Tibetan lineage groups: *Nyingma* ("Ancient Ones") and *Sarma* ("New Ones"). The Nyingma are a single lineage begun in the ninth century C.E. The Sarma are the lineages which restored Tibetan Buddhism after a period of persecution by non-Buddhist kings. There are two original groups, the *Sakya* and the *Kagyu*, both founded in the 11th century and each having many sub-groups. The *Gelug* is a 14th century reform of the Sarma groups. The Dalai Lama belongs to this lineage.

A Tibetan monk or "nun" (the transmission of the Tibetan ordination lineage for nuns has also been broken) wears a habit of heavy maroon wool with a bodice of yellow cotton. A title of respect commonly used for Tibetan teachers of high standing is *Rinpoche* (pronounced RIN-bo-jay), which means "Precious One."

East Asian Mahayana is found in China, Korea, Japan, and regions culturally dependent upon those countries. Whereas Buddhism went to Tibet already synthesized into coherent blocks of teaching and practice, the transmission to China was piecemeal, and the Chinese had to develop their own syntheses. In the 6th century C.E., they developed *Tiantai* and *Huayan*. Tiantai found a place for all of the teachings and practices which had become known to the Chinese and arranged them in a graded sequence called "division of teachings" (*panjiao*) which resembles Tibetan *lamrim* but omits the Vajrayana stage. Tiantai is the mother lineage of later traditions such as Zen and Pure Land (see below). Huayan, which teaches that everything — even dust particles — are the Buddha when seen aright, began and has largely remained as a philosophical structure found in most of the other traditions.

Vietnamese Buddhism is a special case. It has received both Theravada and (Chinese) Mahayana transmissions and contains various syntheses of both. Presently, all lineages are part of the Unified Buddhist Church of Vietnam.

The two most popular forms of Buddhism in East Asia and Vietnam today are Zen and Pure Land. In Japan these are kept separate, but in the rest of East Asia, and in Vietnam, they are synthesized. Zen (known in China as *Chan*, in Korea as *Son* and in Vietnam as *Thien*) concentrates on the experience of enlighten-

East Asian monks and nuns…wear a habit resembling a Christian cassock.   Therevadin Lineage. Laos

A Tibetan nun wearing a heavy maroon wool habit.
                              Inner Asian Mayhayanan Lineage

ment in each and every practitioner. Any other practices, such as liturgy and study, even meditation, are regarded as merely tools for the awakening of the disciple. Pure Land Buddhism downplays, and sometimes rejects, the effectiveness of even these tools for enlightenment. Only by a trusting acceptance of the power of a trans-worldly Buddha known as Amita ("Immeasurable," i.e. "the Buddha of immeasurable Light and Life"), who has vowed to assist any being who calls on his name, can liberation and enlightenment be obtained.

East Asian monks and nuns (the transmission of the Chinese ordination lineage for nuns has been preserved) wear a habit resembling a Christian cassock. Its color is gray, black or very dark brown. Vietnamese monks wear either the Theravadin or the East Asian Mahayana habit, depending on their ordination lineage. Monastics of all traditions have an array of elaborate vestments worn on formal occasions. The Theravadins are the most conservative in their dress. The form of address for East Asian monks and nuns varies according to their country of origin. Japanese Zen masters of high rank are called *Roshi* (pronounced ROE-shee). Officials of the Buddhist Church of America (BCA), a Japanese Pure Land group which has adapted itself to western customs, are not monastics and are addressed as Reverend, in the manner of Protestant ministers.[4]

All major Buddhist lineages are now represented in the USA. Most centers have a web page and can be traced by an internet search.

SCRIPTURES

Buddhist scriptures can be very broadly divided into the word of the Buddha *(sutra)* and the authorized commentaries *(shastra)*. The Buddha gave his teachings in the language of his hearers, and he rebuked those monks who wished to codify his words in a particular language. The experience of enlightenment by the individual Buddhist is more important than the words which are used to bring about that experience, although some words are more effectively enlightening than others and are regarded as more authoritative. Therefore, there is no single canon of scripture, and although texts are classified as authentic and inauthentic by certain traditional teachers, the notion of "canon" as something which is closed and sharply distinguished from apocryphal or commentarial literature is difficult to apply to Buddhist writings with any consistency. There are, however, major authoritative collections in the three quasi-canonical languages of Pali, Tibetan and Chinese. These are, respectively, the scriptures of the Theravada, Inner Asian Mahayana, and East Asian Mahayana. The Theravadin collection, which has been translated into English, is the smallest, and most of its texts are found, in somewhat different editions, in the Tibetan and Chinese collections. Only a few of the many Mahayana texts have been translated into English.

FURTHER READING

Buddhist Scriptures, selected and edited by Edward Conze. Penguin Books. First published in 1959, this remains the single most balanced and accessible anthology.

The Vision of Buddhism: The Space under the Tree, by Roger Corless. St Paul MN: Paragon House, 1989. Arranged by topics rather than historical periods this survey is designed for both the beginning and the more advanced student.

NOTES

This article is revised and updated from "Buddhist Traditions" and "Buddhist Lineages" by Roger Corless, originally published in *Handbook for Interreligious Dialogue*, edited by John Borelli (Morristown NJ: Silver Burdett and Ginn, 2nd edition, revised, 1988), pages 14–19. Extracts appeared as "Buddhist Traditions and Lineages" in *The Catholic World* 233:1395 (May/June 1990), pages 117–120, and an adaptation, "Buddhist Traditions" and "Buddhist Lineages," in *Christians Learning About Buddhist Neighbors* by Roger J. Corless and Lynn de Silva (Occasional Paper #6, Ecumenical and Interfaith Relations Global Missionary Unit of the Presbyterian Church (U.S.A.), Louisville KY: Distribution Management Services, 1992).

1. As explained below, there is no universally recognized sacred language in Buddhism. Sanskrit is recognized as a base language by most Buddhist traditions. Southeast Asian Buddhism is based on texts in Pali, a language which is a close relative of Sanskrit. In this article, technical terms will be quoted in Sanskrit if there is no commonly accepted English equivalent.

2. *Bodhisattva* (Sanskrit) or *Bodhisatta* (Pali) refers in general to a person dedicated to becoming a Buddha. In Theravada (Southeast Asian) Buddhism it is used for the "historical" Buddha (more accurately described as the Buddha for our human space-time continuum) up to the

moment when he achieved *bodhi* (enlightenment) and became a Buddha properly so called. In Mahayana (Inner and East Asian) Buddhism, practitioners are encouraged to take the Bodhisattva Vow, dedicating themselves from then until enlightenment to the welfare and happiness of all beings. Great Bodhisattvas are Mahayana figures of high achievement to whom prayers are offered for assistance in a person's practice.

3. *Dhammapada* ("Verses on the Teaching") is a collection of short, pithy sayings of the Buddha uttered on various occasions. Versions, which sometimes differ significantly, exist in the quasi-canonical languages of Pali, Tibetan, and Chinese, and in obscure dead languages such as Gandhari. There are many English versions, most of them translated from the Pali recension, with the omission of the occasions which gave rise to the sayings. The best version for study, with text, translation, and extensive notes, is *The Dhammapada* by John Ross Carter and Mahinda Palihawadana (Oxford University Press, 1987). A fresh and accessible version is *Dhammapada* by Thanissaro Bhikkhu (Barre MA: Dhamma Dana Publications, 1998) published for free distribution: write to Barre Center for Buddhist Studies, 149 Lockwood Rd, Barre MA 01005. The Penguin Classics version by Juan Mascaró is disappointing and best avoided.

4. In Hawaii the BCA is known as the Honpa Hongwanji Mission of Hawaii and in Canada as the Buddhist Churches of Canada (BCC).

By pausing before action, in a habitual attitude of Bare Attention, one will be able to seize that decisive but brief moment when mind has not yet settled upon a definite course or action or a definite attitude, but is still open to receive skillful directions.

Nyanaponika

UNFOLDING OF A NEW WORLD: THOMAS MERTON & BUDDHISM

Bonnie B. Thurston

INTRODUCTION

It might be helpful to think of this essay as "Merton and Buddhism 101." My modest task is to introduce the origins and extent of Merton's acquaintance with Buddhism. I will say something about the "why" of his interest. Subsequent essays will address branches of Buddhism Merton studied and evaluate his knowledge of the traditions. This essay is the "Freshman Survey;" the subsequent ones are the "Senior Seminars."

In closing a paper on monastic experience and East-West dialogue that he was to have given in Calcutta in October, 1968 Merton outlined four principles of cross-religious dialogue. They provide a useful introduction to his work in Buddhism. They are as follows: (1) Dialogue is reserved for those who "have been seriously disciplined by years of silence and by a long habit of meditation." (2) "There can be no question of a facile syncretism." (3) "There must be a scrupulous respect for important differences." (4) What is essential "is to be sought in the area of true self-transcendence and enlightenment."[1] Happily, Merton followed his own rules in his study of Buddhism and dialogue with Buddhists, both of which were of focal importance in the last decade of his life.

MERTON'S ACQUAINTANCE WITH BUDDHISM

It is useful to think of Merton's acquaintance with Buddhism in three periods: pre-monastic, monastic and Asian.

Pre-Monastic

Buddhism grew from the fertile loam of Hindu thought and practice. Thus Merton's interest in Buddhism dates to his time at Oakham School in England (1928-32) when he argued, and lost, a pro-Gandhi position in a debate. Toward the end of 1937, during

15

his studies at Columbia University in New York, he read Aldous Huxley's *Ends and Means* and, ten years later, devoted several pages to it in his early autobiography, *The Seven Storey Mountain.* He concludes "the most important effect of the book on me was to make me start ransacking the university library for books on Oriental mysticism."[2]

What he found were "the big quarto volumes of the Jesuit Father Wieger's French translation of hundreds of strange Oriental texts." (SSM 229) The result of his reading at the time was not particularly fruitful. Merton reported:

> The only practical thing I got out of it was a system for going to sleep, at night.... You lay flat in bed, without a pillow, your arms at your sides and your legs straight out, and relaxed all your muscles, and you said to yourself: "Now I have no feet, now I have no feet...no legs...no knees." (SSM 229)

Merton pontificated in SSM in 1948, "I suppose all Oriental mysticism can be reduced to techniques that do the same thing, but in a far more subtle and advanced fashion." (SSM 230) Fortunately, Merton, himself, both advanced and became more subtle!

More important to Merton was the meeting in 1937 or 38 with a Hindu monk, Bramachari.[3] Bramachari refocused Merton's religious reading, telling him, "there are many beautiful mystical books written by Christians. You should read St. Augustine's *Confessions,* and *The Imitation of Christ.*" (SSM 242) Shortly thereafter Merton reflected in SSM "my reading became more and more Catholic." (SSM 257) Merton was baptized a Roman Catholic Christian in November, 1938. Brother David Steindl-Rast, another pioneer of Buddhist-Christian dialogue, once remarked he believed Bramachari led Merton to embark "on an exploration not only of Eastern Spirituality, but for the first time in his life on Western . . . as well."[4] As Charles de Foucauld was brought to Christ by Islam, I wonder if Merton were not ferried over by a Hindu monk.

Monastic

Appropriately, in the early monastic years Merton's intellectual and spiritual interests were Christian. But on November 24, 1949, eight years after entering the Trappists, Merton recorded in his journal

> I think I shall ask permission to write to a Hindu who wrote
> me a letter about Patanjali's yoga.... I shall ask him to
> send us some books. A chemist who has been helping us
> with some paint jobs turned out to have been a postulant in
> a Zen Buddhist monastery in Hawaii and he spoke to the
> community about it in chapter.[5]

Brother Patrick Hart reports that it was D.T. Suzuki who stimulated Merton's deep interest in Zen Buddhism. Merton's letters to Suzuki began in the late 1950s and continued until Suzuki's death in 1966.[6] During the monastic years Merton's study focused on the Mahayana tradition of Zen, perhaps because it was most readily available to him in English translations. There is no question but that Suzuki was formative in his understanding of Zen. Buddhist scholars, notably Dr. Roger Corless (whose introduction to Buddhism opens this volume), suggest Suzuki's was not the most accurate rendering of the tradition.[7] But it was the one Merton had. Hopefully, one of the contributions of this volume to Merton scholarship is an accurate evaluation of Merton's understanding of Buddhism by Buddhist scholars. This is long over due.

Merton also corresponded with Fr. Dumoulin, S.J., Dr. John C.H. Wu, Professor Masao Abe, Marco Pallis and others who provided wider knowledge of Buddhist traditions. Merton's largest body of writing on Buddhism is on Zen and includes *Mystics and Zen Masters* (1967) and *Zen and the Birds of Appetite* (1968). (This latter was a primary text in my Buddhist-Christian dialogue class at Harvard in 1983.) Buddhist material also occurs in *Conjectures of a Guilty Bystander* (1966) and in posthumous publications, *The Asian Journal* (1973, included in *The Other Side of the Mountain*, 1998) and *Introductions East and West* (1981), a very rich but under-used book edited by Robert Daggy of blessed memory. Additionally, the effect of Buddhism on Merton's poetry is evident beginning in the 1950s.[8]

Asian

In September, 1964 Merton received a letter from Fr. Heinrich Dumoulin, S.J., the German scholar of Japanese Buddhism.

Dumoulin hoped that Merton might be allowed to visit the Cistercian foundations in Japan to deepen his knowledge of "Oriental mysticism" and to discuss "the possibilities of uniting Eastern and Western Spirituality."[9] Merton immediately wrote to Dom Ignace Gillet, his Father General, and to James Fox, his Abbot, inquiring about the possibility of making the journey, but nothing came of it.[10] By 1968 conditions in the church and the order were different, and there was a new abbot at Gethsemani. When an invitation came for Merton to journey east, he was allowed to accept it. Merton's Asian pilgrimage in the fall and winter of 1968 radically deepened his understanding of Buddhism. In my estimation, the most important aspects of this journey, were his face-to-face, monk-to-monk encounters with Theravadans and Tibetans, especially His Holiness the Dalai Lama in Dharamsala in November, and with Vijarayana and Dzogchen, "schools" of Tibetan Buddhism.

One can hardly overstate the importance of Merton's encounter with the Tibetans, H.H. the Dalai Lama and their monastic tradition in general. Marco Pallis had first introduced Merton to Tibetan Buddhism. By 1963 Merton had read Pallis' *Peaks and Lamas* and had received from him *The Way and the Mountain* and *Born in Tibet*. Merton reported in his Asian journal "I do feel very much at home with the Tibetans, even though much that appears in books about them seems bizarre if not sinister." (AJ 82)

As is so often the case, what we read or hear about people, and what we find when we meet them are very different. In journal entries between November 1 and 8, 1968 Merton becomes more and more enthusiastic about Tibetan Buddhism; this colored his time in Darjeeling (Nov. 12 to ca. Nov. 24) when he met with Chatral Rimpoche with whom he wished to study.[11] Of his meeting with Tibetans Merton says, "...the most significant thing of all [was] the way we were able to communicate with one another and share an essentially spiritual experience of 'Buddhism' which is also somehow in harmony with Christianity." (AJ 148)

Harold Talbott, who accompanied Merton and arranged some of his meetings with Tibetans, reflected that Merton recognized Nyingmapa yogi Chatral Rimpoche "as the embodiment of what he wanted to learn from Buddhism in Asia."[12] Talbott said, "in terms of Tantric or Vajrayana Buddhism Merton was to the manor born.... He took to it as a swan to water."[13] "Merton's reception by each Lama brought an instantaneous mutual recognition in an at-

Merton, Mrs. Lobsang Phuntsok Lhalungpa, Harold Talbott

Brother Patrick Hart

Marco Pallis
Thubden Tenszin, 1895-1989

Gal Vihara, Polonnaruwa, Sri Lanka. 12th Century CE.

mosphere of '*Cor ad cor loquitur.*'"[14] In Talbott's view, part of the reason for this rapport was that by 1968 Merton "had passed through ...the stages of *kenosis*, self-emptying, and was spurning nothing. He possessed something of the 'pure perception' that is developed by practicing...Tibetan Buddhism."[15]

If Tibet represents one trajectory of Merton's Asian experience, Theravada, represented by Merton's visit to the great carved figures at Polonnaruwa, is the other. Merton wrote passionately in his journal about this experience in early December, 1968 and many Merton scholars have exegeted those remarks. What has seldom been noted about those magnificent stone figures is that the standing figure is not Buddha, but his cousin, Ananda.[16] The reclining figure is the dead or dying Buddha, Buddha in the posture of entering Mahaparinirvana as his closest disciple (who later became an Arhat) stands in silent grief nearby. This, and knowing Merton died within a week, casts an interesting light on Merton's reflections:

> Looking at these figures I was suddenly, almost forcibly, jerked clean out of the habitual, half-tied vision of things, and an inner clearness, clarity, as if exploding from the rocks themselves, became evident and obvious. (AJ 233 & 235)

> I don't know when in my life I have ever had such a sense of beauty and spiritual validity running together in one aesthetic illumination. Surely, with...Polonnaruwa my Asian pilgrimage has come clear and purified itself. I mean, I know and have seen what I was obscurely looking for. I don't know what else remains but I have now seen and have pierced through the surface and have got beyond the shadow and the disguise. (AJ 236-236)

Not much more "remained." Merton died by accidental electrocution at a conference of Asian Christian monastics in Bangkok on December 10, 1968. Although it seems untimely, certainly Merton had a good death in the sense that he had seen what he was looking for.

Merton's acquaintance with Buddhism began with the traditions of its Hindu roots. It embraced primarily Mahayana traditions, although Merton's greatest illumination (dare I say his *satori*?) occurred at Polonnaruwa, a fruit of Theravadan Buddhism. At the end of his life Merton's trajectory was clearly toward Tibet. Before Asia, it focused on Suzuki and Zen, in Asia on the Tibetans. Most importantly, throughout his life, Merton had personal contact with practitioners, monks and lamas as well as with scholars of Buddhism. Practice, existential commitment, made all the difference. On December 12, 1964 Merton wrote

> I have no hesitation in saying that the "Buddhist" view of reality and life is one which I find extremely practical and acceptable, and, indeed, I think it is one of the very great contributions to the universal spiritual heritage.... It is by no means foreign or hostile to the spirit of Christianity, provided that the Christian outlook does not become bogged down in a slough of pseudo-objective formalities, as I am afraid it sometimes tends to do.[17]

WHY BUDDHISM?

It is fair to ask why a Christian, a Roman Catholic priest, and a Cistercian monk who loved his own spiritual tradition would be so powerfully drawn to Buddhism? I have seen no convincing evidence that Merton was abandoning Church for Sangha. Nor do any of the persons with whom I have communicated who were with Merton in Asia. I do think, had he lived, he would probably have returned to Tibet for further instruction. In the November 9, 1968 circular letter written from New Dehli that deals with his Tibetan experiences Merton closes, "...in my contacts with these new friends I also feel consolation in my own faith in Christ and His indwelling presence. I hope and believe He may be present in the hearts of all of us." (AJ 325) In an interview in *Tricycle* in 1992 Harold Talbott said simply, "he would never have left the Church."(Interview HT 22)

The aspects of Buddhism which particularly attracted Merton were its articulation of the paths of spiritual development, its "cultural alternative," and its contribution to monastic renewal.

Spiritual Development

From 1951-55 Merton was Master of Scholastics and from 1955-65 Master of Novices at Gethsemani; for nearly 15 years he was constantly involved in the formation of young monks. Because Zen encourages direct, unmediated experience, its language and teaching were particularly valuable to this endeavor. Its preference for the concrete and tangible, its location of meaning in the ordinary tasks and problems of daily life, and its often high spirited, good humored and irreverent approach appealed to Merton. Additionally, the Buddhist tradition is extremely acute psychologically and has developed very precise language to describe interior experience. It provides not only techniques to foster that development, but a language to describe the radical re-ordering of perspective engendered. Merton happily embraced these insights and used this language, and it worked because he had experienced the realities of which they spoke.

Cultural Alternative

Merton's initial understanding of Buddhism and of Asian culture was undoubtedly romanticized. There is a sense in which Buddhism was a metaphor for the antithesis of aspects of Western culture he distrusted: its acquisitiveness, its technological obsessions, it almost universal secularity. He viewed the sorry state of Western society as the outward and visible manifestation of the fact that Western religion had lost its interiority. In a September, 1968 letter he wrote, "Our real journey in life is interior: it is a matter of growth, deepening, and of an ever greater surrender to the creative action of love and grace in our hearts. Never was it more necessary for us to respond to that action." (AJ 296) Buddhism provided models whereby Christians (and this is important, for it means Merton understood Christians could adapt *practices* of other religions in light of their own fidelity to Jesus Christ) could learn the interiority of Christ Who, throughout the gospels, withdraws (Greek, *anachoreo*) to pray, to "commune with his own heart and be still."

More pointedly, Buddhism provided a corrective to the intellectual dualism engendered by Cartesian thought. (Merton thought we all suffered from trying to travel the spiritual path in a broken Descartes!) In *Conjectures of a Guilty Bystander* Merton wrote:

> The taste for Zen in the West is in part a healthy reaction
> of people exasperated with the heritage of four centuries
> of Cartesianism: the reification of concepts, idolization of
> the reflexive consciousness, flight from being into verbal-

ism, mathematics, and rationalization. Descartes made a fetish out of the mirror in which the self finds itself. Zen shatters it.[18]

Monastic Renewal

In his book *Thomas Merton and the Monastic Vision,* Lawrence Cunningham rightly says that everything in Merton's life and thought spirals in toward his monastic vocation.[19] The reason for his Asian pilgrimage was to learn from the great monastic traditions of the East. Dom Jean Leclercq observed, "This journey to the East had been prepared for by thirty years of reading.... All the same, the purpose remained essentially monastic, directed towards inner growth and not to the acquisition of knowledge which later on could be of use in dialogue with non-Christians."[20] In the paper he was to have delivered in Calcutta, Merton wrote of the need to learn in depth from Buddhist or Hindu disciplines. "I believe," he noted, "that some of us need to do this in order to improve the quality of our own monastic life and even to help in the task of monastic renewal which has been undertaken within the Western Church." (AJ 313) (Recall that, at the time, the Roman Church was in the heady first flush of the reforms of Vatican II.) Merton says explicitly that he came to Asia as a "pilgrim" "to drink from ancient sources of monastic vision and experience" "to become a better and more enlightened monk." (AJ 312-313)

Conversion of life is central to the monastic enterprise about which Merton wrote so much and cared so deeply. Central to conversion of life is diminishing the ego, what Merton called the "false self" or "little s" self. One who is self-absorbed cannot be a good monk (or a good Christian!). Merton saw conversion of life, this "egolessness," dramatically incarnated in Tibetan monks and lamas. His earlier studies of Zen gave him a valuable set of practices and teachings to help overcome the problem of self absorption.

CONCLUSION

I conclude with an account Merton gave of a dream he had on November 5, 1968, about a month before he died and during the time he was meeting with H.H. the Dalai Lama. It gives a glimpse of the depth to which Buddhism had penetrated Merton's inner life.

Last night I dreamed that I was, temporarily, back at Gethsemani.
Thomas Merton, *The Asian Journal of Thomas Merton*

> Last night I dreamed that I was, temporarily, back at
> Gethsemani. I was dressed in a Buddhist's monk's habit,
> but with more black and red and gold, a "Zen habit," in
> color more Tibetan than Zen. I was going to tell the cook
> in the diet kitchen, that I would be there for supper. I met
> some women in the corridor, visitors and students of Asian
> religion, to whom I was explaining I was a kind of Zen
> monk and Gelugpa together, when I woke up. (AJ 107)

In the final analysis, "waking up" is what it is all about. In doing
so, the "old world" becomes the "new world" which unfolds like a
flower exactly where one is. So it was for Merton. Buddhism helped
to awaken Merton to the Christ unfolding in the lotus of every
moment.

NOTES

1. Naomi Burton, et al (eds.), *The Asian Journal of Thomas Merton*
(New York: New Directions, 1968/1975) 316. Hereafter in the text as AJ.

2. Thomas Merton, *The Seven Storey Mountain* (New York:
Doubleday/Image, 1970) 228. Hereafter in the text as SSM.

3. For more on this important figure see Francis X. Clooney, S.J.,
"In Memoriam: Mahanambrata Brahmachari (25 December 1904-18
October 1999)," *The Merton Annual* 13 (2000) 123–126.

4. From a ms. "Destination: East; Destiny; Fire" by Brother David.
See *Thomas Merton: Prophet in the Belly of a Paradox* (New York: Paulist
Press, 1978).

5. Thomas Merton, *The Sign of Jonas* (New York: Doubleday/Image, 1956) 237.

6. Merton's letters appear in William H. Shannon (ed.), *The Hidden
Ground of Love* (New York: Farrar, Straus, Giroux, 1985) and with
Suzuki's letters and a record of their 1964 New York meeting in Robert
E. Daggy (ed.), *Thomas Merton and D.T. Suzuki* (Monterey, KY.: Lark-
spur Press, 1988).

7. See Roger Corless, "In Search of a Context for the Merton-Suzuki
Dialogue," *The Merton Annual* 6 (1993) 76–91.

8. See Bonnie Thurston, "Zen in the Eye of Thomas Merton's Poetry," *Buddhist-Christian Studies* 4 (1984) 103-117.

9. Br. Patrick Hart, O.C.S.O. (Ed.), *Thomas Merton The School of
Charity* (New York: Harcourt, Brace, Jovanovich, 1990) 237.

10. The letters appear in *The School of Charity* pp. 237-239. I am
grateful to Erlinda Paguio, past president of the International Thomas
Merton Society and Merton scholar, for reminding me of this material.

11. An Interview with Harold Talbott, "The Jesus Lama: Thomas Merton in the Himalayas," *Tricycle* Summer 1992, 22. Hereafter in the text as "Interview HT."

12. Harold Talbott, from an email of October 13, 2003.

13. Notes of Harold Talbott of December 7, 2000.

14. Harold Talbott, from a letter of September 14, 2000.

15. Notes of Harold Talbott of December 7, 2000.

16. The identity of the figures is disputed. I am quoting Harold Talbott here. Paul Pearson has kindly provided another view, that both figures are Buddhas. For more information, the reader is referred to www.polonnaruwa.org and to the article by David G. Addiss and John J. Albert in the Bibliography.

17. William Shannon (ed.), *Thomas Merton: Witness to Freedom* (New York: Farrar, Straus, Giroux, 1994) 167-168.

Fr. Shannon lists the letter as being to "Mr. Lunsford." But I wonder if this might not be Lunsford Yandell who forwarded to Merton a manuscript on Shen Hui. Brother Patrick Hart's "Editor's Note" to "The Zen Insight of Shen Hui" (see *The Merton Annual* 1/1998, p. 3) suggested as much to me.

18. Thomas Merton, *Conjectures of a Guilty Bystander* (New York: Doubleday/Image, 1965/68) 285. Hereafter in the text as CGB.

19. Lawrence S. Cunningham, *Thomas Merton and the Monastic Vision* (Grand Rapids: William B. Eerdmans, 1999).

20. Jean Leclercq, "Merton and the East," *Cistercian Studies* 8/4 (1978) 312.

PART II
MERTON AND
BUDDHIST TRADITIONS

The world and time are the dance of the Lord in emptiness. No despair of ours can alter the reality of things, or stain the joy of the cosmic dance which is always there. Indeed, we are in the midst of it, and it is in the midst of us, for it beats in our very blood, whether we want it to or not. We are invited to forget ourselves on purpose, cast our awful solemnity to the winds and join in the general dance.

Thomas Merton, *New Seeds of Contemplation*

THOMAS MERTON AND THERAVADA BUDDHISM

James A. Wiseman, O.S.B.

When reflecting on Thomas Merton's encounter with Buddhism, we almost inevitably turn our thoughts to some figure or school within its Mahayana branch, especially Zen and Tibetan Buddhism. One of Merton's few trips outside Kentucky prior to his Asian journey was to visit the Zen scholar Daisetz Suzuki in New York in 1964, while surely the best-known person whom Merton met in Asia was His Holiness the Dalai Lama. Indeed, Merton's secretary, Br. Patrick Hart, has said that of all the other religious traditions in which this Christian monk was interested, Tibetan Buddhism seems to have had pride of place in the final months of his life.[1] It would therefore be wrong to place too much emphasis on the place of Theravada in Merton's life and thought, but that place is nevertheless not negligible. He met with several prominent Theravada monks during his Asian journey, and even though very little has been published about the content of their conversations, the esteem in which he clearly held these monks makes it worthwhile to know something about their life and teaching. This will be the main focus of my article, which will conclude with some reflections on ways in which Merton's own thought parallels theirs and ways in which he might have learned from their teachings.

THERAVADA AND MAHAYANA BUDDHISM

Before turning to that central topic, we should become as clear as possible about the meaning of the terms *Theravada* and *Mahayana*. Granted that these words do designate major branches within the Buddhist religion, just as Roman Catholicism, Eastern Orthodoxy, and Protestantism are the principal divisions within Christianity, textbooks about Buddhism sometimes oversimplify the distinction by implying that the Theravada ideal is a self-centered quest for Nirvana on the part of an *Arhat* whereas Mahayana is characterized by the *Bodhisattva*'s altruistic desire to bring all beings to

31

enlightenment. The effect of this oversimplification is evident in a story told by Sylvia Boorstein, a teacher at a Theravada meditation center in California. She recounts a meeting at a ski resort with a young man who had been taking a world religions course. She told him that she taught at Spirit Rock Meditation Center, whose program was based on the principal meditation practices described by the Buddha in the Pali Canon. The conversation continued in the following way:

> "Oh, I see," he said, "that's Theravada Buddhism, isn't it?"
> "Yes it is," Sylvia replied.
> "Is it true," he asked, "that those were the selfish Buddhists who were only interested in their own enlightenment and not in the liberation of all beings?"

About this exchange, Ms. Boorstein later commented: "I hope I did not wince at what I recognized as a not uncommon survey textbook, shorthand differentiation … [In fact, the Buddha's] message of liberation for 'all beings' is that craving is the cause of suffering, that the end of suffering is possible, that peace is possible in this very life, [and] that insight leads to wisdom, which manifests as compassion on behalf of all beings. This message that Theravada proclaims has remained central to Buddhism for the 2500 years of its evolution through different cultures and different times."[2]

A similar kind of anecdote, this one told by Huston Smith in his best-selling textbook *The World's Religions*, concerns two Germans who, disillusioned by European civilization in the period leading up to World War II, went to Sri Lanka (then known as Ceylon) as young men and became Theravada monks. One of them, taking the name Nyanaponika Thera, remained on that path until he died at the age of 93, while his friend, having learned about Tibetan Buddhism on a trip to north India, switched to that tradition and became known in the West as Lama Govinda. When asked about this years later, Ven. Nyanaponika replied, "My friend cited the Bodhisattva Vow as the reason for his switch to Mahayana, but I could not see the force of his argument. For if one were to transcend self-centeredness completely, as the *Arhat* seeks to do, what would be left but compassion?"[3]

It is true that in past centuries there have been aspersions cast on one of the two main branches of Buddhism by followers of the other branch, but more recently the differences have not loomed so large. Already back in 1966 the World Buddhist Sangha Council was first convened in Sri Lanka with the hope of bridging differences and overcoming animosities and misunderstandings. On that occasion, with leading Mahayana and Theravada monks present, the prominent Theravadin Walpola Rahula drew up a text listing nine basic points upon which he thought the two branches could agree. All nine were approved unanimously. One of them, the fourth, seems clearly intended to avoid the oversimplification that makes wisdom primary for Theravada and compassion most important for Mahayana. This fourth point reads as follows: "Following the example of the Buddha, who is the embodiment of Great Compassion and Great Wisdom, we consider that the purpose of life is to develop compassion for all living beings without discrimination and to work for their good, happiness, and peace; and to develop wisdom leading to the realization of Ultimate Truth."

Similarly, the eighth point leads one to question the widely held belief that the Bodhisattva ideal is unique to the Mahayana branch. This point briefly names the three traditional ways of attaining Enlightenment, namely, by following a humanly established spiritual path (and so becoming an *Arhat*), by attaining Enlightenment without following a path taught by another but nevertheless not communicating this attainment in the form of a teaching (and so becoming a *Pratyekabuddha* or "Solitary Buddha"), and by following the path of a *Bodhisattva* (and so becoming a *Samyaksambuddha* or "Perfectly and Fully Enlightened Buddha"). After listing these three ways, the eighth point concludes with the statement, "We accept it as the highest, noblest, and most heroic to follow the career of a Bodhisattva and to become a Samyak-sam-Buddha in order to save others."[4]

Without denying that there are other differences between the two major branches, perhaps the most objective and non-tendentious way of describing the major difference is to say that the Theravada scriptures are basically limited to those found in the Pali Canon, which consists of three collections of the Buddha's teachings and his rules for the monastic community that were transmitted orally for some centuries and are said to have first been written down in the first century B.C.E. On the other hand, followers of the Mahayana branch recognize and even give priority to certain other scriptures as well, among the best-known of which are the *Perfection of Wisdom Sutras*, whose condensed versions include the *Diamond Sutra* and *Heart Sutra*. This proliferation of scriptures is certainly one reason for greater diversity within Mahayana, where some schools emphasize the "Other power" of celestial beings who can be invoked through rituals and prayers to assist one on the path to Enlightenment, while other schools, such as Zen, place more emphasis on personal effort, as do Theravadins. In fact, one Buddhist scholar, Shanta Ratnayaka, has written an essay arguing that Zen is the Theravada branch of Buddhism in Mahayana countries.[5]

THERAVADA MONKS WHOM MERTON MET IN ASIA

Phra Khantipalo

The previous section of this article mentioned two important Theravada monks, Nyanaponika Thera (later raised to the rank of Mahathera, "Great Elder") and Walpola Rahula. Merton met each of them while in Sri Lanka in late November and early December, 1968, only days before flying to Bangkok after a brief stop in Singapore. It is sometimes overlooked that he also spoke at some length with another Theravada monk in October of that year, when he spent a few days in and around Bangkok upon first arriving in Asia on his way to India. This was an English monk, Phra Khantipalo, who had been born north of London in 1932, had converted to Buddhism as a young man, and had settled in Thailand in 1963, where he lived for the next ten years before moving to Australia and teaching Buddhist meditation in many parts of that country.[6] When Merton met him in Bangkok, Phra Khantipalo was staying at a Buddhist temple in the city but intending within a few days to go to a forest monastery in the northeastern part of the country and study with a meditation teacher. Merton's notes of their conversation were written so rapidly in his small pocket notebook as to have been mostly indecipherable by those who edited his *Asian Journal*, but Phra Khantipalo later composed a summary of the points he made in his talk with Merton. This summary is included in *The Asian Journal* as Appendix II, "On Mindfulness."

Near the beginning of his reflections "On Mindfulness," Phra Khantipalo recounts an anecdote from the Zen tradition, noting that Zen, like the Theravada Buddhism of Thailand, is based upon what is called "the Establishment of Mindfulness." In this story, a certain Zen master was approached by a disciple who wanted to

know the essentials of Buddhist doctrine. Instead of giving an eru-
dite discourse, the master simply said, "When hungry I eat; when
tired I sleep." Disappointed, the disciple replied, "But that is what
ordinary people do. How do you differ?" The old monk answered,
"When they eat, most people think a thousand thoughts; when they
sleep they dream a thousand dreams." Khantipalo goes on to comment that unlike most people, whose minds wander where they
will with very little restraint, one who has reached Enlightenment
will have "no wandering mind, no delusions, no fantasies, but brilliant awareness of *NOW* all the time."[7] He adds that such mindfulness will normally and eventually lead to a loss of the sense of
oneself as an independently existing entity. In his words:

> Although at the beginning of any Buddhist meditation there
> is the concept "I am meditating" or "I am being mindful,"
> if the right path is followed, then this sense of "I-ness" and
> "mine-ness" becomes less marked, or rather its bases in
> mind and body become less identified with "myself," until
> this concept dissolves away completely and not-self (or
> not-soul, as *anatta* may also be translated) is seen with
> penetrative wisdom.[8]

What is especially significant about this teaching is the way in which
the doctrine of *anatta*, not-self, is here grounded not in abstract
reflections but in experience. Phra Khantipalo is saying that through
the persevering practice of meditation one will gradually lose the
sense of "I-ness," so that eventually the very concept of "myself"
will dissolve. For all of Merton's own intellectual acumen, it is
abundantly clear from everything he wrote prior to and during his
Asian journey that he had come to that continent to learn from the
experience of those who, like himself, were dedicated pilgrims on
the contemplative path. Thus, in a letter that he wrote to Erich
Fromm two years earlier, Merton said, "I am not denying the significance of various conceptual frames of reference, but I do believe that when it comes down to the phenomenon of the religious
experience itself, the theological frame of reference is not as crucial as it may appear to be."[9] So, too, in his hastily written "Letter
on the Contemplative Life," composed in the late summer of 1967
at the request of Pope Paul VI, Merton wrote, "I have been sum-
moned to explore a desert area of man's heart in which explanations no longer suffice, and in which one learns that only experi-

ence counts."[10] It was surely the fact that Nyanaponika Mahathera
and Walpola Rahula were experienced contemplatives that led
Merton to arrange meetings with them during his stay in Sri Lanka
from November 29 till December 6.   Who, then, were these two
monks and what did they teach?

Nyanaponika Mahathera

Nyanaponika Mahathera was born in Hanau, Germany, in 1901 as
Siegmund Feniger, the only child of a Jewish couple. He converted to Buddhism while still in his teens and in his early twenties
moved with his parents to Berlin, where he became acquainted
with the writings of Ven. Nyanatiloka Mahathera, a German who
had become a Theravada monk in Sri Lanka and there established
a monastery for Western monks called the Island Hermitage. In
1932 Siegmund's father died, and shortly thereafter Hitler came to
power. As the Nazi persecution of the Jews intensified, Siegmund
arranged for his mother to leave Germany for safer quarters, and
then he himself went to Sri Lanka to join the community at the
Island Hermitage early in 1936. Here he received the name
Nyanaponika, meaning "inclined toward wisdom." Over the next
several decades he completed German translations of major Buddhist scriptures and in 1958 helped found the Buddhist Publication
Society (hereafter BPS), serving as its editor until 1984 and its
president until 1988. His efforts had much to do with making the

BPS a major Buddhist publisher, with outlets in more than eighty countries throughout the world. His own best-known book is entitled *The Heart of Buddhist Meditation*.[11] In addition to this book, Merton had with him two of the Theravada monk's pamphlets: *The Power of Mindfulness: An Inquiry into the Scope of Bare Attention and the Principal Sources of its Strength* and *Anatta and Nibbana: Egolessness and Deliverance*, both published by the Buddhist Publication Society.[12] To help celebrate Ven. Nyanaponika's 93rd birthday on July 21, 1994, the BPS released an edition of his collected essays entitled *The Vision of Dhamma*. A month later his health began failing rapidly. After a brief period of hospitalization he asked to be returned to his residence in the Forest Hermitage near the city of Kandy, where he passed away peacefully in the early morning hours of October 19. His cremated remains were interred at the Island Hermitage in the southern part of the island, where he had spent his formative years as a monk.[13]

It was at the Forest Hermitage that Merton met this monk on November 30, 1968. *The Asian Journal* and the corresponding part of the seventh volume of his published journals contain only two fairly short paragraphs about their meeting, neither of them providing any insight into the content of their conversation. Merton's final sentences about their time together read as follows: "[Nyanaponika Thera's] hermitage is in full jungle, in a reservation, but the jungle is right at the edge of Kandy so he is really not far from town. But it is very wild and quiet. We walked out on the brow of a hill where the jungle has been cleared a bit and there is a fine view of the peaks to the southwest and northwest. I hope my camera caught some of the enchanted beauty of this landscape! Ceylon is incomparable!"[14]

Even though Merton apparently wrote nothing about the conversation he had with this monk, he was definitely familiar with his teaching, not only because he had Ven. Nyanaponika's major book with him but also because the practice of mindfulness taught in that book was precisely the kind he had discussed two months earlier with Bhikkhu Khantipalo in Bangkok, whose published summary of the doctrines they discussed concludes with an explicit recommendation of Ven. Nyanaponika's book.[15] I will here recount some of the major teachings in this work, whose first half contains the Theravada monk's own essay on mindfulness while the last half includes the Buddha's basic discourse on mindfulness

(Nyanaponika's) hermitage is in full jungle…right at the edge of Kandy.

A hot afternoon. I walked alone, glad to be alone, to the Kandy museum, a little up the road past the Temple of the Tooth…after that I walked a little by the lake in the cool breeze thinking of my Advent sermon…Heavy rain. A longer and louder drum continues in the Temple of the Tooth.

Thomas Merton, *The Asian Journal of Thomas Merton*

The temple and shrine of the relic
of the Buddha's tooth.

as found in the Pali Canon plus several related texts from both the Theravada and Mahayana schools.

On the very first page of his introduction Ven. Nyanaponika makes the significant claim that all the methods of mental training to be found in Buddhist literature converge on what he calls "the Way of Mindfulness," referred to by the Buddha himself as "the Only Way" and therefore rightly called "the heart" not only of Buddhist meditation but of the entire doctrine.[16] The Buddha's own major discourse on mindfulness in the Pali Canon, translated in the second half of the book, is known as the *Maha-Satipatthana Sutta*, the Great Discourse on the Foundations of Mindfulness. Ven. Nyanaponika notes that no other discourse of the Buddha, not even his first one, the famous sermon in the Deer Park near Benares, enjoys as much popularity and veneration in Theravada lands as this *sutta*. It is often read and contemplated by both monks and laypersons on full-moon days, is given a place of honor in many homes, and is regularly recited at the bedside of a dying Buddhist so that this "great message of liberation" may provide consolation and conviction in the final hours of one's life (11). Although most of the other texts included in the anthology section of the book come from the Theravada tradition, there are some from the early Mahayana sutras since these, too, show a deep appreciation of the importance of mindfulness in Buddhist doctrine. Ven. Nyanaponika explains that he included these latter texts in order to help foster a sense of common endeavor in the two branches and thereby relegate to the background the differences between them (13). He, like the above-mentioned Buddhist scholar Shanta Ratnayaka, especially singles out similarities between Theravada and Zen Buddhism: direct confrontation with reality (including one's mind), bringing meditative practice into intimate association with everyday life, transcending conceptual thought through direct observation, and living in the present. For this reason, he suggests that Zen practitioners will find much in Theravada teaching on mindfulness that will assist them in their own practice (14).

Following those introductory remarks, Ven. Nyanaponika turns to the teaching of mindfulness itself. In its elementary form, "attention," it is one of the cardinal functions of consciousness, without which there could be no perception of any object at all. From this mere taking notice of an object (whether the object be the body, the feelings, the general state of one's mind, or the specific contents of consciousness at a given moment), one can go on to pay closer attention to details, gradually getting rid of emotional and intellectual prejudices until finally arriving at a clear, undistorted awareness that is the proper domain of Right Mindfulness. This latter, of course, is the seventh category or factor in Buddhism's Noble Eightfold Path leading to the cessation of *dukkha*, the unsatisfactoriness that characterizes the lives of most people.

Ven. Nyanaponika next discusses in some detail the two complementary aspects of mindfulness, namely, Bare Attention and Clear Comprehension. The former he calls "the clear and single-minded awareness of what actually happens *to* us and *in* us, at the successive moments of perception" (30). It allows things to "speak for themselves ... without the narrowing and leveling effect of habitual judgments" and so allows us to see things "ever anew, as if for the first time" (35). Among other advantages, this kind of attention slows down or even stops the usual, fairly rapid transition from thought to action. At this point, "when the mind has not yet settled upon a definite course of action," one will be open to receive helpful advice from others and to ponder the course that will lead to a mature decision characterized by "wisdom, self-control and common sense" rather than by the thoughtless, automatic reactions that can so easily lead to great grief farther down the road (39-40). If, for example, in what is called the practice of Contemplating Mental Contents, one becomes clearly aware that "This is a lustful thought," this "dispassionate and brief form of mere 'registering' will often prove more effective than a mustering of will, emotion or reason, which frequently only provokes antagonistic forces of the mind to stiffer resistance" (42). In short, Bare Attention restores to us the freedom that comes from living attentively in the present, free from rash courses of action, from busy-ness, and from any habitual interfering in matters that really do not concern us (43).

Attention itself, however, is only half of the equation. To use automotive imagery, the inner brakes that it can apply to our tendency to act heedlessly must be supplemented by a steering mechanism to guide us positively through the various choices, decisions, and judgments that face us daily. This guide is Clear Comprehension, whose task is to make our various activities purposeful and efficient, in full accord with our highest ideals. In other words, to the *clarity* of Bare Attention, Clear Comprehension adds the *com-*

prehension of purpose (45-46). Even though one's early training in these two aspects of mindfulness may occur in an intensive retreat setting, where one withdraws from the normal, unpredictable demands of everyday life and focuses on a specific object such as the movement of breath through one's nostrils or the concomitant rising and falling of the abdomen, little by little "the practice of Right Mindfulness should absorb all activities of body, speech and mind, so that ultimately the subject of meditation will never be abandoned" (50). Rather, "the aim to be aspired to by the disciple of this method is that *life* becomes one with the spiritual *practice*, and that the *practice* becomes full-blooded *life*" (50). Possibly anticipating the earlier-mentioned objection occasionally raised against Theravada Buddhism—that it makes the practitioner self-centered—Ven. Nyanaponika concludes his treatment of Bare Attention and Clear Comprehension with the statement that they not only prepare an individual for the final liberation of *nibbana* but, at the very same time, train one "for selfless work in the service of suffering humanity, by bestowing the keen eye of wisdom and the sure hand of skillfulness, which are as necessary for that service as a warm heart" (56).

Leaving for the final section of this article my reflections on what Merton might or might not have appropriated from this teaching, I turn now to the second monk whom he visited in Sri Lanka.

Walpola Rahula

Like Nyanaponika Mahathera, Walpola Rahula lived to be more than 90 years of age. Born in the village of Walpola in the southern part of Sri Lanka on May 9, 1907, he attended the village school for a while but had to leave because of a difference of opinion with his teacher over the issue of corporal punishment. He then entered the Buddhist temple in his village and in his early teens, with his parents' approval, entered the monastic *Sangha* there. After a course of training in the Sinhala, Pali, and Sanskrit languages, together with studies in Buddhist history and doctrine, he became an undergraduate at Ceylon University College. At that time the college was affiliated with the University of London, which awarded him a B.A. Honours Degree in 1941. During his student years he also developed a keen interest in the social and economic welfare of his country, actively supporting the working-class movement and encouraging other Buddhist monks to leave their secluded way of life to work for the good of society. In 1943 he left for India on a Ceylonese government scholarship for post-graduate research at the University of Calcutta, where he worked under the direction of the eminent Sanskritist S.N. Dasgupta. Rahula returned to his homeland in 1945, determined to work on his thesis on the history of early Buddhism there; this was eventually published under the title *The History of Buddhism in Ceylon*. His earlier concern for social issues remained, directed now to the fact that the independence granted his country by the British had in fact done little to improve the economic conditions of the masses or to promote the national culture. Many of his countrymen, unused to seeing him and some fellow monks speaking out on political issues, castigated them for being "political *bhikkhus*," but he held his ground and even published a book defending his understanding of the proper role of a monk in the life of the country.

In 1950 Rahula went abroad once more, this time on a French government fellowship that allowed him to pursue research on Mahayana Buddhism at the Sorbonne. During his years there he became friends with many of the leading Orientalists and Buddhologists in Europe and translated into French one of the most important Mahayana philosophical texts, the *Abhidharma-samuccaya* of Asanga, the first time this treatise had been translated into any modern language. During these years he also wrote his best-known book, *What the Buddha Taught*, first published in English by Grove Press in 1959, with a second and enlarged edition appearing fifteen years later. This second edition has been translated into at least seven European and Asian languages and has become a staple in the curriculum of many colleges and universities.

Walpola Rahula's growing reputation as a scholar led him to be invited in 1964 to fill a newly created professorial chair for the History and Literature of Religions at Northwestern University in Evanston, Illinois, making him the first Buddhist monk ever to hold such a position in the Western world. For the next several years he divided his time between Paris and Evanston, except for an interim period of three years in the late 1960s when he served as Vice-Chancellor of Vidyodaya University in Sri Lanka. He left Paris in 1974 and went to reside in London, where he worked closely with Miss I.B. Horner, president of the Pali Text Society of London. Honorary degrees and visiting professorships were regularly awarded him on several continents. He was also instrumental in encouraging the formation of the first Theravada temple in the United States, the Washington Buddhist Vihara in the District of Columbia. Upon his death in 1998 a fellow monk who had long known him wrote: "While we mourn the passing of this irreplaceable monk, we can't be too sad, since we have the results of his work, a vibrant, living, universally known and admired Theravada Buddhism. His books, his students, his work will be a constant reminder for our generation and generations to come of this key figure in the modern development of Buddhism."[17]

As in the case of Merton's meeting with Nyanaponika Thera, we have very little published material about the content of his conversation with Walpola Rahula in Colombo on December 2. This was the day after Merton's well-known visit to the massive Buddhist statues at Polonnaruwa, about which he later wrote, "I don't know when in my life I have ever had such a sense of beauty and spiritual validity running together in one aesthetic illumination."[18] Indeed, he had found this such a deep experience that he feared he had spoiled it by trying to talk about it at a dinner party, but he did find a certain confirmation of the validity of his experience through his conversation with Rahula: "Yet when I spoke about it to Walpola Rahula at the Buddhist University I think the idea got across and he said, 'Those who carved those statues were not ordinary men.'"[19]

From even the little recounted above about Walpola Rahula, it is clear that his manner of life was in certain respects very different from that of Nyanaponika Mahathera. The latter spent by far the greater part of his time in the forest hermitage where Merton had visited him, while Rahula's adult years were spent largely in academic settings on three continents. His explicit concern for social issues is also much more prominent than Nyanaponika's. On the basic principles of Buddhism, however, the two monks were in agreement, and each one's best-known book is similar in format and length to the other's: Rahula's *What the Buddha Taught* begins with seven chapters giving the monk's own understanding of fundamental Buddhist doctrine, followed by an anthology of selected texts from the Pali Canon.

Rahula's book is so well-known and widely used that there would be no real value in trying to summarize it here. One of its major points should nevertheless be emphasized. Since the author himself was deeply concerned about the social conditions in his country both before and after its independence from Great Britain, it is not surprising that this aspect of his life and thought is prominent in the book. In commenting on the same discourse about mindfulness that has so central a place in Nyanaponika's work, Rahula insists that "the ways of 'meditation' given in this discourse are not cut off from life, nor do they avoid life; on the contrary, they are all connected with our life, our daily activities, our sorrows and joys, our words and thoughts, our moral and intellectual occupations."[20] He notes that some persons automatically associate the practice of meditation with a particular posture, such as the lotus posture, but in fact this is required only for that practice known as "awareness of in-and-out breathing." "For other forms of 'meditation' given in this *sutta*, you may sit, stand, walk, or lie down, as you like," for in such meditation, there is no need to perform any particular action; "you have only to be mindful and aware of whatever you may do" (72). The careful practice of such mindfulness will help one live fully in the present, free from regrets about the past and worries about the future, free also from all the delusions that lead to grasping for power or domination over others. This last point was especially close to Rahula's heart, for his final chapter concludes with the following paragraph:

> Buddhism aims at creating a society where the ruinous struggle for power is renounced; where calm and peace prevail away from conquest and defeat; where the persecution of the innocent is vehemently denounced; where one who conquers oneself is more respected than those who conquer millions by military and economic warfare; where hatred is conquered by kindness, and evil by goodness; …where life in peace and harmony, in a world of material contentment, is directed towards the highest and noblest aim, the realization of the Ultimate Truth, Nirvana. (89)

MERTON'S THOUGHT COMPARED WITH THAT OF THE THREE THERAVADINS

Since we have so very little from Merton's pen concerning the work of the three Theravada monks discussed above—Phra Khantipalo, Nyanaponika Mahathera, and Walpola Rahula—it would be extremely difficult to posit specific influences that any of them may have had on his own thought. It is, however, quite possible to draw some comparisons between their thinking and his on foundational points. At the very least, doing so can point out some genuine agreements among these monks from two religious traditions as well as some abiding differences. To keep the following reflections to a manageable length, I have chosen three prominent points from the work of these Theravadins.

First, if there is one single issue by which early Buddhist thought distinguished itself from the Brahmanic philosophy of that time it is surely the teaching of *anatta*, the doctrine that there is no permanent self or ego, no everlasting entity or separate soul within the ever-changing phenomenal world. In the essay "On Mindfulness" that Phra Khantipalo wrote as a summary of the points he made in his discussion with Merton in Bangkok on October 17, 1968, that monk emphasizes that a sense of self or "I-ness," which comes so naturally to many people, will gradually become less marked with the persevering practice of Buddhist meditation until at last the notion completely disappears. Walpola Rahula likewise addresses this aspect of Buddhist teaching in the sixth chapter of *What the Buddha Taught*, a chapter entitled "The Doctrine of No-Soul: *Anatta*." In the frankest of language, Rahula here draws a sharp distinction between Buddhism and the world's theistic religions:

> Two ideas are psychologically deep-rooted in man: self-protection and self-preservation. For self-protection man has created God, on whom he depends for his own protection, safety and security, just as a child depends on its parent. For self-preservation man has conceived the idea of an immortal Soul or *Atman*, which will live eternally. In his ignorance, weakness, fear, and desire, man needs these two things to console himself. Hence he clings to them deeply and fanatically. (51)

As a convinced Christian, Merton could not have agreed with this statement as such, but his own writings about "the self" nevertheless allow for a certain degree of convergence. In accord with the Gospel's teaching about "losing one's self (*psyche*) to save it" (cf. Mark 8:35 and parallels), Merton regularly wrote about the Christian's call to shed the illusions of "the false self." In *New Seeds of Contemplation* Merton speaks of this false self as "the one who wants to exist outside the reach of God's will and God's love—outside of reality and outside of life," since it "exists only in my own egocentric desires."[21] In another work he describes it as "the machine which we regulate and tune up and feed with all kinds of stimulants and sedatives ... to fit the patterns prescribed by the salesman of pleasure-giving and anxiety-allaying commodities."[22] To the extent that one moves beyond this false self and toward "the true self" willed by God, one may indeed lose a sense of separateness somewhat akin to what Phra Khantipalo described in his reflections on mindfulness. St. Paul spoke of this as living "no longer I, but Christ living in me" (Galatians 2:20); Meister Eckhart (one of Merton's favorite authors in the final years of his life) regularly spoke of his intimate oneness with Christ, and Merton himself, in that well-known and unique letter in which he described his own prayer to Abdul Aziz, spoke of it as "a kind of praise rising up out of the center of Nothing and Silence. If I am still present 'myself' this I recognize as an obstacle."[23] At least in this *experiential* respect, he could surely have agreed with Phra Khantipalo about the loss of a sense of "I-ness" through meditation or meditative prayer.

A second point, especially emphasized by Nyanaponika Mahathera in his treatment of Bare Attention, is the way in which this elementary aspect of mindfulness can help prevent us from pursuing rash courses of action. In his words, "Very often a single moment of mindfulness or wise reflection would have prevented a far-reaching sequence of misery or guilt. By *pausing* before action, in a habitual attitude of Bare Attention, one will be able to seize that decisive but brief moment when mind has not yet settled upon a definite course or action or a definite attitude, but is still open to receive skilful directions."[24] In reading these words, one may well imagine how the practice of such awareness might have spared Merton and the young nurse with whom he fell in love in 1966 a tremendous amount of anguish.

This is not to say that there was nothing positive in their relationship. Like most events in one's life, this episode was neither totally beneficial nor totally harmful. Lawrence Cunningham is surely correct in pointing out one beneficial aspect: "Merton was amazed that he was capable of deep human love, which was crucial for a person who had essentially been brought up as an orphan and whose experiences with women earlier in his life were, by and large according to his own admission, not those of love but—again in his words—'adulterous.'"[25] But Nyanaponika's words about the pause to which Bare Attention gives rise, together with a concomitant openness "to receive skilful directions," are also very much to the point. There is no doubt but that the headiness of falling in love can, as the saying goes, sweep a person off his or her feet. Rare indeed may be the person who can pause at the very onset of this experience, seek the advice of a trusted friend or counselor, and avoid becoming so deeply involved in a relationship that, in a case like Merton's, could have had no satisfactory outcome since his vowed celibacy was an ineluctable obstacle to marriage.

At the beginning of November in 1966, some months after the two of them had ceased seeing each other and she had moved out of state, Merton wrote: "I went for a walk to the Lake Knob, with a great sense of new freedom and discovery—and determination never to get caught again by a love affair and not let this one flare up again. Only now do I begin to see the state of the ruins! What an embarrassing mess! And how completely stupid I have been. At the beginning, like a drunken driver going through every red light—and as a matter of fact only really sobering up now, after seven months of it."[26] It is significant that Merton's image of "going through every red light" represents precisely the kind of rushing ahead that Bare Attention as described by Nyanaponika is able to prevent: "Bare Attention slows down, or even stops, the transition from thought to action, allowing more time for coming to a mature decision. Such slowing down is of vital importance as long as unprofitable, harmful or evil words and deeds possess an all too strong spontaneity of occurrence ... without giving to the 'inner brakes' of wisdom, self-control and common sense a chance to operate."[27]

A third and final point is one much emphasized by both of the Sri Lankan monks, namely, that meditation is not some esoteric practice divorced from the rest of life and does not, for the most part, even require withdrawal from everyday life or the assumption of a particular posture. Like Merton, though at a much earlier stage in his monastic life, Walpola Rahula was convinced that a monk is called to be resolutely concerned about the society around him, including very practical issues of economics and politics. He was roundly criticized for such involvement, even as was Merton once he began writing about race relations and war, but neither man shrank back from what he perceived to be a genuine aspect of his vocation. At the same time, both of them staunchly maintained that such involvement was not merely compatible with the meditative component of their lives but was actually *part* of it. Commenting on the Buddhist sutra, "The Setting-up of Mindfulness," Rahula wrote: "The ways of 'meditation' given in this discourse are not cut off from life, nor do they avoid life; on the contrary, they are all connected with our life, our daily activities, our sorrows and joys, our words and thoughts, our moral and intellectual occupations."[28] Merton would have agreed entirely with this statement, for as he wrote in *Thoughts in Solitude*, "If you want to have a spiritual life you must unify your life. A life is either all spiritual or not spiritual at all."[29] This is also evident in the way he wrote about meditation in his book *Contemplative Prayer*. Merton here goes back to some of the earliest authors of Christian monasticism to illustrate what he means. He writes in particular and at some length about St. Columba, the Irish monk who settled on the island of Iona in the sixth century and, in a poem attributed to him, describes how all of his day's activities form one organic whole, with no separation between holy and profane, sacred and secular:

> That I might bless the Lord
> Who conserves all—
> Heaven with its countless bright orders,
> Land, strand and flood,
> That I might search the books all,
> That would be good for any soul;
> At times kneeling to beloved Heaven,
> At times psalm-singing;
> At times contemplating the King of Heaven,
> Holy the Chief;
> At times at work without compulsion,
> This would be delightful;
> At times picking kelp from the rocks,
> At times fishing,
> At times giving food to the poor,
> At times in a carcair [solitary cell].[30]

For all that we would like to know more about the conversations that Merton had with Phra Khantipalo, Nyanaponika Mahathera, and Walpola Rahula, we could safely say that all four of these monks would have seen something of themselves in those lines from the early Celtic monk. Merton's understanding of the Gospel's "one thing necessary" could not be expressed in the same terms as the three Buddhists' focus on Ultimate Reality in and beyond the multiplicity of ever-changing phenomena, but all four of these monks sought, with varying degrees of consistency, to unify their own lives and, in so doing, to be of compassionate and loving service to others. Each of them continues to be an inspiration to people today.

NOTES

1. Patrick Hart, "Thomas Merton and Interreligious Dialogue," *Bulletin of Monastic Interreligious Dialogue*, Spring 2005, http://www.monasticdialog.org/Bulletins.

2. Sylvia Boorstein, "A Messsage for Everyone," in Donald W. Mitchell, *Buddhism: Introducing the Buddhist Experience* (New York and Oxford: Oxford University Press, 2002), 77.

3. Huston Smith, *The World's Religions* (San Francisco: Harper, 1991), 127.

4. All nine points can be found in Walpola Rahula, *The Heritage of the Bhikkhu* (New York: Grove Press, 1974), 137-38.

5. Shanta Ratnayaka, "Zen Is the Theravada Branch of Buddhism in Mahayana Countries," in *Buddhist Studies in Honour of Walpola Rahula*, ed. Somaratna Balasooriya et al. (London: Gordon Fraser; Sri Lanka: Vimamsa, 1980), 223-33.

6. This information about Phra Khantipalo is taken from Alois Payer, *Materialien zum Neobuddhismus,* Kapitel 14.B (www.payer.de/neobuddhismus/neobuddh14121.gif), accessed on February 4, 2005.

7. Bhikkhu Khantipalo, "On Mindfulness," in Thomas Merton, *The Asian Journal*, ed. Naomi Burton et al. (New York: New Directions, 1975), 298.

8. Ibid., 299.

9. Merton to Erich Fromm, 7 Feb. 1966, quoted by William H. Shannon, *Thomas Merton's Dark Path: The Inner Experience of a Contemplative* (New York: Farrar Straus Giroux, 1981), 212, footnote.

10. Merton, "A Letter on the Contemplative Life," in idem, *The Monastic Journey*, ed. Br. Patrick Hart (Garden City, N.Y.: Doubleday Image Books, 1978), 220.

11. Nyanaponika Thera, *The Heart of Buddhist Meditation: A Handbook of Mental Training Based on the Buddha's Way of Mindfulness* (New York: Samuel Weiser, 1973). This was also published in a slightly different version in German.

12. Merton, *The Asian Journal* (see note 7 above), 186, note 89.

13. The details about Ven. Nyanaponika's life in this paragraph are drawn from Bhikkhu Bodhi, *Nyanaponika: A Hundred Years from Birth*

(Kandy, Sri Lanka: Buddhist Publication Society, 2001), and from the Buddhist Publication Society's obituary notice, published on the Internet (www.buddhanet.net/filelib/therabud/memoriam.txt) and accessed on December 31, 2004.

14. Merton, *The Asian Journal*, 218. The same material can be found in *The Other Side of the Mountain: The End of the Journey*, ed. Patrick Hart, O.C.S.O., vol. 7 of *The Journals of Thomas Merton* (San Francisco: Harper, 1998), 309-10.

15. Bhikkhu Khantipalo, "On Mindfulness," 304.

16. Nyanaponika Thera, *The Heart of Buddhist Meditation*, 7. Subsequent references to this book will be given in parentheses in the text.

17. Ven. Walpola Piyananda, "Remembering Ven. Dr. Walpola Rahula," www.angelfire.com/realm/bodhisattva/rahula.html, viewed January 6, 2005. The other biographical information about Walpola Rahula was drawn from Udaya Mallawarachchi, "Walpola Rahula: A Brief Biographical Sketch," in *Buddhist Studies in Honour of Walpola Rahula* (see note 5 above), vii-x, and from E.F.C. Ludowyk, "Thinking of Rahula," ibid., 133-38.

18. Merton, *The Asian Journal*, 235.

19. Ibid., 230.

20. Walpola Rahula, *What the Buddha Taught*, rev. ed. (New York: Grove Press, 1974), 69. Subsequent references to this book will be given in parentheses in the text.

21. Merton, *New Seeds of Contemplation* (New York: New Directions, 1961), 34-35.

22. Merton, *Faith and Violence* (Notre Dame, Ind.: Univ. of Notre Dame Press, 1984), 112.

23. Merton, *The Hidden Ground of Love: The Letters of Thomas Merton on Religious Experience and Social Concerns*, ed. William H. Shannon (New York: Farrar Straus Giroux, 1985), 63.

24. Nyanaponika Thera, *The Heart of Buddhist Meditation*, 39.

25. Lawrence S. Cunningham, *Thomas Merton and the Monastic Vision* (Grand Rapids, Mich.: Eerdmans, 1999), 139-40.

26. Merton, *Learning to Love: Exploring Solitude and Freedom*, ed. Christine M. Bochen, vol. 6 of *The Journals of Thomas Merton* (San Francisco: Harper, 1997), 156.

27. Nyanaponika Thera, *The Heart of Buddhist Meditation*, 39-40.

28. Rahula, *What the Buddha Taught*, 69.

29. Merton, *Thoughts in Solitude* (New York: Farrar, Straus & Cudahy, 1958), 56.

30. Quoted by Merton, *Contemplative Prayer* (Garden City, N.Y.: Doubleday Image Books, 1971), 32.

THE LIBERTY THAT NOBODY CAN TOUCH: THOMAS MERTON MEETS TIBETAN BUDDHISM

Judith Simmer-Brown

When Thomas Merton began his Asian pilgrimage on October 15, 1968, he wrote that he was "coming home" to a place he had never been, and he rejoiced at "being at last on my true way after years of waiting and wondering and fooling around."[1] His journey was to be a pilgrimage—he chafed at mere tourism, or meeting political leaders, bureaucrats, and patrons. His real passion was to meet the meditation masters and yogis about whom he had heard so much, and to learn from them the oral traditions of meditation practice, what he called "the great affair," as well as finding the "great compassion, *mahakaruna*." (4)

As he arrived in India, he found himself especially attracted to the Tibetans he met, saying "they have a peculiar intentness, energy, silence, and humor. Their laughter is wonderful." (65) Previously he had thought that he might investigate Hinduism, but as his journey evolved, he found Tibetan Buddhism the source of spiritual enrichment he sought.

> It does seem that the Tibetan Buddhists are the only ones who, at present, have a really large number of people who have attained to extraordinary heights in meditation and contemplation. This does not exclude Zen. But I do feel very much at home with the Tibetans, even though much that appears in books about them seems bizarre if not sinister. (82)

It is not surprising that Merton's meeting with Tibetan Buddhism came so late in his life. Prior to the 1959 Tibetan diaspora that was spurred by Chinese oppression, little of substance was known in the west about Tibetan Buddhism. Certainly a few western scholars had done their best to understand the tradition, and it is clear that Merton had done his homework as best he could. Before departing for his Asian pilgrimage, Merton was already reading the available western sources on Tibetan Buddhism: the realization songs of the saint Milarepa, Guiseppe Tucci's work on Tibetan sacred art, and Desjardins' introduction.[2] During his journey he also read T.R.V. Murti's book on Madhyamaka philosophy, and Conze's survey of Indian Buddhism, quoting liberally in his Journal as he read. It was clear that he also loved Shantideva's *Entering the Path of the Bodhisattva* (*Bodhicaryavatara*) written by the 8th century Indian saint, one of the most influential practice texts in all Tibetan Buddhism.

The eighth century Indian saint, Shantideva.

By the mid-1960s, Tibet began to emerge from obscurity as lamas and *tulkus* or "incarnate teachers"[3] emerged from refugee camps to found monasteries, *gompas* or temples, and meditation centers. By 1968, several tulkus had already left India to study and teach in the west. One of the earliest was Deshung Rinpoche, a Sakya[4] lama who in the mid-1960s taught in Seattle with Turrell Wylie at the University of Washington. (Fields 288-289) Merton had corresponded with Deshung Rinpoche through his star student, E. Gene Smith, and Deshung Rinpoche had sent Merton a copy of Gampopa's 12th century classic outline of the bodhisattva path, the *Jewel Ornament of Liberation* (*Tharpa Rinpoche'i-gyen*),

based on Shantideva's classic. In India, Merton was to meet Gene
Smith in Delhi at a dinner at the Canadian Embassy with High
Commissioner James George. Smith had just begun his job with
the Library of Congress in the Delhi office that was to place him as
the curator of Tibetan texts as they emerged in India.

Previously, Merton's interests had been in Zen Buddhism, but
after meeting Tibetans in India he felt an immediate rapport. His
traveling companion Harold Talbott remembered that Merton observed that meeting Tibetans was "heart to heart" rather than "mind
to mind." (Thurston) Very quickly, Merton became especially interested in the formless, advanced meditation traditions of Tibet,
especially Dzogchen.[5] Dzogchen (*dzogpa chenpo*, or *maha-ati*—
"great completion") is sometimes associated with the culmination
of the intricate nine-leveled path of the Nyingma "ancient ones"
school. (Ray 103-129) But more accurately, it is based on the single,
simple point—the direct realization of the naturally abiding enlightenment within one's own experience. This fundamental experience of limitless freedom, clarity, and openness is at the heart
of who we are, and Dzogchen practice merely uncovers this experience. The practitioner "descends from above" with the view—
fruitional, lofty and very simple, summed up in one phrase—"All
things are emptiness." If we realize this, truly, in our moment-to-
moment experience, that is all. It is said not to depend upon study,
reflection, or virtuous conduct. Yet the conduct of Dzogchen "as-
cends from below" with humility, building a foundation for uncov-
ering and realizing this lofty view. The conduct includes foundational practices, meditation retreats, and the practice of discipline.

The Dzogchen tradition has characteristic features. First, it re-
lies on a personal, doubtless and intimate relationship with a qualified teacher, a master who has deep experience in this kind of meditation. Devotion to the teacher and the lineage opens the gates of
the practice, and so the relationship must be one-to-one, not through
books or merely casual contact. Second, Dzogchen practice requires extended and profound resting of the mind in its empty nature, without concepts, words, or movement. It is important not to
fabricate anything, and to rest in naturalness, letting awareness be
completely naked. Then it is possible to experience the true nature
of the mind. For this reason, Dzogchen places strong emphasis
upon solitary retreat. Lastly, Dzogchen is primarily about overcoming any and all bias, especially the bias toward concepts, con-

fusion, and our personal neurosis. Its simplicity is uncompromising and vast, where bias has no capacity to dwell.

Dzogchen is truly simple, too simple for beginners or even experienced meditators. Such simplicity is different from our habitual patterns of conceptual spinning, and requires preparatory training. This means that Dzogchen practitioners usually have extensive background in study of sutra and tantra texts, ritual practice, insight meditation, and service to the teacher. This kind of preparation takes years, and if it works the practitioner develops an open, penetrating mind and heart. Additionally, these practitioners develop conviction in their own awakened nature. Then they may begin the practice of Dzogchen.

The lineages of Dzogchen masters also have their own special qualities.[6] Many of these masters are not monks, but are eremitic meditators—yogis or yoginis—who practice in retreat. They may have consorts or spouses who are co-practitioners with them in Dzogchen meditation; in fact, aspects of the practice are more accessible if one has a mate. These adepts have overcome emotional difficulties and personal obstacles on their paths while engaging in long and arduous silent retreats lasting even decades. Sometimes they face severe illness or meditative illusions that might have undone them if it had not been for the stability of their practice. The great adepts are those who succeeded in their practice, able to manifest tremendous power, formidable confidence, and sometimes-outrageous directness in their beings. It is common for the Tibetan practitioner to unreasonably fear the Dzogchen adept even while feeling irresistible attraction to his or her nonconceptual naturalness and visionary power.

Such realized beings are the rare exception in Tibet, but Merton had the good fortune to meet several of them. In fact, the list of teachers he met served as a kind of "who's who" of Dzogchen masters then in exile in India. And his Dzogchen journey had many of the classic features found in the hagiographies (*namthar*, literally "liberation stories") of the tradition. First he met a guru who pointed out the prerequisite for the view of Dzogchen, the change of motivation that entails the renunciation of "spiritual materialism." Then he met two gurus who discussed the importance of the teacher and the essential nonconceptuality of Dzogchen. Next, he received basic Tibetan Buddhist meditation instruction from His Holiness the Dalai Lama. He met the guru who he felt would be his Dzogchen teacher and investigated the parameters of retreat. And then he went on a short retreat to reflect on his Asian pilgrimage, and to ask the question, should I practice Dzogchen? These stages will form the structure of the sections to follow.

CHOGYAM TRUNGPA, RINPOCHE: UNDERSTANDING SPIRITUAL MATERIALISM

The only Tibetan tulku who was to speak English is the one with whom Merton had the strongest rapport, Chogyam Trungpa, Rinpoche (1940-1987). Trungpa Rinpoche was the youngest tulku with whom Merton spoke, and the only one to have had experience living in the west. Rinpoche was a tulku of the Kagyu school, and before fleeing Tibet in 1959 he was the supreme abbot of Surmang Monastery in Kham in east Tibet. His line of tulkus is associated with both the Mahamudra and Dzogchen lineages of meditation practice. His root teacher was Jamgon Kongtrul of Shechen monastery, but he was also the heart-son of Khenpo Gangshar Wangpo, a Dzogchen master known for his manifestation of the "crazy wisdom" (*yeshe cholwa*) style of unconventional behavior and direct, spontaneous transmissions. Apparently, Khenpo Gangshar was a very learned, traditional master until a serious illness in his late

20s brought him close to death for an extended time. When he miraculously recovered, he underwent a complete transformation, manifesting in the direct, penetrating and outrageous way that spread his fame as a "crazy wisdom" master. It was during this time that Trungpa Rinpoche was his student. Rinpoche and Khenpo Gangshar became separated during the escape from Tibet, and it is unknown what happened to his teacher. Shechen Kongtrul died in Chinese prisons in Tibet.

After Trungpa Rinpoche successfully escaped from Tibet, he was appointed by His Holiness the Dalai Lama as spiritual advisor to the Young Lamas' Home School in Delhi in 1959. In 1963, Trungpa Rinpoche received a Spalding sponsorship to attend Oxford University, where he studied comparative religion, philosophy, history, and fine arts. A Belgian Jesuit named Father DeGives was assigned as Rinpoche's tutor in Bible and western religion. As a result of DeGives' influence, Rinpoche regularly participated in inter-religious dialogues in Britain, and he enjoyed contacts with priests, imams, rabbis, and pandits he met in those years. (Simmer-Brown 2004) By 1966 he had published his first English book, *Born in Tibet*, describing his training in Tibet and his escape with a large group of followers in 1959. In 1967, he co-founded a Samye Ling Meditation Center in Dumfriesshire, Scotland, where he was based at the time he met Father Merton.

On October 19, 1968, Rinpoche and Merton met "quite by chance" at the Central Hotel in Calcutta on the very day Merton arrived in India. In spite of the thirty-five year difference in their ages, they instantly recognized each other as spiritual confreres. During the next several days they dined together, talked, and went on excursions for the Divali holiday. In his journals Merton commented,

> the important thing is that we are people who have been waiting to meet for a long time. Chogyam Trungpa is a completely marvelous person. Young, natural, without front or artifice, deep, awake, wise. I am sure we will be seeing a lot more of each other, whether around northern India and Sikkim or in Scotland, where I am now determined to go to see his Tibetan monastery if I can…. The newsletter he puts out is good. His own meditations and talks, from what I have seen, are extraordinary. (30)

Rinpoche had a similar rapport with Merton. In the 1971 edition of his autobiography, he wrote,

> Father Merton himself was an open, unguarded, and deep person. During these few days, we spent much time together and grew to like one another immensely. He proposed that we should collaborate on a book bringing together sacred writings of the Catholic and Vajrayana Buddhist traditions. (*Collected Works I*, 263)

In another reflection, Rinpoche commented, "Meeting Thomas Merton was wonderful; he was like a child, and at the same time, he was full of energy and life." (Trungpa 1980, 33) Still later, Rinpoche was to conclude, "I had the feeling that I was meeting an old friend, a genuine friend…. [Father Merton] was the first genuine person I met from the West." (*Collected Works III*, 477)

Their friendship involved deep conversations that were significant to them both. Over many gin and tonics and dinner at the Central, Merton and Trungpa Rinpoche shared their disheartenment about the state of spirituality in their respective traditions. Merton commented, "He has the same problems we have with 'progressive' monks whose idea of modernization is to go noncontemplative, to be 'productive' and academic." (31) Rinpoche described the conversations in this way: Father Merton "was in Calcutta attending some kind of collective religious conference, and he was appalled at the cheapness of the spiritual values that various of the conference participants were advocating." (Collected Works I, 263) And later, Rinpoche explained, "He was invited by a group that had a philosophy of spiritual shopping, and he was the only person who felt that it was full of confusion. He felt there was a sense of ignorance there, but nonetheless he joined them." (*Collected Works III*, 477)

Trungpa Rinpoche's meeting with Merton happened at a crucial time in his own life. He was twenty-eight years old, and had been a Tibetan Buddhist monk in Britain for five years. He had become increasingly discouraged and depressed by the prevalence of what he called "materialism" in the west. Materialism, a gloss of the Tibetan word *lalo* that means "barbarian," was the term Rinpoche used for the unquestioning pursuit of wealth that deepens, rather than alleviates, our suffering. In traditional Tibet, material greed for its own sake was deemed as pointless as hoarding wood for one's own cremation, or as bees that gather honey, only to have it taken away. (Cabezon 10) These observations were shared by other Tibetan teachers in exile.

But Rinpoche's concerns were much deeper.[7] He saw that materialism had manifested not only as accumulation of personal wealth, but also infected more subtle levels of experience, and that it was a phenomenon of his own culture as well. Later he commented, "materialism and technological outlook no longer come from the West alone; they seem to be universal. The Japanese make the best cameras; it's a universal situation. Indians make atomic bombs. We are talking in terms of materialism and spirituality in the world at large." (Trungpa 1975, 2) His deepest concerns were focused on what he called "spiritual materialism," in which spiritual practice or life is used to promote and confirm personal status, reputation, and identity. He saw this also at work in his own lost homeland, where the living practice traditions were being lost in monasteries and mountain retreats. During recent centuries, monks performed rituals for patronage, empowerments were collected like souvenirs, and sectarian rivalry flourished. Genuine practitioners were becoming as rare as stars at noontime. How could rampant greed be overcome if it corrupted the very spiritual traditions that could provide a remedy to this suffering? How could he teach the genuine dharma in Asia or the west in this corrupt atmosphere? These were the concerns that he and Merton shared.

Rinpoche was in Calcutta with his English attendant Kunga Dawa (Richard Arthure) having just come from a visit to the kingdom of Bhutan, hosted by the Queen. There he had completed a powerful month-long retreat in a celebrated cave near the city of Paro. This cave was called Taktsang, or "tiger's nest," and is known for its close association with Padmasambhava, Tibet's "precious guru" (Guru Rinpoche), who had transmitted the secret Vajrayana teachings to Tibet in the 8th century. Rinpoche showed Merton a photograph of the cave, revealing a lovely tiered temple perched on a narrow ledge on a vertical and sheer cliff face hundreds of feet above the valley floor. He recommended it to Merton as a good place for retreat. (31)

The Taktsang retreat had been a turning point for Rinpoche. He had gone into retreat troubled by spiritual materialism, and hoped for inspiration about how best to teach and alleviate suffering.[8] For the first several weeks nothing seemed to be happening, and

Rinpoche fell into a depression. Then, near the end of the retreat, potent new inspiration appeared in the form of a *sadhana* text that arose in his mind as *terma*, or "discovered treasure." (Ray 2000, 113-117) The terma tradition, inaugurated by Guru Rinpoche, introduces in prophetic form new perspectives and teachings fresh from the heart of the lineages of enlightened gurus. They are received in visionary form by the *terton* (treasure discoverer) while in meditative state. Taktsang had been a renowned *terma* site, and for Rinpoche, this new *sadhana* provided impetus for overcoming materialism in meditation and life. Quickly he recorded the text in Tibetan, and creatively translated it into English with the help of Richard Arthure. While *sadhanas* are usually restricted texts, given only to properly initiated disciples, Rinpoche insisted at the outset that it be shared widely. When he and Merton met in Calcutta, he gave him a copy of the *sadhana*, signifying their close connection on these vitally important spiritual issues.[9]

The Sadhana of Mahamudra is known as a ritual practice that completely joins the visions of the Mahamudra and Dzogchen lineages, invoking the wrathful form of Guru Rinpoche, Dorje Trollo, as both a father of our enlightened minds and protector against the lords of materialism.[10] It suggests that the degradation of spirituality has enraged his enlightened lineages, and that they are prepared to come to the aid of the authentic practitioner. The ultimate protection provided by this lineage is the recognition of the true nature of our obstacles—they have no more ultimate reality than the "imprint of a bird in the sky." The degraded forces at work in the world and in our spirituality dissolve when we see the true nature of the mind, which is the realm of the Mahamudra and Dzogchen forefathers, vast and luminous emptiness. Access to this realm is found through renunciation and devotion, merging our minds with the guru. Then spirituality recovers its vitality, openness, and joy.

The sadhana has become a favorite practice by Trungpa Rinpoche's students in the decades since 1968, and is practiced on the new-moon and full-moon days every month. It is also practiced by Buddhists of other teachers and traditions, and by non-Buddhists, for Rinpoche felt that it provided the necessary impetus to counteract the powerful forces of materialism. The opening of the sadhana speaks of signs of the degradation of spirituality in Buddhist terms, calling it the "dark age" in which "sectarian bitterness," "intellectual speculations," the loss of insight meditation, and "performing little ceremonies for material gain" are primary symptoms. (*Collected Works V*, 303) It laments that "the Buddha's teaching is used merely for political purposes and to draw people together socially"; because of this, "the blessings of spiritual energy are being lost." The *sadhana* was written to "enable individuals to ask for the help [of the buddhas of the three times and the great teachers] and to renew spiritual strength." The *sadhana* introduces the practitioner to the antidote to spiritual materialism, a genuine spirituality that awakens the naked and luminous mind.

While Merton did not mention the *sadhana* in the published version of his journals, it is clear that the content of their conversations set the tone for his Indian pilgrimage. He was skeptical about political or bureaucratic situations in his travels, and several times mentioned his desire to inquire about spirituality rather than politics. His passion for Dzogchen indicated the directness and purity of his spiritual interests, and the conversations he recorded detailed these interests. In his November circular to his colleagues, Merton wrote,

> I can say that so far my contacts with Asian monks have been very fruitful and rewarding. We seem to understand one another very well indeed. I have been dealing with Buddhists mostly, and I find that the Tibetans above all are very alive and also generally well-trained. They are wonderful people.... But they are also specialists in meditation and contemplation. This is what appeals to me most. It is invaluable to have direct contact with people who have really put in a lifetime of hard work in training their minds and liberating themselves from passion and illusion. I do not say they are all saints, but certainly they are men of unusual quality and depth, very warm and wonderful people. (324)

Merton continued to speak fondly of Trungpa Rinpoche in the months to follow. They met again, briefly, a month later in Calcutta at a garden party at the Canadian High Commissioner's home.[11] He remembered Rinpoche in his November circular, in which he referred to him as "interesting," "successful," and "talented." On the morning of his death, in his paper on Marxism and monasticism to the Bangkok conference, Merton spoke enthusiastically of

Trungpa Rinpoche, referring to him as "a good friend of mine—a very interesting person indeed," and he expressed his desire to visit him later in Scotland. (337-338) Elsewhere in the paper, he drew from Rinpoche's advice, "From now on, everybody stands on his own feet"(338), as a key to monastic life in the contemporary age.

As for Trungpa Rinpoche, after receiving the Sadhana at Taktsang, his profile as a dharma teacher underwent a complete transformation, following the example of his outrageous Dzogchen teacher, Khenpo Gangshar. Upon returning to Scotland, he gave up his monastic robes and married a young Englishwoman, Diana Pybus. Together they left the Scottish retreat center, Samye Ling, and immigrated to North America. His teachings became fresh and direct, pointing to meditative experience and realization, and his methods were often experimental and daring. In North America, he exhibited charisma and immediacy that both attracted and frightened the hippie generation he encountered there. His English vernacular improved quickly, and within a few years he was traveling widely in the United States, drawing large crowds in every venue. These radical changes were shocking and unsettling to his students in the United Kingdom, but Rinpoche felt that the dharma must be transmitted without the cultural trappings and spiritual exoticism employed by many in the "spiritual supermarket" of the 1970s. When Rinpoche founded Naropa Institute (now University) in 1974, he was to establish a series of Buddhist-Christian dialogues on meditation practice in Merton's name, remembering the significance of those conversations. (Simmer-Brown 2005; 2005)

Trungpa Rinpoche became the pioneer in bringing Tibetan Buddhism to the West, and in his short life accomplished a great deal. He founded a network of meditation centers under the banner of Shambhala that extends throughout North America, Europe, South America, and Japan. He founded a university in Boulder, Colorado, the largest fully accredited "Buddhist-inspired" university outside of Asia. He authored thirty-five books that have brought countless western students to the dharma. After a long illness,Trungpa Rinpoche died in 1987 at the age of forty-seven at his home in Halifax, Nova Scotia.

KHAMTRUL RINPOCHE AND CHOKLING RINPOCHE:
THE NEED FOR A GURU

Later in Dharamsala, Merton was to meet Sonam Kazi, who served as official interpreter assigned to the Dalai Lama by the government of India. Kazi had interpreted for high-profile talks between His Holiness and Nehru, Chou En Lai, and other political leaders. Merton's meeting him was significant, because Kazi was a Sikkimese lay adept in the Nyingma tantra, especially the Dzogchen tradition of meditation. While Kazi was not then a teacher, his descriptions ignited Merton's curiosity about the living and vital meditative traditions of Tibet. When Kazi suggested that Merton seek a Tibetan guru in the tantric lineage of "direct realization and dzogchen," asking if he "were willing to risk it," Merton responded, "why not?"(82) In the weeks to follow he eagerly read Tucci's writings on the *mandala* principle (the Tibetan "sacred systems" theory), and recorded questions about the "child mind" discovered through meditation. He reflected also on the significance of his dreams, and on Kazi's opinions about mixing traditions, world-evasion followed by some Buddhist schools, and the meaning of vows.

It is important to remember that throughout his journey Merton had to rely on whatever interpreters were available in his conversations, and those interpreters may or may not have been familiar with the meditation practices about which Merton was inquiring. It was fortunate that Sonam Kazi served as his translator in Dharamsala, with the exception of his meetings with His Holiness, because of Kazi's meditation experience. While Merton's other translators were likely not experienced in meditation, certainly his later translated meetings with His Holiness the Dalai Lama, Chadral Rinpoche and Kalu Rinpoche would have included profound communications having little to do with words, as each was a celebrated adept who radiated directly the peace and diamond-like clarity of the mind.

Kazi aided in Merton's meetings with Dzogchen meditation masters near Dharamsala. Khamtrul Rinpoche Dongyu Nyima (1930-1980) was a Drukpa Kagyu master, the 8th in his line of tulkus, who was the traditional head of the eastern Tibetan branch of his lineage. One of his renowned teachers was the great Dilgo Khyentse Tashi Paljor (1910-1990) of Shechen Monastery, with whom he

Karlu Rinpoche

studied Dzogchen meditation. In 1958, Khamtrul Rinpoche received early indication of the disaster brewing in Tibet, and approached Trungpa Rinpoche, asking him to flee India with him. When Trungpa Rinpoche demurred, Khamtrul departed with a group of followers and a caravan of sacred items and texts. He was one of the only lamas to successfully leave Tibet with the precious texts and relics of his lineage. (Trungpa 1966, 138-9) In India he moved from one refugee camp to another, looking for an auspicious place to begin again. In 1969, shortly after meeting Merton, he was to establish an exile community and Khampagar monastery in Tashi Jong ("auspicious valley"), one of the earliest Kagyu centers outside of Tibet. He served as powerful teacher, monk, leader, and guide for Tibetan lay people, *togdens* or lay yogis, and monastics. As a Dzogchen master, he served as root guru to the well-known contemporary master, Ven. Tsoknyi Rinpoche, the son of the great Kyabje Tulku Ugyen Rinpoche of Nagi Gompa, on the rim of the Kathmandu Valley in Nepal.

Khamtrul Rinpoche

Khamtrul Rinpoche was known as a very traditional, penetrating meditation teacher. Popularly known in the West as the root guru of the English nun, Tenzin Palmo, who did nine years of retreat in a "cave in the snow," Khamtrul Rinpoche was described this way in her accounts of that time.[12]

He was a tall man, heavily built, but like many big people he was surprisingly light on his feet. He was an excellent 'lama dancer' and a very accomplished painter as well. Quite famous among his own people. He was also a poet and a grammarian. His presence was also very big but he was extremely sweet and gentle, with a very soft little voice. I was terrified of him. It's interesting that one felt this kind of awe. He was considered to be one of the fierce forms of Guru Rinpoche…, and sometimes people would see him in that form. So I guess that's what it was. On the outside he was very sweet but you sensed this great force that was inside him. (47)

When Khamtrul Rinpoche met Merton, they sat on the ground amid young tea plants and pines in a place with a fine view of the mountains, near Dharamsala. Merton wrote of their conversation:

Khamtrul Rinpoche spoke about the need for a guru and direct experience rather than book knowledge; about the union of study and meditation. We discussed the "direct realization" method…. And about the need of a guru. "And," he asked, "have you come to write a strange book about us? What are your motives?" (89)

This kind of questioning is quite traditional in the yogic schools of Tibetan meditation. Khamtrul wanted to know, why was Merton investigating meditation? He had authored many books, and a Tibetan meditation teacher like him would not consider "research" a sufficient motivation to warrant sharing the precious oral instructions. Khamtrul Rinpoche was serving as a protector of the esoteric teachings with this line of questioning. Rinpoche was to die a decade later of diabetes at the age of forty-nine, leaving a large and prosperous community in Himachal Pradesh, near Dharamsala.[13]

A few days later, Merton met with yet another Dzogchen teacher, the Nyingma lama Chokling Rinpoche.[14] The 3rd Neten Chokling Pema Gyurme (1928-1974) was a disciple of the great Dzogchen master Dzongzar Khyentse Chokyi Lodro of Dzongzar monastery in Tibet. After escaping from Tibet in 1959, he established a monastery in northern India, in Bir near Dharamsala. As a young man, he was a fully ordained monk, but for most of his adult life he was a yogi married to a famous yogini. Several of their children are Nyingma tulkus, each Dzogchen adepts in their own right.[15] At the age of forty-seven he had an automobile accident on the road from Delhi and died instantly from a skull fracture, six years after his meeting with Merton.[16]

Harold Talbott described Chokling Rinpoche as "a way-out yogi, a very wild man who was an incredible kick-over-the-traces, irresponsible-type person, a tremendous troublemaker, and extremely rollicking in an unpredictable way, a top-flight, wonderful Nyingmapa yogi."(18)   In another Tibetan refugee camp on a tea plantation, Chokling Rinpoche asked Merton whether he believed in reincarnation before he would answer any questions about enlightenment. When Merton demurred, Chokling Rinpoche refused to give him the teachings on enlightenment he requested. Still, he did provide Merton with guidance for the next step of his journey.

> Like everyone else, he spoke of masters, and the need of finding one, and how one finds one—of being drawn to him supernaturally, sometimes with instant recognition. He asked me a koanlike question about the origin of the mind. I could not answer it directly but apparently my nonanswer was "right," and he said I would profit by "meeting some of the tulkus that are in India." Sonam Kazi said, "You have passed the first test," and he seemed pleased. (97)

This was the ideal next step in Merton's journey, to be tested directly about his experience of the nature of the mind. Now he was being taken seriously as an earnest pilgrim. But he must find a teacher if he would like to continue on the journey. Neten Chokling Rinpoche's testing and interrogation of Merton was excellent preparation for his later meeting with Chadral Rinpoche.

MEETING THE DALAI LAMA: LEARNING TO MEDITATE

Next, Merton was formally introduced to Tibetan Buddhist meditation. This occurred in Dharamsala as part of his official meetings with His Holiness[17] the Dalai Lama and officials from the Tibetan government in exile. When Merton arrived in India, he was steadfastly opposed to meeting with His Holiness, saying "I'm not going. I've seen enough pontiffs."(Tworkov 31) Given his years dealing with authority and obedience in the Trappist order,

Merton "didn't trust organized religion and he didn't trust the big banana," remembers Talbott. "He did not come to India to hang around the power-elite of an exiled central Asian Vatican." (Tworkov 17) But, with Talbott's encouragement, Merton agreed to meet with His Holiness and a few top officials of the government in exile.

His first practical conversations on meditation in Dharamsala did not impress him. He met with Rato Rinpoche, a Gelukpa lama who was head of the Ministry of Religious Affairs for the Tibetan government in exile. Oddly enough, this meeting did not make the published version of Merton's journal. By Talbott's account, Rato Rinpoche spoke of calm abiding (*shamatha, shi-ne*) meditation, commenting especially on the phenomenon experienced by beginners of the constant presence of the "watcher." Merton seemed unimpressed by this teaching, telling Talbott, "We know that already, and we don't want the watcher to watch it, so that's of no use to us. So let's see what *is* useful around here." (Tworkov 17) The fact that Merton already understood this phenomenon indicates his familiarity with the fundamentals of meditation that must be traversed before genuine and profound practice can begin.[18]

He was not to receive actual Tibetan Buddhist meditation instruction until the second meeting with His Holiness. Little did he know of His Holiness' vast experience and training in the esoteric schools of Tibetan Buddhist meditation, especially Dzogchen. The Gelukpa school, of which the Dalai Lamas are the principal lamas, has not historically emphasized Dzogchen training. But, even before his escape from Tibet, His Holiness had received transmissions of Mahamudra and Dzogchen practice, and in India he continued to study with one of the most important masters of the twentieth century, Kyabje Dilgo Khyentse Rinpoche, who became one of his main teachers. The Dalai Lama has become a Dzogchen teacher in his own right. (Dalai Lama 2000) Additionally, Dzogchen perspective has introduced an ecumenical sensibility that has served His Holiness well in exile, where broad, unbiased training of this kind has helped ameliorate the sectarianism that had become rife in Tibet.[19] His Holiness was uniquely qualified to introduce Merton to this meditation.

Merton's meetings with His Holiness were a delightful surprise, as was immediately evidenced when they met. Here he had met a "pontiff" who was accessible, frank, and deeply interested in meditation. He wrote:

> The Dalai Lama is most impressive as a person. He is strong and alert, bigger than I expected.... A very solid, energetic, generous, and warm person, very capably trying to handle enormous problems—none of which he mentioned directly. There was not a word of politics. The whole conversation was about religion and philosophy and especially ways of meditation. (101)

Years later, in his autobiography, His Holiness remembered vividly Merton's striking appearance in white robe and black scapular and wide, rough leather belt.

> But more striking than his outward appearance, which was memorable in itself, was the inner life that he manifested. I could see he was a truly humble and deeply spiritual man. This was the first time that I had been struck by such a feeling of spirituality in anyone who professed Christianity. Since then, I have come across others with similar qualities, but it was Merton who introduced me to the real meaning of the word 'Christian.' (Dalai Lama 1991, 189)

Immediately upon meeting His Holiness, Merton made it clear that his interest was Dzogchen meditation. The Dalai Lama responded with traditional, appropriate concerns. Merton wrote, "It is important, the Dalai Lama said, not to misunderstand the simplicity of dzogchen, or to imagine it is 'easy,' or that one can evade the difficulties of the ascent by taking this 'direct path.'" (102) His Holiness was deeply concerned that Merton establish a good grounding in Buddhist metaphysics first, especially from the Madhyamaka "middle way" school that serves as the sutra foundation of the practice.

In the second meeting, His Holiness moved right to the point, appropriate for a meditation teacher: he spoke of the mind. Here is one of the most striking scenes of Merton's Asian journey. His Holiness actually sat down on the floor and taught meditation in the customary way a student is instructed. Merton wrote, "he demonstrated the sitting position for meditation which he said was essential. In the Tibetan meditation posture the right hand (discipline) is above the left (wisdom). In Zen it is the other way around."

The Dalai Lama emphasized taking the mind itself as a meditation object.... Then we got on to 'concentrating on the mind.' Other objects of concentration may be an object, an image, a name. But how does one concentrate on the mind itself? There is division: the I who concentrates...the mind as object of concentration ...observing the concentration...all three one mind.

Thomas Merton, *The Asian Journal of Thomas Merton*

Dzogchen—"great completion"…is based on the single, simple point—the direct realization of the naturally abiding enlightenment within one's own experience. This fundamental experience of limitless freedom, clarity, and openness is at the heart of who we are, and Dzogchen practice merely uncovers this experience.

Judith Simmer-Brown

(112) This is where all Tibetan meditation begins, emphasizing correct posture. Talbott remembered, "he showed Merton the lotus meditation posture and the hand position and the posture of the back." (Tworkov 19) Later His Holiness expressed surprise about what he learned from Merton about Christian meditation.

> He told me a number of things that surprised me, notably that Christian practitioners of meditation do not adopt any particular physical position when they meditate. According to my understanding, position and even breathing are vital components to its practice. (Dalai Lama 1991, 189)

It is particularly striking that His Holiness sat on the floor, for as Talbott observed, in Tibet such an act would be unthinkable. Dalai Lamas are expected always to remain physically above others, seated on a throne.

After an introduction to meditation posture, His Holiness moved into the appropriate object of focus in meditation. Here we see his responsiveness to Merton's interest in Dzogchen practice, for he emphasized taking the mind itself as a meditation object. This kind of focus is not the customary one for a beginning student, who starts with emphasis on mindfulness of breathing, or of a visual object such as a stone. Another customary object of meditation is a guiding dharmic phrase or sentence, that forms a foundation for the practitioner to more deeply understand its meaning. It is customary to introduce the mind as object only after years of preliminary practice with more accessible objects.

> Then we got on to "concentrating on the mind." Other objects of concentration may be an object, an image, a name. But how does one concentrate on the mind itself? There is division: the I who concentrates…the mind as object of concentration…observing the concentration…all three one mind. He was very existential, I think, about the mind as "what is concentrated on." It was a very lively conversation and I think we all enjoyed it. He certainly seemed to. (112-113)

It is difficult to get a full flavor of what His Holiness taught Merton about the mind, especially as the journal notes the difficulties of the translator, Tenzin Geche,[20] who was likely inexperienced in this kind of meditation instruction. Talbott remembers:

And he gave us very, very clear, sound meditation instructions that would be completely familiar to vipassana practitioners. He was leading up to teachings on emptiness and compassion and then went on to a gentle explanation of tantra as a field of Mahayana Buddhism that is a very, very strong practice throughout history. And then at some point he gave a summation of the schema of Nyingmapa Buddhism starting with some Theravada teachings. (Tworkov 19)

Most likely, the instruction was very introductory, with simplicity and sophistication, designed to give Merton a place to begin in his practice. No doubt the powerful atmosphere of sitting with His Holiness introduced more than words could express. As the journal concludes the description—"at the end he invited us back again Friday to talk about Western monasticism. 'And meanwhile think more about the mind,' he said as we left him." (113) In his November Circular, Merton wrote of their meetings,

We spoke almost entirely about the life of meditation, about samadhi (concentration), which is the first stage of meditative discipline and where one systematically clarifies and recollects the mind. The Tibetans have a very acute, subtle, and scientific knowledge of "the mind" and are still experimenting with meditation.... The highest mysticism is in some ways quite "simple"—but always and everywhere the Dalai Lama kept insisting on the fact that one could not attain anything in the spiritual life without total dedication, continued effort, experienced guidance, real discipline, and the combination of wisdom and method (which is stressed by Tibetan mysticism). (322)

While Merton greatly enjoyed his meetings with His Holiness, his interests continued to be in the areas of meditation and the yogic path. Talbott remembers Merton encouraging him to leave Dharamsala to seek a meditation teacher:

What the Tibetan tradition has to offer us is dzogchen and that's where it's at and the sooner you get out of the Himalayan Vatican the better. If you want to spend the rest of your life being trained to be a curial diplomat and reading

sutras and tantras for the next forty years before you even
get to start really practicing shamata [sic] go right ahead
and stay in Dharamsala. But if you want to know where
it's at, find a dzogchen yogi. (Tworkov 18)

KYABJE CHADRAL RINPOCHE: MEETING THE GURU

Shortly after his meetings with His Holiness the Dalai Lama, Merton
continued his pilgrimage with a visit to Darjeeling, a hill station in
northeast India where he planned a short retreat. Nawang Jinpa
Rinpoche, a young Gelukpa tulku educated and ordained in Lhasa,
served as his translator for this portion of his journey. (135, 181)
On a daytrip near Ghoom, Merton sought out Chadral Rinpoche, a
renowned Dzogchen teacher who had a small hermitage there. This
November 16, 1968, meeting was significant, for Merton was to
declare that this would be his Dzogchen guru.

Kyabje Chadral Sangye Dorje Rinpoche (1913-) is one of the
last great living masters of Dzogchen trained in Tibet, a holder of
the "heart essence" tradition of Longchenpa (*Longchen Nyinthik*).
Chadral Rinpoche grew up in a nomadic family in the Nyak-rong
province of Kham in east Tibet and soon migrated to Amdo in the
northeast with his tribal group. At fifteen, he abandoned his family to dedicate his life to dharma practice, giving up riding and
traveling only on foot. His root Dzogchen teachers were all renowned masters: Kathok Khenpo Ngawang Palzang (1879-1941),
Dzongzar Khyentse Chokyi Lodro (1893-1959), and Kyabje
Dudjom Rinpoche (1904-1987). (Thondup 196-297) He has spent

Merton and Chadral Rinpoche, 1968.

his entire life in retreats, caves, or hermitages, avoiding householder life; thus, he earned his name *chadral* that means a practitioner who abandons ordinary activities and conventional life. He has always avoided the spotlight, choosing retreat and solitude as his lifestyle. Rinpoche is not a monk, but practices as a tantric yogi, and he and his consort Kamala have two daughters.

Upon leaving Tibet, Rinpoche was the first Tibetan lama to build a three-year retreat (*druppa*) center near Ghoom; at the time of his auspicious meeting with Merton eight hermits had just completed a three-year retreat, with eight more just beginning. After seeking him there, Merton was to meet him at the nearby nunnery, supervising the painting of a fresco in the oratory.

> Chatral[sic] looked like a vigorous old peasant in a Bhutanese jacket tied at the neck with thongs and a red woolen cap on his head. He had a week's growth of beard, bright, eyes, a strong voice, and was very articulate, much more communicative than I expected. We had a fine talk and all through it Jimpa, the interpreter, laughed and said several times, "these are hermit questions…this is another hermit question." [21] (143)

While Merton did not note anything threatening, Harold Talbott described Chadral Rinpoche as a true Dzogchen master.

> I wouldn't dream of studying with him, or anybody remotely like him, because he is totally and completely unpredictable. He is savage about the ego and he will put you on the spot and I am not prepared to up the ante to that degree…. That [was] an opportunity for me to hide behind Merton's skirts and also meet Chadral Rinpoche who I'm terrified of. He could throw stones at you—as he does do—and so I [would] use Merton as a front. (Tworkov 21)

Merton immediately found Chadral Rinpoche magnetic, "the greatest rinpoche I have met so far and a very impressive person."(143) For two hours, they spoke about Dzogchen, "the ultimate emptiness, the unity of shunyata and karuna, going 'beyond the dharmakaya' and 'beyond God' to the ultimate perfect emptiness." (143) Their rapport was strong, as can be seen from Merton's description.

The unspoken or half-spoken message of the talk was our complete understanding of each other as people who were somehow on the edge of great realization and knew it and were trying, somehow or other, to go out and get lost in it—and that was a grace for us to meet one another. (143)

Chadral had questions about Christianity, wondering how a religion could be based on a man who comes back to life after death, and Merton explained the resurrection in a kind of tantric terminology, "about the overcoming of fear and the utter and complete power of liberation which is the center of Christianity."(Tworkov 22) This satisfied Rinpoche, who was surprised at getting on so well with a Christian. He called Merton a *rangjung sangye* or "naturally arisen Buddha," a Dzogchen compliment indicating natural realization.

It is clear from Merton's and Talbott's comments that this communication was extraordinary. Chadral Rinpoche spoke to Merton with a rare collegiality. Earlier Rinpoche commented that he had meditated in solitude for thirty years or more and had not attained to perfect emptiness—and Merton said he hadn't either. Later Rinpoche commented that perhaps both of them would "attain to complete Buddhahood in their next lives, perhaps even in this life, and the parting note was a kind of compact that we would both do our best to make it in this life."(144) Merton asked him to be his teacher, and Rinpoche outlined the required four preliminary practices of *ngondro*[22] for him, saying that he could do his retreat in a hermitage in Bhutan, continuing the theme begun with Trungpa Rinpoche in Calcutta. In his journal Merton wrote, "If I were going to settle down with a Tibetan guru, I think Chatral [sic] would be the one I'd choose. But I don't know yet if that is what I'll be able to do—or whether I need to." (144)

Chadral Rinpoche now practices in retreat at Parpheng on the edge of the Kathmandu Valley in Nepal. He has few students, but has a reputation for direct, uncompromising teaching, and for his emphasis on personal solitary retreat. His other famous passion is for saving the lives of animals. Annually he goes to the city of Calcutta and purchases animals destined for slaughter, and releases them. He collects donations for the entire year, and on a recent trip bought thousands of fish from the fishing fleet and released them back to the Indian Ocean. (Scales 65) In a sample teaching, he requested:

I passionately appeal to humanity at large, irrespective of nationality, caste, or religion to practice this most simple but profound virtue of compassionate love. We can praise and please our Lord Buddha in no better way than by doing all we can to save the lives of innocent, mute and defenceless animals and birds, fish and insects and thereby grant them the precious gift of life. Moral values abjure us from taking anything which we can not give to others. We can not give life to anybody; it is the sole discretion of the Lord. So it will be shameless arrogance and heinous sinfulness on our part if we snatch life from others. It is my firm belief that if people adopt this practice by universal consensus, everlasting peace and all round happiness will descend on this earth, and human suffering in all its forms will become a thing of the past.[23]

Later, before departing from India, Merton had an opportunity to learn more specifics about the three-year retreat from Kalu Rinpoche (whom Merton erroneously called "Karlu"), a renowned Shangpa Kagyu master who lived in Sonada. Kalu Rinpoche (1905-1989) was raised in east Tibet and trained as a monk at Palpung, a great center of the nonsectarian *Ri-me* (ree-may) movement, with the greatest teachers of his day. At age twenty-six, he embarked on a retreat of almost twenty years in the mountains of east Tibet, and became renowned as a genuine yogi, very popular among the local villagers. He became one of the major teachers at Palpung monastery, mentoring great meditation masters like the 16th Karmapa, always emphasizing personal retreat and direct realization of the nature of mind. When he escaped from Tibet in 1959, he became an early meditation teacher in North America, and established the first three-year retreat center for western students. Kalu Rinpoche died at Sonada in 1989 at the age of eighty-four. His successor was born in 1990 and was enthroned at Sonada in 1993. A vivacious young child, he is particularly fond of musical instruments.

Kalu Rinpoche established his first exile three-year retreat center in Sonada, near Darjeeling, and that was the center that Merton visited. Merton commented on Kalu Rinpoche's distinctive, birdlike appearance:

He is a small, thin man with a strange concavity in the temples as if his skull had been pressed in by huge thumbs.

> Soft-spoken like all of them, he kept fingering his rosary,
> and patiently answered my many questions on the hermit
> retreat. (164)

In the journal Merton recorded the details of the retreat and schedule. Candidates were screened by Rinpoche after their foundational training, examined "on their capacity to undertake the retreat and each case is decided on its own merits." (164) He described the progression of the *ngondro* (the foundational practice Chadral Rinpoche had asked him to complete) that begins the first segment of the retreat. *Ngondro* is followed by an initiation, and then the last two years are taken up with the Dzogchen practice itself.[24] The hermits see only their teacher—all practices are done in solitude. The hermit's day begins at 2 or 3 a.m.; tea is served at 5; the first meal is served at 11. It is clear that Merton was checking out the schedule in detail, including a question about whether firewood would be available. Kalu Rinpoche invited Merton to do his retreat there at Sonada, or to write later with his meditation questions. He also presented Merton with somewhat primitive hand-colored wood-block prints of Tibetan deities, which still hang in the Merton Library at Bellarmine University. In his journal, Merton concluded: "That was very kind of him. With my reaction to this climate at its best and the noise of the Indian radio in a cottage across the road from the hermitage, I guess it's still Alaska or California or Kentucky for me." (166) By this time he had decided that an Asian retreat may not have been the best idea. This conclusion probably came from his retreat in Darjeeling the week before.

KANCHENJUNGA: MERTON'S SEVENTH MOUNTAIN[25]

What would have happened if Merton had lived? Would he have returned to Bhutan to do retreat with Chadral Rinpoche? Would he have pursued his earlier plans to build a new hermitage in Alaska or California, or return to Gethsemani? Would he have built a western retreat center in New Mexico, based on the meeting of Tibetan Buddhism and Catholicism, as he discussed with Sonam Kazi?

There is no way of knowing exactly what might have happened to Merton if he had lived. But his retreat in Darjeeling gives clues about his digestion of the encounter with Tibetan Buddhism, especially Dzogchen. On November 17, shortly after his meeting with

In the clarity of limitless awareness, without conceptuality, the mountain shines beautifully as the inseparability of the observer and the observed, the glamour of things as they are (yatha-bhutam). She is, inseparably, SEEN.

Judith Simmer-Brown

The full beauty of the mountain is not seen until you too consent to the impossible paradox, it is and is not. When nothing more needs to be said, the smoke of ideas clears, the mountain is SEEN.

Thomas Merton, *The Asian Journal of Thomas Merton*

Chadral Rinpoche, Merton began a short personal retreat at the Mim Tea Estate in view of the majestic mountain Kanchenjunga.[26] The mountain came, in his journal entries, to symbolize that which he had sought on his Asian pilgrimage—its grandeur, its mystery, its tendency to recede into the distance when sought and to emerge in all its immensity and power when ignored. Five days earlier, upon entering Darjeeling, he was struck by its beauty. Within days he was entranced by it, finding its loveliness hard to capture in photographs. By the first day of his actual retreat, he was tired of Kanchenjunga, relieved that it was veiled by clouds. The next day, when acknowledging his annoyance with the mountain, "its big crude blush in the sunrise," he reflected on his entire Indian experience.

> Reassessment of this whole Indian experience in more critical terms. Too much movement. Too much "looking for" something: an answer, a vision, "something other." And this breeds illusion. Illusion that there *is* something else. Differentiation—the old splitting-up process that leads to mindlessness, instead of the mindfulness of seeing all-in-emptiness and not having to break it up against itself. Four legs good; two legs bad. (148)

While meeting all the Tibetan lamas had been so exhilarating and significant, what was the next step? Hermit in India or Bhutan? Gethsemani? Temporary or permanent? Merton also reflected on the "real" Asia—and in the context of the famous Madhyamaka "middle way philosophy" dialectic, he knew what kind of question that was. Was Asia an illusion? What was permanent?

> I want this all to be permanent. A permanent post card for meditation, daydreams. The landslides are ironic and silent comments on the apparent permanence, the "eternal snows" of solid Kanchenjunga.... Nothing is to be decided; nor is "Asia" to be put in some category or other. There is nothing to be judged. But it must be cold for the lamas, at night, in their high, draughty little gompas! (150-151)

The next night, still on retreat, Merton had a dream about Kanchenjunga that seemed to indicate a shift in his perspective. In the dream, a voice said, "There is another side to the mountain," and he saw the mountain rotated and now he was seeing it from its

Tibetan side. The other side was the one that had never been seen or photographed or turned into postcards. And Merton remarked, "That is the only side worth seeing." (153)

Several others have found this moment of Merton's Asian journey significant; for this author, its significance has to do with the fundamental teachings of Dzogchen. The true nature of reality cannot be touched by concept or anything voyeuristic. It cannot be seen conventionally or dualistically. The true nature of reality must be discovered within our experience, and we can never really know in advance what that discovery might yield. In his journal, Merton commented that we must step beyond the "picture postcard" way of seeing the mountain in order to see it at all. This means that we must "go to the other side." This is a fascinating image, very traditional as Merton would have known from his reading of Edward Conze's work on the *Prajna-paramita-sutras*. "Prajna-paramita" ("wisdom gone-beyond") refers to the direct, nonconceptual wisdom developed in meditation that "goes beyond" the limits of conceptuality. This is the kind of wisdom Dzogchen meditation cultivates. The Heart Sutra, the most famous of the Prajna-paramita texts, closes with the mantra recitation in Sanskrit: *Gate gate, paragate, parasamgate, bodhi, svaha!*—"gone, gone gone beyond, gone completely beyond, awake—wow!" This mantra expresses the true discoveries of Dzogchen meditation, the completely awake limitless and empty awareness that is our own Buddhahood.

Ironically, Kanchenjunga does have another mysterious and dangerous side. As a contemporary Darjeeling travel news site explains,

> Kanchenjunga is not a calm and serene mountain as it appears to be when viewed from Darjeeling. Both ice and rock avalanches of incredible dimensions frequently thunder as they roll down precipitous slopes of this mighty massif. Last but not the least is wind of hurricane force, one of the deadliest of Kanchenjunga's weapons which plays a havoc with any intruder who ventures "to walk the heights of gods."[27]

Probably Merton did not know this about the mountain. The "other side" that is not the "picture postcard" Kachenjunga was quite different from the one that Merton viewed from Darjeeling. Could he have envisioned this about Tibetan Buddhism? His beautiful introduction to the tradition might have been quite different once he actually began the pith practices. The serene beauty might have been replaced by the precipitous slopes, the hurricane force winds, and the avalanches of intensive practice that reveals the naked nature of reality. There is something in Merton that would have been attracted to the dangerous mystery of this. Perhaps that is the "other side" of which he spoke.

Merton's reflections on Kanchenjunga did not end with the "other side" dream. Later he developed a kind of devotion for her, and sang to her as "Tantric Mother Mountain" a free soliloquy, much as Buddhist adepts sang to the Prajna-paramita the Mother of Wisdom in 5th century India:

> Kanchenjunga this afternoon. The clouds of the morning parted slightly and the mountain, the massif of attendant peaks, put on a great, slow, silent dorje dance of snow and mist, light and shadow, surface and sinew, sudden cloud towers spiraling up out of icy holes, blue expanses of half-revealed rock, peaks appearing and disappearing with the top of Kanchenjunga remaining the visible and constant president over the whole slow show. It went on for hours....The full beauty of the mountain is not seen until you too consent to the impossible paradox: it is and is not. When nothing more needs to be said, the smoke of ideas clears, the mountain is SEEN. (155-157)

Here was another glimpse of her mystery. In her absolute nature, she does not independently, inherently exist. And yet she appears, as all phenomena appear when they are seen as without inherent existence. When we actually see the beauty of the world around us, the russet oak leaves, the glisten of dew on grass, the sudden blueness of the sky, there is no duality between seer and seen. In the clarity of limitless awareness, without conceptuality, the mountain shines beautifully as the inseparability of the observer and the observed, the glamour of things as they are (*yatha-bhutam*). She is, inseparably, SEEN.

As he closed his Mim retreat, Kanchenjunga receded into a cloudbank for over three days, and Merton got one final glimpse on the wild taxi-ride down the main road. "A last sight of Kanchenjunga, bright and clear in the morning sun, appearing over the hills of Ghoom…a surprise." (170)   Shortly later he left India for good.

There is another profound dimension to Merton's early Indian meetings with the Dzogchen teachers Khamtrul Rinpoche and Chokling Rinpoche that emerges once the sources are examined. Both of these great masters independently and unexpectedly presented an advanced meditation practice associated with dying and death to Merton. First, Khamtrul Rinpoche introduced Merton to the possibility of direct realization through *phowa*, or ejection of consciousness, at the moment of death. At that time, Merton noted in his journal that Khamtrul Rinpoche had taught "some curious stuff about working the soul of a dead man out of its body with complete liberation after death—through small holes in the skull or a place where the skin is blown off—weird!" (89) Several days later, Neten Chokling Rinpoche first asked him if he believed in reincarnation and then, without an explicit request, gave Merton actual *phowa* transmission. (Tworkov 19) That two powerful meditation masters, known for their yogic clairvoyance, chose to introduce Merton to an esoteric practice associated with realization of the ultimate nature at death was significant to Harold Talbott, who years later made this observation.

> The reason Chokling Rinpoche taught Merton phowa practice—say I—is that he saw that Merton was going to be dead in a couple of weeks. He needed the teachings on death. He did not need teachings of karma and suffering, calming the mind, insight meditation. He needed to be taught how to dispose his consciousness at the time of death because this was the time of death for him. And Merton scribbled in his journal: "I'm not sure about all this consciousness and shooting it out the top of the head. I'm not sure this is going to be very useful for us."[28] (Tworkov 19)

This view was confirmed by Chokling Rinpoche's son Dzigar Kongtrul Rinpoche, who commented about this transmission, "Maybe Rinpoche saw what was coming and gave the transmission to help him."[29]

Dzogchen teaches that there are special opportunities for direct realization at the time of death. Highly realized beings who have completely realized and accomplished their experience of the fundamental limitless awareness (*rikpa*) die naturally, without any concerns or conscious methods of meditation or instructions from teachers. Others who have practiced Dzogchen and have attained a high level of stability may practice at death, following specific instructions they have been given in how to die. One of these practices is called *phowa*, or ejection of consciousness. At a strategic moment, the practitioner visualizes his consciousness as a white syllable "*A*" (in Tibetan form) and ejects it through the central channel out to merge with the realized mind of the Buddha, symbolized as a purified awareness realm. In Tibet, such a practice was viewed as a "method of attaining enlightenment without a lifelong experience of meditation practice."[30] For the accomplished Dzogchen adept, this practice can be accomplished alone. For others, the presence of a qualified teacher at the moment of death is critical, even if one has received the transmission. It would be unusual for the transmission of this type of esoteric practice to be given to a non-Buddhist, especially one who did not directly request it.

A month later while Merton gazed at the magnificent huge sculptures of the peacefully dying, reclining Buddha at Polonnaruwa, one wonders at the power of his realization and premonition there:[31]

> Looking at these figures I was suddenly, almost forcibly, jerked clean out of the habitual, half-tied vision of things, and an inner clearness, clarity, as if exploding from the rocks themselves, became evident and obvious.... The thing about all this is that there is no puzzle, no problem, and really no "mystery." All problems are resolved and everything is clear, simply because what matters is clear. The rock, all matter, all life, is charged with dharmakaya...everything is emptiness and everything is compassion. I don't know when in my life I have ever had such a sense of beauty and spiritual validity running together in one aesthetic illumination (233-235).

The imagery in this observation is so full of Dzogchen themes— the sudden jerk out of habitual mind, the clarity and simplicity of the realization, the inseparability of compassion and emptiness.

Perhaps Merton had found what he was looking for, the great affair, the great compassion—perhaps this was his own "great completion" of this Asian journey and of his life. On the morning of Thomas Merton's tragic death in Bangkok in 1968, he presented a paper to a Bangkok conference of Cistercian monks. One of the most striking features of this presentation was the following statement—Tibetan Buddhism and Christianity share the view

> that if you once penetrate by detachment and purity of heart to the inner secret of the ground of your ordinary experience, you attain to a liberty that nobody can touch, that nobody can affect, that no political change of circumstances can do anything to…. [Behind these two traditions is] the belief that this kind of freedom and transcendence is somehow attainable. (342)

Several hours later, Merton died in the bathroom of his Bangkok hotel bungalow.

Among native Tibetan communities in India and the west it is often whispered that Merton has, of course, reincarnated as a Tibetan monk. He could never, in his previous life, have left his beloved order or tradition. His fidelity to his vows and his Trappist order was too strong. Yet, they say, he saw a vision of what he might do to continue his practice in the Dzogchen tradition. Some say they know he is at this monastery, or another, a promising monk practicing the essential teachings of the "great completion" tradition. Others say he is a yogi in solitary retreat in the caves of the Himalayas. Perhaps he is even on the lower slopes of Kanchenjunga, radiating the limitless vastness of pure awareness.

NOTES

1. This reference (4-5) and the others to follow from *The Asian Journal of Thomas Merton* are referenced only by page number from the 1968 edition.

2. It is not clear how Merton had obtained these two books by Tucci and Desjardins, as they were first published in 1969. He mentioned them frequently and included numerous quotes from them on his Asian journey, and so somehow he must have received advance copies.

3. The Tibetan tradition holds that highly realized teachers have the ability to consciously incarnate in an auspicious situation after death, continuing their spiritual journeys and their compassionate activity with-

out forgetting the accomplishments of their previous lives. These beings are called *tulkus* that literally means "incarnate Buddhas." *Tulkus* are commonly referred to as *rinpoche* which means "precious jewel," signifying their high status as teachers and guides on the spiritual path. Occasionally other great teachers who have developed realization in this life are also called "rinpoche"—so it is not a term applied only to *tulkus*. The measure of the value Tibetans have placed on *tulkus* can be found in how they responded to the Chinese occupation. While they systematically smuggled texts and sacred relics and ritual implements from the country into India, they especially insisted that the living holders of the oral instructions of meditation lineages be escorted out of the country, living treasures of Tibet.

4. Sakya is one of the four major schools of Tibetan Buddhism, along with Nyingma, Kagyu, and Gelukpa.

5. The other such tradition is closely related, coming from the Kagyu lineage as opposed to the Nyingma. It is called Mahamudra, or Chakchen, the "great seal." Its methods closely parallel the Dzogchen. Merton's interest in Dzogchen grew from the influences of the western scholar Gene Smith; Sonam Kazi, the lay Sikkimese practitioner who served as Merton's interpreter in the Dharamsala area; and Lopsang Lhalungpa, who was a Tibetan translator in Delhi. For further exploration of Dzogchen, see Ray 2001, pp. 294-325; for teachings from Dzogchen masters, see Schmidt 2002 and Schmidt 2004.

6. The lore concerning Dzogchen teachers is found in sacred biographies called *namthar*. For a classic collection of Dzogchen namthar, see Tulku Thondup.

7. The level of Trungpa Rinpoche's concern is evident from the title of his first popular book on meditation published in 1973, *Cutting Through Spiritual Materialism*, in which he describes the "three lords of materialism" with special emphasis upon spiritual materialism. This concern was to permeate all of his teachings, especially from the mid-1960s through the 1970s. See *Collected Works*, Vols. II and V.

8. Detailed descriptions of this retreat are given by Trungpa Rinpoche (1975) and by his attendant Richard Arthure (*Collected Works V*, pp. xxii-xxvii.) See also Midal, 18-24.

9. Personal communication, 2004, Richard Arthure. Also Trungpa, *Collected Works V*, pp. xxii-xxiii.

10. The subtitle of the sadhana liturgy expresses the full purpose of the text: "The Sadhana of Mahamudra Which Quells the Mighty Warring of the Three Lords of Materialism and Brings Realization of the Ocean of Siddhas of the Practice Lineage." Trungpa, *Collected Works V*, p. 303. An excerpt of the original translation of the Sadhana appears

here. For the joining of Mahamudra and Dzogchen, see "Joining Energy and Space," *Collected Works V*, pp. 310-314.

11. Merton 1968, p. 129. Trungpa Rinpoche was to remain close to James George, who helped him obtain a Canadian visa as he emigrated to first Canada and then the United States.

12. Mackenzie 1998. See chapter five for Tenzin Palmo's account of meeting her root teacher. She may very well have been serving as Khamtrul Rinpoche's secretary at the time of this meeting with Merton.

13. Mackenzie 1998, p. 104-5. Tenzin Palmo describes the death of her teacher, very suddenly, and the subsequent miracles associated with his death. These are consistent with Dzogchen teachings on death and dying. The 9th Khamtrul was born in 1981.

14. There are two incarnation lines of Chokling Rinpoches in the Nyingma tradition, both traced from Chogyur Lingpa, the great *terton* of the early part of the 18th century. The other Chokling is Tsikey Chokling, son of the great Tulku Ugyen, Rinpoche, the Dzogchen master of Nagi Gompa on the rim of the Kathmandu Valley. Tsikey Chokling is father of the *yangtsi* or reincarnated tulku of Dilgo Khyentse Rinpoche, who served as teacher of both Choklings.

15. Their children include Orgyen Tobgyal Rinpoche and Dzigar Kongtrul Rinpoche, both Dzogchen masters. Dzigar Kongtrul taught for many years at Naropa University in the Religious Studies department, and now heads Mangala Shri Bhuti, a network of meditation centers and two retreat centers in Vermont and in Crestone, in Southern Colorado, dedicated to the Longchen Nyingthik teachings.

16. Gyurme Dorje, the fourth Chokling of Neten, was born in Bhutan to a poor family, was discovered as the tulku, and taken to his monastery in Bir near Dharamsala at age seven. In addition to directing his monastery, he has co-directed a high-profile film, *Himalaya* (2000).

17. There is no Tibetan term that is translated as "His Holiness." From the impetus of Tibetan Buddhism in exile, this term used for the Catholic Pope was used for the heads of the four major schools of Tibetan Buddhism—and so from the 1960s, there were always four "His Holiness"—His Holiness Karmapa, Sakya Trinzin, Dudjom, and the Dalai Lama—they are all referred to in English as "His Holiness." The term in Tibetan is more often given Kyabje, which means "Lord of Refuge," which means the teacher has been recognized by his peers to embody all the qualities of enlightenment in his manifestation and his compassionate teaching. There is no legislative body that makes this decision. The term begins to be used over time, especially for the genuine elders of a tradition. So, you will notice, Kyabje is applied to several other teachers in this essay.

18. Talbott was shocked by Merton's response. At that point he was a beginner in Buddhist meditation himself, and he was surprised that Catholic contemplation had included such insight.

19. Dzogchen has been closely connected with the "non-sectarian" (Ri-me, "without bias" pronounced Ree-May) movement in Tibet that grew in strength and popularity in the 19th century. Ray 2000, 207-208; Simmer-Brown 2004.

20. Merton mistakenly spelled his name "Geshe"—but this was kindly corrected by Robert Thurman, who explained that this monk had not earned the "geshe" monastic degree.

21. Later in the Journal, Merton met Dr. Pemba, a medical doctor from Tibet, who also admired Chadral Rinpoche and commented that he wore "unconventional clothes" because he put all money he was given into the retreat center, nunnery, and temples around Ghoom. p. 162.

22. Ngondro, or foundation ritual practices, include the completion of prostrations and refuge; the 100-syllable purification mantra; the mandala offering; and the guru-yoga practice. Each practice requires 100,000 repetitions, and the last requires 1,000,000 repetitions. Doing this practice intensively on retreat may take five to eight months.

23. See www.purifymind.com/SaveBeings.htm.

24. Merton 1968, p. 66. Kalu's retreats would have emphasized Mahamudra practice instead, but this practice is so similar, especially at the beginning, that these distinctions were probably put aside in Rinpoche's descriptions.

25. This is what Kanchenjunga is called in Mott 1984, chapter 7.

26. Kanchenjunga (28,169 feet or 8598 m tall, the world's third highest mountain) was named from the Tibetan "kan-chen-dzo-nga" that literally means "five treasures of the great snow" as it has five peaks sacred to the peoples of the Himalayas. It is located on the border of Nepal and Sikkim, just 46 miles northwest of Darjeeling. The first non-Asian climbers to reach the summit were British, in 1955, and they did not mount the very top, out of respect for Sikkimese beliefs.

27. This quote is taken from a Darjeeling news site, www.darjeelingnews.net/kanchenjunga.html.

28. Talbott's comments are limited to the actions of Chokling Rinpoche, but Khamtrul Rinpoche also taught Merton *phowa*. Private communication, Harold Talbott.

29. Verbal communication, Dzigar Kongtrul Rinpoche, October 19, 2003, at Drupchu teaching.

30. Sogyal , p. 232. For more information on this practice and its Dzogchen context, see chapter fourteen of *The Tibetan Book of Living and Dying*.

31. Thurston. Talbott noted the powerful influence of the reclining Buddha on Merton, but observed that most likely Merton did not realize that this was Buddha on his deathbed.

WORKS CITED

Burton, Naomi, Brother Patrick Hart, and James Laughlin, ed. *The Asian Journal of Thomas Merton.* New York, N. Y.: New Directions, 1968.

Cabezon, Jose. "Singing Bowls and Power Beads: On the Commodification of Tibet." Unpublished paper for symposium, "Representing Tibet: A Symposium on the Representation of Tibetan Culture in the U.S." January 2000, University of Colorado, Boulder.

Chang, Garma. *The Hundred Thousand Songs of Milarepa.* Boulder, Co.: Shambhala Publications, 1977. Originally published by Oriental Studies Foundation, 1962.

Conze, Edward. *Buddhist Thought in India.* Ann Arbor: University of Michigan Press, 1967.

Dalai Lama. *Freedom in Exile: The Autobiography of the Dalai Lama.* San Francisco: Harper & Row, 1991.

Dalai Lama. *Dzogchen: The Heart Essence of Great Perfection.* Ithaca: Snow Lion, 2000.

Desjardins, Arnaud. *The Message of the Tibetans,* translated from the French by R. H. Ward and Vega Stewart. London: Stuart & Watkins, 1969.

Fields, Rick. *How the Swans Came to the Lake: A Narrative History of Buddhism in America.* Boulder: Shambhala Publications, 1981.

Mackenzie, Vicky. *Cave in the Snow: Tenzim Palmo's Quest for Enlightenment.* London: Bloomsbury Press, 1998.

Midal, Fabrice. *Trungpa, His Life and His Vision.* Boston: Shambhala Publications, 2004.

Mott, Michael. *The Seven Mountains of Thomas Merton.* New York: Houghton Mifflin, 1984.

Murti, T. R. V. *The Central Philosophy of Buddhism.* London: Allen & Unwin, 1960.

Ray, Reginald. *Indestructible Truth: The Living Spirituality of Tibetan Buddhism.* Boston: Shambhala Publications, 2000.

Ray, Reginald. *Secret of the Vajra World: The Tantric Buddhism of Tibet.* Boston: Shambhala Publications, 2002.

Scales, Sandra. *Sacred Voices of the Nyingma Masters.* Berkeley: Padma Publishing, 2004.

Schmidt, Marcia Binder, ed. *Dzogchen Essentials.* Hong Kong: Rangjung Yeshe, 2004.

Schmidt, Marcia Binder, ed. *The Dzogchen Primer.* Boston: Shambhala Publications, 2002.

Simmer-Brown, Judith. "Heart to Heart: Interreligious Dialogue," in Fabrice Midal, ed., *Recalling Chogyam Trungpa.* Boston: Shambhala Publications, 2005. Originally published as *Chögyam Trungpa: Pour chaque moment de la vie au éditions du Seuil.* Paris, 2004.

Simmer-Brown, Judith. "Preface to the Second Edition," in Susan Szpakowski, ed., *Speaking of Silence: Christians and Buddhists in Dialogue.* Halifax: Vajradhatu Publications, 2005, pp. 3-10.

Sogyal Rinpoche. *The Tibetan Book of Living and Dying.* San Francisco: HarperSanFrancisco, 1992.

Thondup, Tulku. *Masters of Meditation and Miracles: The Longchen Nyingthig Lineage of Tibetan Buddhism.* Boston: Shambhala Publications, 1996.

Thurston, Bonnie. "The (Almost) Final Days of Thomas Merton: A Conversation With Harold Talbott." Louisville, KY: Thomas Merton Center Foundation, 2000.

Trungpa, Chogyam. *Born in Tibet,* as told to Esme Cramer Roberts. London: Allen & Unwin,1966.

Trungpa, Chogyam. *The Sadhana of Mahamudra Sourcebook.* Boulder: Vajradhatu Publications, 1975.

Trungpa, Chogyam. Hinayana-Mahayana Seminary Transcripts, 1980. Boulder: Vajradhatu Publications, 1981.

Trungpa, Chogyam. *The Collected Works,* Vols. I-VIII. Edited by Carolyn Gimian. Boston: Shambhala Publications, 2003-4.

Tucci, Giuseppe. *The Theory and Practice of the Mandala.* New York, N. Y.: Samuel Weiser, 1969.

Tworkov, Helen. "The Jesus Lama: Thomas Merton in the Himalayas, An Interview with Harold Talbott," *Tricycle* (Summer 1992), 14-24.

HEARING THE CRIES
OF THE WORLD:
THOMAS MERTON'S
ZEN EXPERIENCE

Ruben L.F. Habito

John Wu, Jr. has noted, somewhat ironically, that "Merton seemed
to have become less Zen and more academic when he wrote seriously about the subject to D.T. Suzuki, my father (Dr. John C.H.
Wu), and others." (Wu Jr. 1996) Taking this cue, I would like to
focus my treatment not on Merton the intellectual and academic
who wrote about Zen based on the knowledge available at the time
from books of D.T. Suzuki and others, but on Merton the man who
in his own life and writings, singlemindedly pursued a vocation as
a Christian contemplative, yet who also engaged passionately in
the affairs of the world of his time. Our interest here is not "Merton
on Zen," but rather, "Zen on Merton."

The "Zen" I refer to here is primarily, though not exclusively,
the Zen as taught and practiced in the Sanbo Kyodan Lineage, which
incorporates elements from the Soto and Rinzai traditions of Japanese Zen. It is based on the practice guidelines set by Harada Daiun
Sogaku (1870-1961), transmitted to Yasutani Hakuun (1885-1973)
and Yamada Koun (1906-1989). The latter, who established a center of practice adjacent to his home in Kamakura, Japan, where he
led Zen practitioners for nearly three decades, authorized a number of Japanese and non-Japanese disciples who practiced under
his guidance for many years. These Zen heirs of Yamada now form
a worldwide living community of practitioners, with its mother
Zendo in Kamakura and with sister communities of practice in Asia,
Europe, and North America. In addition to these communities, Robert Aitken's Diamond Sangha lineage, and the Rochester Zen Center, established by the late Philip Kapleau (1912-2004), a longtime
student of Yasutani, with its affiliate centers led by Kapleau's students, offer Zen training in the Sanbo Kyodan tradition. The heirs

of the late Maezumi Taizan, who founded the White Plum lineage, also generally follow similar lines of teaching and practice. (See Maezumi and Glassman, eds. 2002.) As they guide their own communities of practice in different localities, teachers of these lineages join together with those of Soto, Rinzai, and Korean lineages of Zen in annual gatherings of the American Zen Teachers' Association (AZTA) for mutual encouragement and learning.

The book *Three Pillars of Zen,* which has found wide readership in the Western hemisphere, compiled, translated and edited with the cooperation of Yamada Koun and Philip Kapleau, presents the basic structure and offers vignettes of Zen practice in the Sanbo Kyodan style, though its living heirs have taken new strides in their Zen teaching and practice since the 1960s when *Three Pillars* was compiled. Other books are also now available describing Zen perspectives that come out of the matrix of Sanbo Kyodan. (Aitken 1982, 1984, 1990; Habito 2001, 2004; Maezumi and Glassman 2002; Yamada 2004)

In this essay, I will first outline key features of Zen practice, way of life and worldview as reflected in the Sanbo Kyodan tradition, but which may be recognized by practitioners and teachers of the various living Zen lineages as shared features in their own respective traditions as well. With this in the background, we will seek glimpses into Thomas Merton's inner world, and mark themes that possibly resonate with a Zen outlook. We will not rely so much on what Merton wrote about Zen as such in his well-known works, but rather pay closer attention to accounts of experiences and events in the various stages and contexts of his much celebrated life as he shared them with us through his journals and published writings.

WHAT IS ZEN?—THE FRUITS OF A ZEN LIFE

What is Zen?

Instead of a pat definition that may perhaps satisfy our inquisitive intellect and give it something to hold on to, but which would serve only to sidetrack us further from our subject matter, I offer a heuristic principle from the Christian New Testament as our starting point: "By their fruits ye shall know them." (Mt.7:16) Let us then look at the fruits of the Zen life, that is, those features that come to fruition in the life of one who engages in Zen practice, as a roundabout way of addressing our question, what is Zen?

As a person takes up this practice of sitting with a steady posture, facing a wall or in a direction with a line of sight that will not be distracting, breathing in a mindful way, and letting one's mind be focused in the here and now, there are things that come to fruition in one's awareness of oneself in relation to the world and which can begin to make their mark on one's life. This is so especially as a person takes this on as a regular form of practice, whether it be for ten minutes, twenty minutes, thirty, or more, in one's daily life.

One of the things that can happen as a person undertakes this practice and continues it on a regular basis is that the disparate elements in a person's life come to a greater sense of cohesion and unity. In other words, one may be able to see the varied dimensions of one's life in greater focus from the standpoint of an inner center. This is a fruit of practice that we can call "centering of one's being."

A more familiar term in this regard is "concentration," but this word in English has connotations that may be misleading for us. For example, the famous statue by Rodin, named "The Thinker," may be for many people a model of concentration, but this is not what we refer to in the context of Zen practice. If we hold on to the use of this word, which we can also find in many books as a standard translation for the Buddhist term in Sanskrit, *samadhi*, it might be helpful to render it with a hyphen between "con-" and "centration" (thus, *con-centration*) to bring home point, that is, of the process of things coming together in greater focus from a unified center of awareness.

Incidentally, the word in Sanskrit that expresses the impetus that led Siddhartha Gautama to leave his secure and affluent life for a life in search of inner peace, which opened the way for the experience of awakening that marked his becoming a Buddha, is *duhkha*. This term has also been enshrined as the first of the Four Ennobling Truths realized by the Buddha and said to have been preached by him soon after the event of awakening. Traditionally translated as "suffering," or "dissatisfactoriness," as well as "unease" or "dis-ease," the word *duhkha* comes from a compound that refers to an image of a wheel that is mal-aligned, a wheel that is not properly "centered" and is thereby "dysfunctional."

We take this etymological excursus to give us a better angle from which to understand the first fruit of Zen practice, that is, "the centering of one's being." In short, those who come to this practice may be motivated by different kinds of factors, but one key factor leading individuals to it is this sense of "dislocation" in one's life, a sense of inner unease, or "dis-ease," that "things are not quite all right" with oneself and with the world. Engaging in this practice of seated meditation, or *zazen,* not only helps one see things in better light, but also enables one to live one's life in a less disparate, scattered, disorganized way, as a person situates oneself closer, or comes home, to the center of one's being, and thereby overcomes the effects of *duhkha.*

As a person continues in this process of coming home to the center of one's being, giving oneself to the practice of seated meditation, and taking steps to cultivate a recollected mind throughout the day, there may occur an event that can stand out and become pivotal in a person's entire life journey. This may come in an unexpected moment, whereby one suddenly "sees" the world, oneself, everything, in a totally different light, from a totally different perspective than the conventional one of a subjective "I" looking out into the world as "out there." This is an event that in Zen is called "seeing into one's own true nature," which thereby turns a person into an awakened one, a Buddha. This is what we refer to as the second fruit of Zen practice.

This is an inner event that can mark a veritable turning point in the life of a person, and in some cases can be accompanied by an intense emotional outburst, with laughter, tears, convulsions, and so on. For others, it may be an unobtrusive, unemotional, externally unnoticeable, quiet event that is nonetheless revolutionary and life-changing. This kind of experience is to be distinguished from "insight" or "intellectual realization," as well as from emotional reactions or affective responses to such insights or to images, real or conjured. Insights and affective reactions may come in different ways to an individual, through reading, reflection, or quiet meditation on various facets of one's life or of reality, and may indeed inform and transform the way a person relates to oneself and to the world.

But there is a distinctive character in an awakening experience: this is not based on a conceptual grasp of reality, but is a recognizably palpable *event* that leaves its mark in the life of a person, one that occasions a shift in the fulcrum of one's being.

What does a person come to "see" or "realize" in this experience? Although the Zen tradition proclaims such an experience to be beyond words or concepts, in claiming that "it does not rely on words or letters," in the centuries of Zen tradition there is no dearth of letters, words, and concepts attempting to describe such an experience or its "contents," and volumes and volumes have been written in this attempt. Among the terms used in this regard are "Emptiness," "Absolute Nothingness," "the interconnectedness of all reality," and a host of others. Numerous books, including those written by D.T. Suzuki and others who followed him, have dealt with these kinds of experiences or events from different angles, exploring their psychological, philosophical, literary, artistic, and other implications. Such treatments have succeeded mainly in romanticizing or idealizing Zen, thereby causing the proliferation of misleading, or outright mistaken assumptions about it.

Some Zen lineages have developed, through centuries of tradition, systematic procedures for "checking" whether reported experiences or events are genuine or not. The Lin-chi or Rinzai lineage, from where the Sanbo Kyodan also in part derives its mode of training and procedure for checking, stands out in this regard. Other lineages, such as the Soto, do not "make a fuss about" nor monitor or accentuate such experiences or events as such, but focus on how one's Zen practice throws light on and transforms one's entire life.

This aspect, that is, how Zen practice throws light and transforms one's entire life, refers directly to the third fruit of Zen. This can be called "the embodiment of awakening in one's daily life." Whereas the second fruit can be realized in an instant, this third takes one whole lifetime for its fruition. It is also the most reliable checkpoint on whether what is claimed to be an awakening experience is a genuine one or not.

What are the features of this third fruit? An individual person who has been drawn to Zen by the experience of *duhkha*, or dissatisfaction, an existential awareness of one's dis-eased condition, of a state of separation, alienation, disparateness of one's being, experiences this third fruit as an overcoming of the sense of alienation and separation, and thereby as a "coming home." Upon coming home, a person finds all that one can ever really want or need, truly, and thereby discovers genuine inner satisfaction and inner peace. This is what is referred to by the phrase attributed to Master Lin-chi—"true person of no rank." Such a person lives in the ordinariness of daily life, eating when hungry, drinking when thirsty, going to work, getting tired, enjoying (or getting bored at) parties, washing the dishes, taking out the garbage, and so on. And in this ordinariness, one is fully at peace. At peace, indeed, but not smugly content.

Lohan, a realized Arhat.

In this place of peace, one is not thereby rendered passive and indifferent to the rest of the world. Rather, as the second fruit is an experience of emptying of one's self-centered delusions, an overcoming of the barrier that separates one's "self" from the "world," and an awakening to one's interconnectedness with all, one comes to realize that what the world is, is precisely what one is.

"We are the world; we are the children." This is the title of a song that evoked a deep chord worldwide in the 1980s, and was also used for various political ends at the time. This is also an expression that can emerge out of that place of "coming home" in the Zen context. A person finds one's home in this world, and yet in opening one's eyes, sees this world that is one's home in tatters. One comes to realize all the pains and sufferings, but also the hopes and joys, of everyone in the world, as one's very own pains and sufferings, hopes, and joys.

The third fruit of the Zen way of life then is a way of embodying this realization of oneness with all the pains and sufferings of one's fellow sentient beings in this world, in a life of com-passion. Here is another word that is more effectively rendered with a hyphen after "com-." The English usage of the word "compassion" often is no different from "pity" or "commiseration" or the etymologically parallel term "sympathy," emotional responses to situations of misfortune or tragedy in others. This is not what we are referring to in the context of the third fruit of Zen. Placing a hyphen after "com-" calls our attention to its more fundamental sense, of "suffering-with. "

The realization of this dimension of one's own being, that is, the dimension of com-passion, awakens and draws one out of indifference, smugness, or perhaps a sense of privilege, tempting one to say for example, that "fortunately I am not like those others." It also draws one from a sense of powerlessness, that overwhelming feeling that the problems of the world and the sufferings of people are so enormous that any efforts on one's part are bound to be futile, and therefore be tempted to passive resignation or worse, despair. The com-passion that is part of the third fruit of Zen rather becomes a source of empowerment, enabling one to give all that one has and all that one is, in the capacity that one is able, in the particular way one is given within one's life circumstances, toward the alleviation of the world's pain, toward the healing of the Earth's wounds.

A point to note here is that these three fruits of Zen practice are not necessarily manifested in linear succession, or appear in chronological order, but are to be seen as intertwined elements that reinforce one another in the life of a practitioner in an ever deepening spiral movement to one's center, a center that is dynamic and always shifting, yet also intimately accessible as one's mind settles in stillness and silence.

In sum, the Zen way of life can be described as a life of awakening to the dynamic reality of the present moment. It is a life that opens one to the fullness of what it is to be human, with the pathos and the glory, the complexity and the simplicity and all else that this implies.

MERTON'S PATH:
FROM CHAOS TO CONTEMPLATION TO COMPASSION

The Seven Storey Mountain is a delightfully moving account of a spiritual pilgrimage whereby the writer is led, through different twists and turns of circumstance, from a state of inner chaos, toward a life of contemplative silence. Referring to his student days at Columbia, Merton writes:

> Now my life was dominated by something I had never really known before: fear. Was this something altogether new? No, for fear is inseparable from pride and lust....
>
> ...I had at last become a true child of the modern world, completely tangled up in petty and useless concerns with myself, and almost incapable of even considering or understanding anything that was really important to my own true interests.
>
> ...I...walked out into the world that I thought I was going to ransack and rob of all its pleasures and satisfactions. I had done what I intended, and now I found that it was I who was emptied and robbed and gutted. What a strange thing! In filling myself, I had emptied myself. In grasping things, I lost everything. In devouring pleasures and joys, I had found distress and anguish and fear....
>
> I...was bleeding to death. If my nature had been more stubborn in clinging to the pleasures that disgusted me: if I had refused to admit that I was beaten by this futile search for satisfaction where it could not be found, and if my moral and nervous constitution had not caved in under the weight of my own emptiness, who can tell what would eventually have happened to me? Who could tell where I would have ended?
>
> I had come very far, to find myself in this blind alley: but the very anguish and helplessness of my position was something to which I rapidly succumbed. And it was my defeat that was to be the occasion of my rescue. (SSM 163-165)

The inner vacuity, the distress and anguish and fear that Merton describes, needless to say, is an all-too-common experience of so many of us who, seeking true happiness, pursue it in all the wrong places and end up in its opposite. This acknowledgment of one's own helplessness, of defeat, is a turning point in the pilgrimage, the very "occasion of my rescue." In Buddhist terms, experiencing *duhkha,* recognizing it, accepting it, one is launched into the path of awakening. From this point on, the path is an ascent to truth, and *Seven Storey Mountain* concludes where Merton's life of solitude and contemplation begins, as he is admitted to the Cistercian monastery of Our Lady of Gethsemani near Louisville, Kentucky, on December 10, 1941.

> Now my sorrow is over, and my joy is about to begin: the joy that rejoices in the deepest sorrows. For I am beginning to understand. You have taught me and have consoled me, and I have begun again to hope and learn.
>   I hear you saying to me:
>   *I will give you what you desire. I will lead you into solitude. I will lead you by the way that you cannot possibly understand, because I want it to be the quickest way.*
> (SSM 421-22)

Having come to the stark realization that the true happiness he was desperately seeking with his entire being was not to be found in the pursuit of worldly gains and pleasures, Merton is led to a renunciation of such a world, and enters the realm of contemplative silence.

There is an anecdote, recorded as Case No. 7 in the collection known as the *Gateless Gate (Wumen-kuan),* that comes to mind.

> A monk asked Joshu in all earnestness. "I have just entered the monastery. I beg you, Master, please give me instructions."
> Joshu asked: "Have you eaten your rice gruel yet?"
> The monk answered, "Yes, I have."
> Joshu said, "Then wash your bowls." (GG 40)

Merton's earnestness is evident to anyone who peruses his journals. His entries during the monastic years from 1941 up to 1960 (ES; SS) attest to his total dedication to this vocation to silence and solitude. It is in the midst of this silence that a seeker on the ascent

Our Lady of Gethsemani, Trappist, Kentucky. Monastery (above)
and Merton's hermitage (below).

In short, as one finds true peace, one no longer feels any need to seek anything of worldly gain or honor or glory. If there is anything one glories or finds joy in, it is the very matter-of-fact events of everyday life, in their ordinariness: "of trees that say nothing, of birds that sing, of a field in which nothing ever happens (except that a fox comes and plays, or a deer passes by)."

Thomas Merton, *Learning to Love*

The Christ we seek *is* within us, in our inmost self, is our inmost self, and yet infinitely transcends ourselves.

From Thomas Merton's letters to D.T. Suzuki, 1959, *Encounter*

to truth can arrive at one's center. It is here where he receives tastes of his "rice gruel," spiritual nourishment that gives true inner satisfaction. After many years of living the monastic life himself, Merton is able to write the following advice to those who seek a life of contemplation.

> The first thing that you have to do, before you even start thinking about such a thing as contemplation, is to try to recover your basic natural unity, to reintegrate your compartmentalized being into a coordinated and simple whole and learn to live as a unified human person. This means that you have to bring back together the fragments of your distracted existence so that when you say "I," there is really someone present to support the pronoun you have uttered. (IE 3-4)

This comment of Merton's brings to mind another anecdote from the *Gateless Gate*. This is entitled "Joshu examines the hermits," Case No. 11.

> Joshu went to a hermit hut and asked, "Anybody in? Anybody in?"
> The hermit thrust up his fist.
> Joshu said, "The water is too shallow for a ship to anchor." Thereupon he left.
> Again he went to a hermit's hut and asked, "Anybody in? Anybody in?" The hermit too, thrust up his fist.
> Joshu said, "Freely you give, freely you take away. Freely you kill, freely you give life." He made a profound bow. (GG 59)

It is only as one arrives at the center of one's being, and is able to utter "I" with the fullness of responsibility (response-ability), in being totally "present" in each here and now, that one can cast that "I" into the fiery altar of sacrifice and be able to celebrate its dissolution, its "emptying." Emptying oneself of this "I," one is able to wash one's bowls in unrestricted freedom, as one discovers a divine fullness in the everyday tasks of life.

Merton continued to feast on his "rice gruel," and continued to drink from the fountains of divine presence in silence and solitude in the context of the regulated life of a Cistercian monk. And then, seventeen or so years into this life, something happens to him during a visit to the city. This interior event was to mark another turning point in his journey. In an entry in his personal journal dated March 19, 1958, Thomas Merton wrote the following lines.

> Yesterday, at Louisville, at the corner of Fourth and Walnut, suddenly realized that I loved all the people, and that none of them were or could be totally alien to me. As if waking up from a dream—the dream of my separateness, of the "special" vocation to be different. My vocation does not really make me different from the rest of men, or put me in a special category except artificially, juridically. I am still a member of the human race, and what more glorious destiny is there for man, since the Word was made flesh and became, too a member of the Human Race!
>
> Thank God! Thank God! I am only another member of the human race, like all the rest of them. I have the immense joy of being a man! As if the sorrows of our condition could really matter, once we begin to realize who and what we are—as if we could ever begin to realize it on earth....
>
> God is seen and reveals himself as a *man,* that is, in us, and there is no other hope of finding wisdom than in God-manhood: our own manhood transformed in God! (IM 124)

Readers of Merton will note that he has presented another account of this same experience in *Conjectures of a Guilty Bystander*, published in 1966, with additional descriptive and reflective comments (CGB 140-42). Having written how "I was suddenly overwhelmed with the realization that I loved all those people," he adds:

> ...that they were mine and I theirs, that we could not be alien to one another even though we were total strangers. It was like waking from a dream of separateness, of spurious self-isolation in a special world, the world of renunciation and supposed holiness. The whole illusion of a separate holy existence is a dream. Not that I question the reality of my vocation, or of my monastic life: but the conception of "separation from the world" that we have in the monastery too easily presents itself as a complete illusion: the illusion that by making vows we become a different

species of being, pseudo-angels, "spiritual men," men of interior life, what have you.

Certainly those traditional values are very real, but their reality is not of an order outside everyday existence in a contingent world, nor does it entitle one to despise the secular, though "out of the world." We are in the same world as everybody else, the world of the bomb, the world of race hatred, the world of technology, the world of mass media, big business, revolution, and all the rest....

...This sense of liberation from an illusory difference was such a relief and such a joy to me that I almost laughed out loud.... To think that for sixteen or seventeen years I have been taking seriously this pure illusion that is implicit in so much of our monastic thinking. (CGB 140-142)

In this later, revised account, Merton has been able to reflect on further implications of that "event" that may have lasted for no longer than a fleeting moment. The affirmation that "all these things" in the world, which he thought he had renounced when he entered the monastic life, also *belong to God* was a radical rediscovery of a dimension he may have known all along and accepted on a conceptual level, but only now came to fully appreciate and realize experientially.

The lines toward the end of *Seven Storey Mountain* come up once more.

> *I will give you what you desire. I will lead you into solitude. I will lead you by the way that you cannot possibly understand, because I want it to be the quickest way.* (SSM 421-22)

The quickest way it may indeed be, but it took Merton all of sixteen or seventeen years to arrive, ending up at the very place where he started and knowing the place for the first time. (With apologies to T.S. Eliot.)

This new realization does not thereby lead Merton to abandon or doubt his own vocation to silence and solitude. Rather, it enables him to affirm:

> My solitude, however, is not my own, for now I see how much it belongs to them—and that I have a responsibility

for it in their regard, not just in my own. It is because I am
one with them that I owe it to them to be alone, and when
I am alone they are not "they" but my own self. There are
no strangers! (CG 142)

Followers of Thomas Merton's life journey will readily note that
from around this time on, the focus of his life and the tone of his
writings take on new directions, opening to wider horizons and
interests. The editors of his journals have given apt expression to
this new focus, in the titles of the fifth and sixth volumes, covering
the years 1960 to 1965: *Turning Toward the World,* and *Dancing in
the Water of Life.*

Another striking way of describing Merton's inner life from
this point on is in the title of another collection, that of his social
essays, edited and introduced by William Shannon: *Passion for
Peace* (Crossroad, 1996). In these essays we read Merton no longer
as the sensitive and artistic young man seeking interior peace from
the chaos of a worldly life, inviting others to solitude and silence
(though he never ceased doing the latter). We now encounter Merton
the citizen of the world, who, on behalf of all his fellow human
beings, is indignant at and protests the folly and stupidity of those
whose minds are caught in the stereotypes received from tradition,
from mass media, as well as from prejudice and ignorance.

The passionate conviction that permeates these essays, de-
nouncing war, exposing racial prejudice, espousing non-violence,
appealing to all peoples, especially the political, economic, civic,
and religious leaders, comes from the heart of a citizen of the world,
a human being whose heartbeat throbs with each and every fellow
human caught in the whirlpool of a violent and chaotic world. The
following is from "The Root of War is Fear," a piece he sent to
Dorothy Day, and published in *The Catholic Worker* in September
of 1961.

The present war crisis is something we have made entirely
for and by ourselves. There is in reality not the slightest
logical reason for war, and yet the whole world is plunging headlong into frightful destruction, and doing so *with
the purpose of avoiding war and preserving peace!* (Italics Merton's) This is a true war-madness, an illness of the
mind and the spirit that is spreading with a furious and

subtle contagion all over the world. Of all the countries that are sick, America is perhaps the most grievously afflicted....

The root of all war is fear, not so much the fear men (and women) have of one another as the fear they have of *everything*. It is not merely that they do not trust one another; they do not even trust themselves....

...For only love—which means humility—can exorcise the fear which is at the root of all war. (PP 11-19)

The following is from an essay entitled "Christian Action in a World Crisis," which appeared in *Blackfriars,* a journal published by Dominicans in Oxford, England, in June 1962.

Two things are clear, first the enemy is not just one side or the other. The enemy is not just Russia, or China, or Communism, or Castro, or Krushchev, or capitalism, or imperialism. The enemy is both sides. The enemy is in all of us. The enemy is war itself, and the root of war is hatred, fear, selfishness, lust....

As long as we arm only against Russia, we are fighting for the real enemy and against ourselves. We are fighting to release the monster in our own soul, which will destroy the world. We are fighting for the demon who strives to reassert his power over (hu)mankind. We have got to arm not against Russia but against war. Not only against war, but against hatred. Against lies. Against injustice. Against greed. Against every manifestation of those things, wherever they may be found, and above all in ourselves....

We cannot pretend to have a full understanding of what is going on in ourselves and in our society. That is why our desperate hunger for clear and definite solutions sometimes leads us into temptation. We oversimplify. We seek the cause of evil and find it here or there in a particular nation, class, race, ideology, system. And we discharge upon this scapegoat all the virulent force of our hatred, compounded with fear and anguish, striving to rid ourselves of fear by destroying the object we have arbitrarily singled out as the embodiment of all evil. Far from curing us, this is only another paroxysm which aggravates our sickness. (PP 80-91)

"The enemy is us." This well-cited dictum, attributed to the cartoon character Pogo, was Merton's. He perceives world events not, as it were, as a detached onlooker protected by the walls of his monastery, but as one immersed right in the midst of these events, and who shares its pains and concerns, its hopes and joys.

> As long as I assume that the world is something I discover by turning on the radio or looking out the window I am deceived from the start. As long as I imagine that the world is something to be "escaped" in a monastery—that wearing a special costume and following a quaint observance takes me "out of this world," I am dedicating my life to an illusion....
>
> ...That I should have been born in 1915, that I should be the contemporary of Auschwitz, Hiroshima, Vietnam and the Watts riots, are things about which I was not first consulted. Yet they are also events in which, whether I like it or not, I am deeply and personally involved. The "world" is not just a physical space traversed by jet planes and full of people running in all directions. It is a complex of responsibilities and options made out of the loves, the hates, the fears, the joys, the hopes, the greed, the cruelty, the kindness, the faith, the trust, the suspicion of all. In the last analysis, if there is war because nobody trusts anybody, this is in part because I am defensive, suspicious, untrusting, and intent on making other people conform themselves to my particular brand of death wish. (CWA 160-161)

While identifying himself with all of those who are victims of war and hatred and racial prejudice and hunger and persecution and all the violence in the world ("...they were mine, and I theirs"), and raising his voice in protest, at the same time Merton identifies in his very own self the causes of all these evils, and thus acknowledges complicity with the perpetrators of all these evils. In this confession of complicity, in his admission of being a "guilty bystander," Merton finds resonance with a Vietnamese Buddhist monk he came to regard as his brother, Thich Nhat Hanh (PP 260-62). The latter expresses similar sentiments in a poignant poem entitled "Please Call Me by My True Names."

…I am the child in Uganda, all skin and bones,
My legs as thin as bamboo sticks
And I am the arms merchant,
Selling deadly weapons to Uganda.

I am the twelve-year old girl,
Refugee on a small boat,
Who throws herself into the ocean
After being raped by a sea-pirate.
And I am the pirate,
Not yet capable
Of seeing and loving…

Please call me by my true names,
So I can hear all my cries and laughter at once,
So I can see that my joy and pain are one…. (Hahn 2001, p. 81)

One who hears the cries of the world in distress and anguish and suffering, who recognizes and embraces the world's wounds as one's very own, is thereby faced with momentous choices. "What is to be done?" "How may I live my life fully in a way that is true

Thomas Merton and Thich Nhat Hanh.

to this calling, as I continue to hear the cries of the world?" Each one can only discern for oneself, listening to the call from the depths of one's being.

For Thomas Merton, it was not so much a matter of "what to do," but of "how to be." The call he heard, with greater clarity than ever before, was for him to plunge more deeply into his silence and solitude, as his way of giving himself to the world healing. His request to live as a hermit, made to his superiors even in his earlier years as a contemplative monk, is at last granted in summer of 1965.

> In the last analysis what I am looking for in solitude is not happiness or fulfillment, but salvation. Not "my own" salvation, but the salvation of everybody. (June 24, 1966. LL 345)

This echoes the lines already cited above from the revised account of his experience at Fourth and Walnut.

> My solitude, however, is not my own, for I see how much it belongs to them—and that I have a responsibility for it in their regard, not just in my own. It is because I am one with them that I owe it to them to be alone, and when I am alone they are not "they" but my own self. (CGB 142)

This time his entry into solitude is not an escape from, a turning back upon the world, but rather, a decisive act of plunging oneself right in the midst of the wounded world, to partake in the tasks of its healing, in the particular way he was called. And with a clear and eloquent voice emerging out of that silence and solitude, he continues to call upon his fellow human beings, together to hear the cries of the wounded world and to join hands in the tasks of healing from the different contexts and states of life each one may find oneself to be.

His exchanges with Rosemary Radford Reuther, who challenged him about his choice to remain inside the cloister rather than to go out and make himself accessible and of greater service to the world, and questioned whether it was a choice of "complacency," provide us with glimpses of his discernment of his own particular calling. (HGL 497-516) Very candidly, he writes:

About monasticism, my vocation and all that...I always tend to assume that everyone knows I have had a monumental struggle with monasticism as it now is and still disagree violently with most of the party-line policies. I am a notorious maverick in the Order and my Abbot considers me a dangerous subject, always ready to run off with a woman or something, so I am under constant surveillance. If I am allowed to live in a hermitage, it is theoretically because this will keep me more under wraps than otherwise. So when I say I "have no problem with my vocation," I just mean that I am not for the moment standing over the Abbot with a smoking gun in my hand. In other words, I have the usual *agonia* with my vocation but now, after twenty-five years, I am in a position where I am practically laicized and de-institutionalized, and living like all the other old bats who live alone in the hills in this part of the country and feel like a human being again. My hermit life is expressly a *lay* life. I never wear the habit except when at the monastery and I try to be as much on my own as I can and like the people around the country. Also I try as best I can to keep up valid and living contacts with my friends who are in the thick of things, and everyone knows where my real "community" is. I honestly believe that is the right place for me (woods, not Gethsemani) insofar as it is the right battleground. It is a sort of guerilla-outpost type of thing if you like. But from my experience I would be leading a less honest and more faked life if I were back in the cities. This is no reflection on anyone else. In staying here I am not just being here for myself but for my friends, my Church, and all those I am one with. Also, if there is one thing I am sure of too, it is my need to fight out in my own heart whatever sort of fight for honesty I have to wage and for fidelity to God. I am not by any means turning my back on other people, I am as open as the situation (of overcontrol) permits and want to make this more open as time goes on. Lots of people would like me to get out and join them in this or that, but I just don't see that I could do it without getting into some absurd role and having to act a dumb part or justify some nonsense or other that I don't really believe in. I know I firmly disbelieve all the favorite cliches about monasticism, and the community knows it too. I can say where and how my life is eschatological, because as far as I can see I am a tramp and not much else. But this kind of tramp is what I am supposed to be. This kind of place is where I am finally reduced to my nothingness and have to depend on God. Outside I would be much more able to depend on talk. Maybe I am just protesting too much, but that is the way I feel about it. I assure you that whatever else it is not complacency, because there is ample material for not being complacent, I assure you.... (February 14, 1967. HGL 503-4)

The young man who, experiencing the fear and chaos of a worldly life, "turned his back on the world—the man who spurned New York, spat on Chicago, and tromped on Louisville, heading for the woods with Thoreau in one pocket, John of the Cross in another, and holding the Bible open at the Apocalypse" (CWA 159), came back full circle, embracing the world, acknowledging responsibility for it, giving himself and seeking to do all he could to be at its service. And yet for Thomas Merton, this "re-turn to the world" was not a setting aside of the path of silence and solitude that he was called to as a young man and which he pursued for over two decades of his life. It was rather a reaffirmation of his particular calling, now no longer as separating himself from the world, but rather in a way that affirmed his oneness and solidarity with the multitudes of his fellow human beings, while affirming the possibilities of the human, in the midst of a chosen life of silence and solitude as a hermit living in the woods.

His was a calling to live in the ordinariness of being human, "reduced to nothingness," in his own words, like a tramp, communing with the earth and with the trees "who say nothing," listening to the birds, to the wind, as well as to the sounds of the world in his own heart. His life of solitude in the woods was his battleground against the forces of greed, enmity, and selfishness based on ignorance, poisons that afflict us all.

There is a verse in the *Gateless Gate* that speaks to Merton's situation most aptly.

Far better than realizing the body is to realize the mind and be
   at peace.

If the mind is realized, there is no anxiety about the body.
If both body and mind are completely realized,
A holy hermit does not wish to be appointed lord. (GG 52)

Another translation of the last line is "A saintly hermit declines to be a noble." (Aitken 1990, p. 64) In short, as one finds true peace, one no longer feels any need to seek anything of worldly gain or honor or glory. If there is anything one glories or finds joy in, it is the very matter-of-fact events of everyday life, in their ordinariness: "of trees that say nothing, of birds that sing, of a field in which nothing ever happens (except that a fox comes and plays, or a deer passes by)." (LL 341)

INCONCLUSIVE CONCLUSION: MERTON'S LIVING *KOAN*

Thomas Merton's reaffirmation of his calling to solitude comes in the context of an intense inner struggle brought on by his encounter with M., who figures prominently in his journals from April of 1966 on until about the end of the same year. One cannot do justice in a few lines to this extremely important period of Merton's life wherein he falls deeply and passionately in love with a young woman who also professes her deep love for and devotion to him. (Mott 1984, Griffin 1993)

> M. Her little, clear, determined voice coming to me through all the cold and snow, in a letter, saying she has carefully considered it, and she really, powerfully loves me, and she is never going to stop. So definite. I read the letter out there in a field of snow, weeping, looking through hot tears at the icy hills, the frozen wood, where we were Ascension Day. And she is right. Without getting carried away (or wishing that I were not, seeing that I don't *have to be*) I have to admit our love as a basic and central truth about which there can be no nonsense. And will have to try somehow to reconcile it with contemplative liberty (after all she explicitly accepts this situation)....
>
> The fact of passion has to be faced, and I must not let it get too disruptive. The fact of my vocation to a deep mystical life has to be faced—though I am helpless to account for it or cope with it and am in danger of being terribly unfaithful. The fact of M's love has to be faced and

met with my own most serious gift and trust. God alone
can reconcile all that has to be reconciled. I have simply
been torn by it. Reduced, and walking in the sun and snow
and renouncing any hope of quick answers. (LL 157)

In Zen terms, Merton is here faced with a living *koan* that cut right
through the core of his very being. A *koan*, as is generally known,
involves a word, phrase, anecdote, or situation presented before a
Zen practitioner that defies conceptual thought or logical reasoning, and which calls for a response from the depths of one's being.
In Merton's case, here was the dilemma of a man who on the one
hand is solemnly committed to the monastic life and to lifelong
vows of celibacy, and on the other has fallen deeply and passionately in love with a woman who also loves him as deeply and passionately.

His journal entries (LL 37ff.) provide us a glimpse of how he
faced this living *koan* headlong, and continued to struggle with it
in varying degrees of intensity.

In any case I know in my heart that my true call is to solitude with God, however much I love her. She knows this
too.

The objective fact of my vows, more than a juridical
obligation. It has deep personal and spiritual roots. I cannot be true to myself if I am not true to so deep a commitment.

And yet I love her. There is nothing for it but to accept
the seeming contradiction and make the best of it in trust,
without impatience or anxiety, realizing that I can't realis-
tically manipulate things for us to meet, etc. Yet if God
wants us to be together somewhere it will be possible. But
there is no use in fostering a lot of illusions.

Apart from that—the whole thing makes me ache
through all the regions of my being, and at times I am close
to sheer desperation. (LL 162)

For Merton, this love was not simply something to be dismissed as
a deviation from his vows, least of all from his fidelity to the God
of love.

If God has brought her into my life and if God has willed
our love, then it is more His affair than ours. My task con-

The Zen life is after all nothing but one lived in fidelity to each moment, wherein "just being there is enough." (LL 341) It is a life, lived in each moment, "just being there," wherever that may be, or in whatever circumstances one may find oneself, totally open, hearing the cries of the world, and responding to the call that each moment brings.

Ruben L.F. Habito

sists in not forcing my love into a mold that pleases and reassures me (or both of us), but in leaving everything "open"—and not trying to predetermine the future. (LL 312)

A *Koan* cuts right through a human being seeking to discover one's True Self, taking away all one's certitudes, making one unable to rely on any pre-established pattern, rule, or doctrine. It invites a human being to become totally naked before God, to plunge oneself, amidst contradictions, at the heart of the Mystery of life itself. Merton plunged himself headlong into this living *koan* and continued to struggle with it until the end.

Thomas Merton's life on earth was abruptly cut, in the midst of his Asian journey, in an accident that left the world in shock and in sorrow. From our earthly point of view, his was an unfinished life, as it still had so much promise, so much waiting to be accomplished, totally "open" to new possibilities that could have been. We are left with questions of "what if..." or "if only..." and have only our imaginations to fill in the blanks on "what could have been."

And yet, perhaps, from another point of view, his was a life that was complete, replete, even in his "untimely" death. For from all indications, he lived to the full, giving himself totally to what was called of him, through the different twists and turns and the manifold encounters of his life journey, and embodying in this life the joys and pains, the glories and the struggles, of what it is to be human.

The Zen life is after all nothing but one lived in fidelity to each moment, wherein "just being there is enough." (LL 341) It is a life, lived in each moment, "just being there," wherever that may be, or in whatever circumstances one may find oneself, totally open, hearing the cries of the world, and responding to the call that each moment brings.

ABBREVIATIONS:

CGB *Conjectures of a Guilty Bystander* (New York: Doubleday, 1966)

CWA *Contemplation in a World of Action.* (New York: Doubleday, 1973)

ES *Entering the Silence* (Journals, Vol. 2)

GG   *The Gatelesss Gate* (Yamada 2004)
HGL *The Hidden Ground of Love*. (Shannon, ed., 1984)
IE   *The Inner Experience, Notes on Contemplation* (Shannon, ed., 2003)
LL   *Learning to Love* (Journals, Vol. 6)
PP   *Passion for Peace* (Shannon, ed., 1996)
SS   *A Search for Solitude* (Journals, Vol.3)
SSM *The Seven Storey Mountain*. (New York: Harcourt, Brace & Co., 1948)

References

Aitken, Robert. 1982. *Taking the Path of Zen*. San Francisco: North Point Press.

———. 1984. *The Mind of Clover*. San Francisco: North Point Press.

———. 1990. *The Gateless Barrier*. San Francisso: North Point Press.

Griffin, John Howard. 1993. *Follow the Ecstasy: The Hermitage Years of Thomas Merton*. Maryknoll: Orbis.

Habito, Ruben. 2001. *Healing Breath Zen Spirituality for a Wounded Earth*. Dallas: MKZC Publications.

———. 2004. *Living Zen, Loving God*. Boston: Wisdom Publications.

Hahn, Thich Nhat. 2001. *Essential Writings*. Ed. by Robert Ellsberg. Maryknoll: Orbis Books.

Kapleau, Philip. 1965. *The Three Pillars of Zen*. Boston: Beacon Press.

Maezumi, Taizan, and Bernard Glassman, eds. 2002. *On Zen Practice: Body, Breath, and Mind*. Boston: Wisdom Publications.

Merton, Thomas. 1995-1998. *The Journals of Thomas Merton*. Patrick Hart, O.C.S.O., General Editor. San Francisco: HarperSanFrancisco.

———. Vol. 1: *Run to the Mountain*. Ed. by Patrick Hart.

———. Vol. 2: *Entering the Silence*. Ed. by Jonathan Montaldo.

———.Vol. 3: *A Search for Solitude*. Ed. by Lawrence S. Cunningham.

———. Vol. 4: *Turning Toward the World*. Ed. by Victor A. Kramer.

———. Vol. 5: *Dancing in the Water of Life*. Ed. by Robert Daggy.

———. Vol. 6: *Learning to Love*. Ed. by Christine M. Bochen.

————. Vol. 7: *The Other Side of the Mountain*. Ed. by Patrick Hart.

Mott, Michael. 1984. *The Seven Mountains of Thomas Merton*. Boston: Houghton Mifflin.

Shannon, William H., ed. 1985. *The Hidden Ground of Love. The Letters of Thomas Merton on Religious Experience and Social Concerns*. New York: Farrar Straus Giroux.

————. 1996. *Thomas Merton: Passion for Peace. The Social Essays*. New York: Crossroad.

Wu, John Jr. 1996. "The Zen in Thomas Merton." Originally presented as "Thomas Merton and the Spirit of Zen," at the first general meeting of the Thomas Merton Society in Southampton, England, May 1996. *Thomas Merton Society Homepage*.

Yamada, Koun. 2004. *The Gateless Gate: The Classic Book of Zen Koans*. Boston: Wisdom Publications.

Zen: not abstract at all the way I see it. I use it for idol cracking and things like that. Healthy way of keeping one's house clean. Gets the dust out quicker than anything I know. I am not talking about purity, just breathing, and not piling up the mental junk.

> Thomas Merton, *At Home in the World: The Letters of Thomas Merton and Rosemary Radford Ruether*

THE LIMITS OF THOMAS MERTON'S UNDERSTANDING OF BUDDHISM

John P. Keenan

When I was fifteen years old I entered St. Charles Borromeo Seminary in Philadelphia to study for the diocesan priesthood. It was a new world to me, entirely new, with norms and expectations so very distinct from my previous world of teenage struggle and conformity. I liked it—up at five o'clock in the morning, silent meditation and prayer, early Eucharist, friends and companions dressed in cassocks, the consummate skill one had to have to fold a surplice along its pleats so that it would fit into the cylindrical bag. The practice today is not to take boys in their mid-teens into the seminary, for they are as yet too unripe emotionally. But for me—having just lost my father and feeling dissatisfied with the life prospects before me—it was like finding a lost home. The values expressed in the life there were entirely different from those of my old life, for the viewpoint of reality had shifted. Indeed, if God is, then everything changes—and should change.

Shortly after entering seminary, I began to read the books of Thomas Merton. First I read his mountain story and identified with his move, although I had never experienced the social world of young adults that he described and cannot today remember many of the details—only that Merton had turned his back on the world and aimed his heart toward the silence of God. I read *The Sign of Jonas* and *The Waters of Siloe* and became convinced that I too should seek that higher calling to the cenobitic life, hidden in the love of God, praying and laboring.

This conviction was at odds with my seminary existence, for we studied many hours a day, learning history and Latin, and even Greek, while the Merton I read seemed to bypass all that to dive into the darkness of God. Why was I learning all about declined agricolas when I could have been tasting the ineffable experience of the godhead? I consulted my spiritual director, and he pointed

118

out that, while monks were fine, we diocesan priests actually worked for the Kingdom in the give-and-take of the world, although not determined by it. Besides, he pointed out, I was only seventeen. So I settled in and completed the full ten years of praying in the early morning and studying all the day long.

But still I read Merton for still he wrote—a constant stream of books on the spiritual life. They led me into the practice of the faith and guided me into the early Church fathers and their theology of union with Christ and the indwelling of the Spirit. I indeed desired to be a "new man," one formed in the close and direct love of Christ. Merton himself had been formed in the *via negativa*, so cherished by Catholic thinkers and spiritual adepts: Only in the way of negation does one meet God in the darkness of unknowing, in a silent experience beyond words. One was to ground oneself in that darkness and open oneself to the darkness that surrounds us all, as does Moses on Mt. Sinai when he meets God in the absolute dark night of his upward journey. Gregory of Nyssa, Dionysius— sometimes pseudo—and a host of Christian thinkers in that apophatic tradition from Augustine to the writer of *The Cloud of Unknowing* prepared the way. Merton claimed them all and focused my attention on their spirituality.

MERTON AND THE DISCOVERY OF BUDDHISM

During my eighth year of training, in scripture class, Dr. John J. O'Rourke mentioned a book he had just read called *Zen Catholicism*, by Dom Aelred Graham, a Benedictine monk and writer. O'Rourke observed in passing that this volume might be the most important book of the year. I read the book and saw how Dom Aelred made use of Zen practices and spiritual advice to deepen the very same spiritual practices that Merton prized so much: silence, quietness, withdrawal, peace, transformation.

Merton, too, discovered Zen during those years. He saw in the east a wondrous mystic tradition that could act as a counteragent to the intellectual approaches of our so-familiar west. And I went with him, for I also had studied and learned the philosophies and theologies of the Church, the Neo-Thomist discourse on being and the Lonerganian focus on the insightful mind. By contrast to the Asian religions, the mystic strain in Christianity seemed almost to be eclipsed by these more cerebral theologies, or at least shunted to the periphery. It was always there, of course, and Lonergan and

Gilson knew well enough that at times one was to withdraw into the unmediated realm of falling in love with God. But it seemed to me that all too many theologians practiced an interrupted love, spending most of their time in weaving theological edifices that would relate to modern people.

In the period when Merton first encountered Buddhism and began to read about that tradition, we in the Christian world in the United States were profoundly ignorant on the subject. Indeed, my seminary history professor, having consulted the *Oxford English Dictionary*, announced to us that the proper pronunciation of the term was "'Bud'-ism," rhyming with "bud" in "buddy." None of us questioned the professor, for he had looked it up. I remember reading in 1963 or 1964 a scholarly article in *The Thomist*, I believe it was, about the Buddhist doctrine of emptiness. The author demonstrated how negligent Buddhist thinkers were, for again and again they violated the basic principle of logical contradiction. All of which showed us the need for grace, even to be rational. Today we know how narrow-minded and parochial our understanding was then.

My own first personal encounter with Buddhism, which occurred in 1958, illustrates this parochialism all too vividly. That summer I was engaged in seeking out potential Catholics by going door to door in the city, asking questions about people's religious roots and hopes. Near 4th and Girard in Philadelphia, when I knocked on the front door of a nondescript house, a smiling Oriental man answered. To my questions, he replied that he was Buddhist and invited me up into the front room on the second story of his house. I did not quite understand why, for his English was none too clear, but, being polite and somewhat curious, I followed; it was obvious that he wanted to show me something. And there, with my own eyes and much to my consternation, I beheld a golden idol sitting serenely upon an altar. The afternoon sun coming through the window illumined the image in its slanting rays so that it sat glimmering in the splendor of pagan quietude, suggesting to me realms of demonic evil. With hardly a word, quickly and spontaneously, I quitted the scene of such idolatry and, fearing the presence of the devil, fled down 4th Street, away from that Buddha.

Against such a background—and I was a model child of my time and place—Merton's writing on his encounter with Buddhism came as an enlightening ray of understanding. Merton began to stretch our minds. He was not in fact the first to write about Buddhism in the west, for of course there had been many scholars of Buddhism and some Zen teachers long before him. But they were either far off in Japan or Europe or too scholarly for easy access. Here, as in his other trail-blazing efforts to limn a path of engaged contemplation, Merton embodied the new openness of Vatican II. He was our light-bearer. He had read the works of D.T. Suzuki, met a few times with that well-known Japanese proponent of Zen, met once with Vietnamese Zen monk Thich Nhat Hanh, and eventually even elicited an expression of admiration from the Dalai Lama. His inquiring mind crossed boundaries, and he—a Trappist monk—introduced us to the Zen experience. So, thanks to Thomas Merton and to the new spirit of Vatican II and its dreams for interfaith understanding and dialogue, I no longer needed to run from the Buddhists and their "idols." Now I could understand that the Buddha image glowing on that altar in North Philadelphia was symbolic, in function no different from images of Jesus in my suburban home parish of St. Denis, or in the chapel of St. Charles Borromeo Seminary.

That was then, but today, some decades later, I feel that it is important for us to consider the source and nature of the Buddhism that Thomas Merton introduced to us, and to identify it within its historical context of the 1960s and 1970s, so that we may take more mature steps into Buddhist Christian dialogue and doctrine. I will argue in this paper that Merton's understanding of that tradition—welcome and mind-stretching though it was to his contemporaries—is quite insufficient today for any dialogue with Buddhism, or with Zen. I will agree here with the major thrust and most of the conclusions of Roger Corless in his article written some twelve years ago on the Merton-Suzuki dialogue ("In Search of a Context"). During the last decade, Buddhist critiques of D.T. Suzuki have left little doubt that the Buddhism he presented in 1960s America was tailor-fitted to that time and place. Corless saw this earlier; it is even clearer now. Finally, I would like to present a few thoughts on silent, wordless experience and its role in interfaith dialogue.

D.T. SUZUKI AND THOMAS MERTON'S UNDERSTANDING OF BUDDHISM

In the 1960s, in this culture, it was D.T. Suzuki and his western companion Alan Watts who were the popularly authoritative voices

on Zen, and indeed on all of Buddhism, which was perceived to
have come to its apex in Zen, in Japanese Zen. As a seminarian and
young curate, I read all that they wrote and watched Watts on tele-
vision. I signed up to take a course in Zen at Temple University
under Professor Richard DeMartino, who espoused the teachings
of Suzuki. In all of this, I felt that I was faithfully following the
injunctions of the Vatican Council, which had adopted a new attitude toward other traditions, confidently open and fearlessly engaged.

Thomas Merton, like many in those days, also took D.T. Suzuki
as his guide and his authority on Zen Buddhism. In *Mystics and
Zen Masters* he writes: "Daisetz Suzuki is certainly the most authoritative and accomplished interpreter of the Rinzai [Zen] tradition" (p. 41). Suzuki provides, Merton claims, "without question
the most complete and the most authentic presentation of an Asian
tradition and experience by any other man in terms accessible to
the West" (Merton, "D.T. Suzuki: The Man and his Work"). He
read Suzuki with wonder, perceiving there the same *via negativa*
he knew from his previous practice. Suzuki's influence is unmistakable when Merton writes:

> Zen is not theology, and it makes no claim to deal with
> theological truth in any form whatever. Nor is it an ab-
> stract metaphysic. It is, so to speak, a concrete and lived
> ontology which explains itself not in theoretical proposi-
> tions but in acts emerging out of a certain quality of con-
> sciousness and of awareness. Only by these acts and by
> this quality of consciousness can Zen be judged. The para-
> doxes and seemingly absurd propositions it makes have
> no point except in relation to an awareness that is unspo-
> ken and unspeakable (*Mystics and Zen Masters*, ix-x).

Following Suzuki, Merton presents the heart of Zen as a wordless
experience of pure consciousness, beyond intellectual approach and
yet present at the center of our being. One cannot judge Zen by the
work of thinking, he tells us, for that merely misleads. One is to
pass directly from experience to Zen discourse, skipping over the
demands of intelligent insight and dispensing with rational adjudi-
cation.

Merton again echoes Suzuki in explaining that "Zen is therefore not a religion, not a philosophy, not a system of thought, not a

doctrine, not an ascesis.... The truth is, Zen does not even lay claim to be 'mystical,' and the most widely read authority on the subject, Daisetz Suzuki, has expended no little effort in trying to deny the fact that Zen is 'mysticism'" (*Mystics and Zen Masters*, 12). Clearly, Merton was attracted to this simple and bare experience that was presented by Suzuki as the heart of Zen.

Merton writes that one "might say that Zen is the ontological *awareness of pure being beyond subject and object*, an immediate grasp of being in its 'suchness' and 'thusness'" (*Mystics and Zen Masters*, 14). Here, he seems to be blending meanings. I wonder if he had in the back of his mind not only the mystic tradition of darkness, but also the pure ontological intuition into the being (*esse*) of being as celebrated by Neo-Thomist philosophers like Étienne Gilson. It does seem to me that he was trying to sketch approaches to that which cannot be approached, to offer words that lead to silence. In doing so, he sought out parallels and analogies between Zen and his Christian mystic tradition. (See *The Inner Experience*, which sketches his ongoing thought on the topic.) Suzuki criticizes the west for being abstract and discriminative, and Merton follows along: "We have habitually taken Western metaphysical concepts as equivalent to Buddhist terms, which are not metaphysical but religious or spiritual, that is to say, expressions not of abstract speculation but of concrete spiritual experience" (*Mystics and Zen Masters*, 16).

Based as his works are on D.T. Suzuki's Zen teachings, I think we must recognize that we cannot look to Merton for any adequate understanding of Buddhism. Because of the limitation of sources available to him in his time, his understanding of Zen Buddhism as presented for example in *Zen and the Birds of Appetite* and in *Mystics and Zen Masters* was imperfect and incomplete. It is not enough—as Merton learned to do from Suzuki—to appeal to a simple, non-discriminative experience of truth and reality as if that were the core experience behind all our varied and sorry words and doctrines.

RECENT CRITIQUES OF SUZUKI

After I left the Roman clergy in 1969, I attempted to follow Merton's model of the celibate secular monk, at least for as long as I could maintain the conviction of being an eschatological sign that nobody else noticed. (It was initially Ivan Illich's treatise on "The

Vanishing Clergyman" that had encouraged my move back into the secular world.) But still I was taken with theology and with prayer, and I wanted to study a new language in which to think, not so much seeking new answers as new questions. At least, I wanted new ways to formulate questions of faith. And so I took up the study of Chinese and Japanese, and then of Buddhism (along with its other canonical languages of Sanskrit and Tibetan).

Before I began my academic studies of Buddhism, I—along with Thomas Merton and many of my fellow students in the Buddhist Studies Program at the University of Wisconsin—regarded D.T. Suzuki as an enlightened *roshi*, or master. But I soon noticed that my academic mentor Professor Minoru Kiyota very consciously kept his distance from enlightened masters, and I learned that, in Japan at least, Buddhist monks and masters were not very highly regarded. Then, as scandals around some Buddhist masters here in the United States became public, the authenticity of once-and-for-all enlightenment (*satori*) began to be questioned. And, finally, a few years later, Robert Sharf began to write about D.T. Suzuki, critiquing the latter's teaching of Zen as naively simplistic, indeed as chauvinistic in celebrating Zen not only as the heart of Japanese culture but as the inner core of *all* authentic religious experience. At one point, Sharf showed me an early draft of an article he had written on Suzuki and asked for my comments ("The Zen of Japanese Nationalism"). As much as it surprises me today, I told Robert then that I thought he was being too harsh on Suzuki and his presentation of Buddhism. I had no hesitancy in criticizing Catholic bishops and cardinals but shrank back in timidity at even seconding a critique of a Buddhist teacher.

But Sharf was right on the point. As demonstrated by Buddhist scholars in recent years, Suzuki was not a very good guide to Zen history or even to the actual Zen practice of his time and place (Victoria, Faure). It appears now that he presented an "export Zen" to the west, tailored in caricature for an audience that was then ready to question and go beyond its own philosophical and religious inheritance. Suzuki wrote voluminously but idiosyncratically. And, importantly, he did not have Zen credentials or the weight of any Zen institution behind him. As Robert Sharf writes:

[S]o many of those responsible for popularizing Zen in the twentieth century lacked formal institutional sanction themselves. D.T. Suzuki, Nishitani Keiji, and Abe Masao, to

name but a few, all lacked formal transmission in a Zen
lineage, and their *intellectualized* [italics mine] Zen is often held in suspicion by Zen traditionalists. We should be
cautious before uncritically accepting their claim that Zen
is some sort of nonsectarian spiritual gnosis, for such a
claim is clearly self-serving: by insisting that Zen is a way
of experiencing the world, rather than a complex form of
Buddhist monastic practice, these Japanese intellectuals
effectively circumvent the question of their own authority
to speak on behalf of Zen. But there is something more
pernicious at work here than the attempt of a few "outsid-
ers" to appropriate the authority of the tradition, for in insisting that Zen could be, and indeed should be, distinguished from its monastic "trappings" these writers effectively severed Zen's links to traditional Buddhist
soteriological, cosmological, and ethical concerns ("Whose
Zen?," 43).

Although Zen was indeed a tried and tattered school of Chinese
and Japanese Buddhism, Suzuki and others began to characterize
it as transcending sectarian boundaries. Sharf points out that this
understanding of Zen is "largely a twentieth century construct,"
formulated to meet the apologetic needs of the modern age ("Whose
Zen?," 44).

He identifies four moves that are made in presenting this type
of Zen. The first involves positing "a distinction between the 'essence' of a religious tradition and its 'cultural manifestations,'"
thus enabling one to speak of the essence apart from any cultural
embodiment of that essence. In the second place, one identifies
that "essence as a type of 'experience.' The heart of Zen thus lies
not in its ethical principles, its communal and ritual practices, or
its doctrinal teachings, but rather in a private, veridical, often momentary 'state of consciousness,'" which allows one to skip the
labor of careful thought and proceed directly from bare experience
to spiritual affirmation. Thirdly, and importantly, one can then uni-
versalize the "'Zen experience' by denying that Zen is a school or
sect of Buddhism per se, or even a 'religion.' Rather, partisans
would insist that the term 'Zen' properly understood denotes the
universal experiential core of all authentic religious traditions, both
Eastern and Western. In short, Zen is truth itself, allowing those

with Zen insight to claim a privileged perspective on all the great religious faiths." Finally, and of nationalistic import, this view claims "that the universal religious experience of Zen is the ground of Japanese aesthetic and ethical sensibilities" ("Whose Zen?" 44-46).

It was precisely this version of Zen Buddhism as presented by D.T. Suzuki in the 1960s that Merton (along with many others at the time) accepted as normative: That beyond all the words of all the traditions there lies the silent experience of awakening, of abandoning oneself to the ocean of God. Words are not important, only the practice that leads to silence is important. This constitutes a pluralist theology in which all traditions and all teachings are seen as leading their practitioners to a similar direct experience, "a metaphysical intuition" enabling them to see—perhaps like the insight into the "to be" of being.

It is based on an appreciation that the wisdom of all Mah y na practice is explained to be quiescent and non-discriminative, the silence of the saints, beyond the realms of logic and reasoning. But this perfection of silent wisdom, in all the Mah y na teachings, must be accompanied by a subsequently attained, discriminative and enunciable wisdom (Nagao). But Suzuki stressed the first without bothering with the second; he championed the silence of ultimate awakening while denigrating the worldly conventions of the teachings and engagements of the tradition. His Zen was just too pure and too naïve, too simplistic, for it distorts both the Chan/Zen tradition and the broader Buddhist tradition. Bernard Faure, in his book *The Rhetoric of Immediacy*, demonstrates that Zen indeed does engage in extensive theological and doctrinal discourse. It is not, and never has been, anything but a teaching that seeks to encourage practitioners to enter into meditation (*zen*), meditation that itself is directed by Mah y na themes, even when these themes are presented in enigmatic *kōans*. The Zen tradition is no less literate, and no more rarified, than any other religious tradition; it abounds in all manner of Chinese rhetorical moves. It prizes scripture, and it values the study of philosophy, complicated philosophy (both traditional and Kyoto school). Zen practitioners in some cases even honor their past teachers by preserving their mummified remains in the back rooms of temples. In a word, Zen is not the bare and pure experience of the ultimate that is beyond all words and doctrines. The Zen notion that one must go beyond doctrine is itself a

Zen doctrine! Moreover, Zen is but one school of Buddhism among many, and in Japan it is not even the largest (which is Pure Land).

THE PRESENT DIALOGUE WITH BUDDHISM

The problem, in short, is that the simplistic, bare bones understanding of Zen Buddhism is just not a remotely adequate understanding of Buddhism, or of Zen. Zen is a school of Buddhism, embedded in its Chinese and Japanese history and drawing on the Indian sources of all Buddhism. Buddhist scholar Edward Conze is reported to have quipped, "Zen is just *prajñ -p ramit* (the 'perfection of wisdom' tradition) with jokes." The early Mah y na movement arose from these *Perfection of Wisdom* scriptures—*The Heart Sutra, The Diamond Sutra*, and a number of other texts that were written to counter the very metaphysical, theoretical, and abstract Abhidharma writings on Buddhist philosophy, which they regarded as too intellectual. Zen (Chan) is a Chinese school of Mah y na that developed a rhetoric of immediacy within a specific cultural and doctrinal context. Zen tradition glories in words and double-backs, highlighting paradox and parable. It certainly is aimed toward awakening, as are all forms of Buddhism, but it is clearly discourse, volumes and libraries of discourse. And Zen thinkers, like all Buddhist thinkers, did and do argue constantly about the interpretation of Buddhist scripture and tradition.

But the Zen that Merton encountered in the writings of Suzuki had been styled to catch the attention of a western world that heretofore had been so assured of its own theologies and ideologies that it consistently ran from other religious traditions. It is quite the safer course to run away from Buddhas and abide in the security of assured truth; and, to their credit, both Suzuki and Merton were attempting to counter such sectarian isolation. But I do not think theirs is a skillful approach in the long run. It is attractive, for it allows one to recognize brothers and sisters across faith lines as well as to discover inspired scriptures never before inspected, rich traditions addressing the same issues that bother us all—life and death, salvation and sin, wisdom and delusion. But this strategy for breaching interreligious barriers functions only by retreating from any attempt at insight or rational judgment, and thus from any shared effort to cross-fertilize our traditions.

Merton, although limited by his environment, did break free from the bounded world of intra-Christian faith and practice. He expanded the horizon to encompass truth and practice in all the traditions, especially in the Zen Buddhism he encountered in 1960s America. He could not have been expected to engage Buddhism on any but a spiritual and shallow level, for that is what his "authorities" offered. We, however, have more knowledge available to us and so can be expected to go deeper. Buddhism is not just the pure experience of awakening, but also the entire complex of words and ideas that make up its many traditions. Its varied teachings and practices are meant to lead one to awakening, embodying as they do an entire cultural heritage with all its literature and all its architecture and all its liturgies as expressed among men and women throughout Asia and in these latter days even in the West. Its doctrinal histories are as complex as anything we find in western religions. Its institutional embodiments are as varied as the peoples who construct them. And its doctrine is both simple and immeasurably complex, shifting perspectives as the Dharma (the Buddhist teaching) moves from country to country. Buddhism is a multicultured missionary religion without a central institutional force and without a commonly accepted canon of scriptures.

For over a thousand years no Buddhist ever heard about Zen, for it emerged only in medieval (Tang) China, but earlier Buddhists knew well enough that the wisdom of the Buddha was non-discriminative, beyond imagination, and ineffable. They practiced meditation (chan-na, i.e., Zen-na, dhy na) to personally experience the awakening of the Buddha and realize that wisdom. But they also knew that it was not enough to retreat to ineffable experience, in N g rjuna's words, to cling to emptiness ineptly. They were to live in this world and preach the Dharma. So they discoursed at length and in depth on the "wisdom attained subsequent" to awakening, the rich and culturally alert wisdom of skillfully enunciating the path of awakening, of leading people to practice. Whenever they faced challenges from other religions—which was often—and whenever they needed to address issues within the Buddhist community—which was always—they talked and wrote, held councils and developed commentaries.

EXPERIENTIAL SAMENESS AND THE ECLIPSE OF DIALOGUE

Buddhism is a rich and varied tradition, offering many avenues of ingress. Its deepest experiences are colored by the many teachings and practices that dispose, engender, trigger, and suggest them. As

Buddhism, Zen has an honored place among these traditions, but it is far from a simple experience that people can have if they somehow slough off their language and culture to reach a desired mental equipoise. All Buddhists speak of experience beyond language and without words, for that is the negative limning of the truth of ultimately meaningful cessation. There is no need for Suzuki to have looked elsewhere for his teachings about immediate and nondiscriminative experience (pace Roger Corless). But immediately, all schools stress, a subsequently attained wisdom of discriminative wisdom must go hand in hand with that quiescence. All the Mah y na texts teach this, in detail and repeatedly. And so we need to conduct a textured dialogue with Buddhism, as with other traditions, a dialogue that goes beyond easy camaraderie and fellow feeling, even beyond spiritual silence, to the creative tension of shared approaches to our traditions, both cultural and overarching, and doctrinal and specific.

After forty years of conversation, people tire of dialogue, because it so often rehearses the same old ground about our common humanity, offering no new insight and no new approach. We bow to one another and cooperate on social issues. All well and good, but that does grow tedious. At the same time, old Buddhist caricatures of God as baby-sitter pop up and ask to be taken seriously (Pema Chödrön). And Christian canards—most canards and caricatures catch something real before distorting beyond recognition—about other-worldly detachment and easy karmic explanations of human events still appear. All this goes without any delving into the actual teachings of these traditions, as if we had never trained ourselves to read scriptures and commentaries, to converse, argue, and enjoy the creative tension. All our creative trials and challenges are slipping into a numbing cup of soporific wine of dialogic oblivion. Perhaps so afraid of past sectarianism, this age of ours seems to have become enamored of a new type of unitarian sameness. This is not the recognized and cherished tradition of Unitarian Universalist thought and practice, but a naïve belief that no doctrine or directed practice is any more valuable than any other. It is Suzuki's version of the pure Zen experience lying at the heart of all religions and traditions.

But no pure experience, by the very fact that it is ineffable and unmediated, can ever serve as a source of any insight or judgment about anything. Mystic insight serves as data to nothing. It grounds no discourse and warrants no doctrine whatsoever, even the doctrine that there is no doctrine. Appeals to direct experience do encourage meditative practice and foster a mind of no thinking. They are spiritual practice and do constitute a deep spiritual formation (*paideia*). They indeed lead to awakening and wisdom. But they are not useful for talking. The point is everyday and obvious: Talking is not silence and silence is not talking. Dialogue does not move in withdrawal from the world of mediated meanings into silent wonder, but takes place through language, in realms of history, culture, philosophy, and theology (Lonergan, *Method*, 112).

There is an ongoing discussion of whether "pure experiences" do in fact occur. And—if they occur—whether such pure experiences, unmediated by any work or sign, are all identical, or whether perhaps they are different. Some maintain that all experiences are formed by culture and language. So, do we all climb the same mountain and share the same experience? Or are we climbing different mountains, from which maybe we might catch a glimpse of one another across the wide divides of inhabited valleys? These are, I think, imponderables.

I do think that unmediated experiences exist. Most often they are simply experiences of everyday living that we do not attend to and do not gain insight into. A host of unnoticed sensations swirl through our nervous systems and consciousness. Others indeed are experienced as spiritually profound, as profoundly transformative. Some follow upon meditative practice and long sitting. Still, I want to argue that, precisely because such experiences are ineffable there is no way to adjudicate anything about them, whether they be the same or different, and there is no way to employ them as the base support for a shared dialogue, simply because there is no way to employ them at all—unless one translates them into language. In that case, they will be Englished, or Japanized, but never more ineffable. In dialogue, it is enough—and indeed a goal devoutly to be cherished—to ground ourselves, not in primal experiences, but in our histories, to embark upon a deep and detailed engagement with other traditions, not just a heady and warming intermingling.

To reach across boundaries, to "see" beyond borders, is one of the deepest human experiences. But it is rather like flying in airplanes: However grand the perspective from up there, sooner or later one has to land on the ground. So in interfaith dialogue we may fly over to inspect the territory, but unless we land, nothing comes into clear perspective. Better for participants to stand their ground and confess belief heartily and with conviction. Not as if that doctrine itself were absolute, but as it flows from the revealed word into our all too human cultures and languages. As it flows from the Dharma realm, from God, into the lives we in fact lead. Words do mean their meanings. Insights do envisage patterns and relationships between things. Judgments do entail commitments to culturally tried and true spiritual orientations.

There is nothing to be further discovered in focusing on the silent, for when we come together to dialogue, why would we want to remain silent? We can do that at temple, or in church, or in the quiet of our own rooms. We can withdraw from the entire realm conditioned by mediated meaning into and above airplane clouds of unknowing. We can fall in love with God unrestrictedly, and abide in the liminal presence that envelopes the earth. But we cannot dialogue there, and we cannot incite one another toward deeper insight without challenging one another on doctrinal issues. What is no-self? Who has a soul? Who is God? Is God refuted by the traditional arguments against a Creator Deity? Does the inexorable law of karma parallel Christian notions of providence? Is that law really inexorable? What about forgiveness? How can Zen be Buddhist if Pure Land is Buddhist? What do we have to say to Presbyterians? And to their rationalist offspring, the Unitarians? What about power? What is religious language? Is it different from any other language? No? Then how can it speak about what everyone admits is beyond word and image? What on earth is Christian Zen? How can a Jesuit Zen master confer a Zen warranty (*inka*) upon a Trappist Zen practitioner?

Merton touched on many of these issues, but he was so taken by his discovery of so many new brothers and sisters and so many new horizons, and his life was cut off so abruptly, that he never had a chance to pursue them in depth. He never was able to delve into the textual and historical sources of Buddhist thought and practice. He was hopeful, for it was indeed an age when we hoped that peace and love would abound. And Thomas Merton's hopes have not been disappointed: Some of my best friends are Buddhist. But we must go beyond Merton's understanding of Buddhism to engage in the tasks of dialogue that remain before us.

REFERENCES

Chödrön, Pema. *When Things Fall Apart: Heart Advice for Difficult Times.* Boston: Shambhala, 2000.

Corless, Roger. "In Search of a Context for the Merton-Suzuki Dialogue." In *The Merton Journal* , vol. 6 (1993), pp. 76-90.

Faure, Bernard. *The Rhetoric of Immediacy: A Cultural Critique of Chan/Zen Buddhism.* Princeton: Princeton University Press, 1991.

———. *Chan Insights and Oversights: An Epistemological Critique of the Chan Tradition.* Princeton: Princeton University Press, 1993.

Gilson, Étienne. *The Christian Philosophy of St. Thomas Aquinas.* New York: Random House, 1956.

———. *Being and Some Philosophers.* Toronto: Pontifical Institute of Medieval Studies, 1952.

Graham, Dom Aelred. *Zen Catholicism.* Reprint by Crossroad Publishing Company, 1994. First published: Harcourt, Brace, & World, 1963.

Lonergan, Bernard F. *Insight : A Study of Human Understanding.* Volume 3 of *Collected Works of Bernard Lonergan.* Toronto: University of Toronto Press, 1997. First published by Longmans, Green, & Co., 1957.

———. *Method In Theology .* New York: Herder and Herder, 1972.

Merton, Thomas. "D.T. Suzuki: The Man and his Work," *Eastern Buddhist* , n.s. 2, 1 (1967): 3-9.

———. *The Inner Experience.* San Francisco: Harper SanFrancisco, 2003.

———. *The New Man.* New York: Farrar, Straus &Giroux, 1961.

———. *Mystics and Zen Masters.* New York: Farrar, Straus and Giroux, 1961.

———. *Seven Storey Mountain.* New York; Harcourt, 1949.

———. *The Sign of Jonas: The Journals of Thomas Merton .* New York: Harcourt, Brace, 1956, as Image Books. First published by Harcourt, Brace, and Co., 1953.

———. *The Way of Chuang Tzu.* New York: New Directions, 1965.

———. *Zen and the Birds of Appetite.* New York: New Directions, 1968.

Nagao Gadjin. *The Foundational Standpoint of M dhyamika Philosophy.* Trans. John P. Keenan. Albany: State University Press of New York, 1989.

Sharf, Robert H. "Buddhism and the Rhetoric of Experience" paper given at AAR conference, Nov. 22, 1992, reincarnated as "The Zen of Japanese Nationalism." In *Curators of the Buddha: The Study of Buddhism under Colonialism* . Ed. Donald Lopez. Chicago: University of Chicago Press, 1995.

———. "Whose Zen? Zen Nationalism Revisited." In James W. Heisig and John C. Marlado, eds., *Rude Awakenings: Zen, the Kyoto School, and the Question of Nationalism.* Honolulu: University of Hawaii Press, 1994, pp. 40-51.

Suzuki, D.T. *An Introduction to Zen Buddhism.* New York, Grove Press; first published by Evergreen, 1964.

Everything wants to return to it and cannot. For who can return "nowhere"? But for each of us there is a point of nowhereness in the middle of movement, a point of nothingness in the midst of being: the incomparable point, not to be discovered by insight. If you seek it you do not find it. If you stop seeking, it is there. But you must not turn to it.

Thomas Merton, *Cables to the Ace*

PART III
BUDDHIST TRADITIONS
AND THOMAS MERTON'S ART

MERTON, SUZUKI, ZEN, INK: THOMAS MERTON'S CALLIGRAPHIC DRAWINGS IN CONTEXT

Roger Lipsey

In his memorial essay of 1967 honoring D.T. Suzuki, Thomas Merton wrote these layered, haunting words: "Pseudo-Dionysius says that the wisdom of the contemplative moves in a *motus orbicularis*—a circling and hovering motion like that of the eagle above some invisible quarry, or the turning of a planet around an invisible sun."[1] He applied this figure, drawn from its seclusion in early Christian mysticism, to Suzuki's long faithfulness to Zen Buddhist tradition. Over the half century and more of Suzuki's authorship in English, ideas had come and gone in the West while Suzuki continued to bear witness to Zen, "inexhaustibly new," as Merton wrote in the same essay, "with each new book."

Merton himself, from the mid-1950s until nearly the end of his life, moved in *motus orbicularis* around the sun of Suzuki's writings and the larger Zen literature to which they point. He corresponded with Suzuki, co-authored with him on one occasion, exchanged gifts with him, and for two days in the spring of 1964, in New York City, at last met him. More than anyone he had known, Suzuki embodied for Merton the ideal of the desert father, which he had encountered in early Christian sources and revered. The *abba* or spiritual father in the desert tradition, whom Merton had been unable to find in his own monastic world, had at last appeared in the person of the diminutive, smiling, urbane, quite ancient Dr. Suzuki. It was an enriching detail that Suzuki was Buddhist. By the time they met, Merton was no longer easily deluded by appearances. He could see and feel that Suzuki "understands what interior simplicity is all about and really lives it. That is the important thing, because without contact with living examples, we soon get lost or give out."[2]

The project of this essay is dual: to chronicle and interpret Merton's experience of Zen Buddhism and to explore Merton's practice of brush-drawn calligraphy in the 1960s, modeled in part on the practice of Zen priest-artists. The word "experience" is deliberately chosen to indicate a focus on Merton's reception of Zen as a religious seeker rather than on his expository writings about Zen.[3] Although the period we need to consider is limited—some fourteen years from 1955 to 1968—the density of experience of those years in Merton's life is so great that we will need to exercise care. In the end, Merton is not an academic subject. He is still looking at us.

RECOGNITION AND RESERVE

In mid-winter 1955, Merton wrote to his friend and publisher, Jay Laughlin at New Directions Books: "Have you ever run across any books by D. Suzuki (I think that is how you spell him) on Zen Buddhism? I am anxious to track some of them down and have them."[4] The mixed tentativeness and urgency of the inquiry are touching; the spelling of Dr. Suzuki's name would not long remain in doubt. From published documents it's unclear whether Laughlin, always helpful, sent a good batch of books, but a year later Merton was thoroughly engaged in reading and assimilating not only Suzuki's writings but also the wider range of classic Zen sources. In May 1956, well past his first round of reading and now seeking rarer texts, Merton told Laughlin, "...I have finally found the Zen books I was looking for in the Library of Congress and am borrowing them from there. Zen is fierce, but terrifically practical. I think after all I am innately Chinese (Zen is really Chinese—combination of Taoism and Buddhism, reduced to its practical essence, all doctrines thrown out, naked contact with reality)."[5] In the summer of that year, inviting his lifelong friend Ad Reinhardt, the New York painter, to visit him at Gethsemani, Merton wrote:

> The very name of Suzuki produces in me electric currents from head to foot. If you come here you will have to answer such questions as "Why did Bodhidharma come from the west?" You will be given a cell in which to meditate on Joshu's Mu. Etc etc.
>
> My favorite answer to all questions is "The wooden man sits at the loom and the stone man at night throws in the shuttle."

> My favorite character—Hui Neng, the 6th patriarch.
> My roots: Wu-chu, which is to say not abiding anywhere.
> My philosophy: Wu nien, or in plain English, "Leave
> them all be: they are okay the way they are."[6]

The letter leaves no doubt that by summer 1956 Merton was—
with some ferocity of his own—reworking his approach to the inner life in light of his readings in Suzuki and the classic texts of
Zen. At much the same time he was also exploring the teachings
of the desert fathers in Latin editions and preparing to translate
outstanding passages for publication. The two themes—Zen and
the desert fathers—were closely bound in his mind: the living Zen
tradition, news of which was reaching the West through Suzuki
and a very few others, mirrored not so much the monastic spirituality of Merton's day as it mirrored the teachings of the desert fathers, with whom monasticism originated in fourth-century Egypt.
It was as if some great bird, presumed to be extinct and known
only through naturalists' reports, had been discovered in the forest. Now it was singing again.

Yet some years more would be needed for Merton to abandon
trace reservations. The full ecumenical embrace that was so characteristic of him in his later years snagged in one place until the
mid-1960s. When he turned directly toward participants in other
faiths and practices, he was free of reservations; he could not have
been more open and welcoming. In the private reflections recorded
in his journal he unreservedly recognized a new aspect of his vocation: to contribute to the integration of Christian and Buddhist
insight and practice. But in certain published writings and correspondence with fellow Catholics, he continued for some years to
assert or imply, without zeal, the primacy of Christian revelation.
For example, in an article on monastic spirituality published in
1957, he wrote:

> A Zen Buddhist, in Japan…may enter a monastery to seek
> a life of retirement and spiritual discipline. He is perhaps
> seeking the highest reality. He is seeking "liberation." Now
> if we enter the monastery seeking the highest reality, seek-
> ing perfection, we must nevertheless realize that for us this
> means something somewhat more than it can ever mean
> for a Zen Buddhist.… It makes much more sense to say,
> as St. Benedict says, that we come to the monastery to

seek God than to say that we come seeking spiritual perfection.[7]

"Something somewhat more...." Merton would retain this reserve
a while longer—for example, accepting uncritically the traditional
Catholic distinction between "natural" and "supernatural" contemplation. Even for Merton, a man of immense scope and capacity
for fellowship, there was a journey to be made between the familiar notion that salvation lies exclusively within the Church and
unreserved acknowledgment that the Lord is more generous than
that—that one's own church and tradition, unspeakably grand, exist alongside other religious institutions and traditions, no less grand.

It isn't easy to detect Merton growing and changing. We can
see him grown and see him changed—how different he was in each
decade. But to see him growing and changing, ambivalent and at
times in contradiction with himself, asks something more. The
sound of Merton in a mixed attitude of recognition and reserve
toward Buddhism can be heard as late as spring 1963, in a letter
that affirms the value of Buddhist meditative practice while almost
casually setting a limit around its reach:

> I don't hold with these extreme liturgy people for whom
> all personal and contemplative prayer is suspect. If you
> make a meditation they think you are a Buddhist. I have
> been writing an article on Zen, and I think there is a lot to
> be learned from the Buddhists, as regards the natural and
> psychological side of contemplation, especially some of
> the most obvious psychological blocks, which we blithely
> ignore, and to our cost.[8]

Even in 1965, the year in which he published his vivid and loving
study of the early Taoist patriarch, Chuang Tzu,[9] he retained that
slight reserve, inherited from generations of Catholic missionaries
doing the salvific work of the Church in Asia. "Chuang Tzu seems
to have been on the right track in many respects," he wrote in that
year, "though without the theological depth that would come with
true faith: still, he grasped the nature of things and of our orientation to God in silence."[10]

Merton's residual reserve through these years was a small tear
in an otherwise whole garment. And in his last year, 1968, he
encountered in Asia the mirror image of his attitude, equally un-

derstated but real. Many years after meeting Merton in Dharamsala, the Dalai Lama recalled, "I could see he was a truly humble and deeply spiritual man. This was the first time that I had been struck by such a feeling of spirituality in anyone who professed Christianity.... It was Merton who introduced me to the real meaning of the word 'Christian.'"[11] Thomas Merton among Tibetans knew that he was among brothers.

THE SENGAI CALENDARS

Merton rarely hesitated long to initiate dialogue through an exchange of letters with writers, thinkers, participants in the religious life, activists, and serious people of influence in world affairs. He had a realistic notion of his reputation: it was altogether sufficient to ensure a good possibility that persons he invited to correspond would welcome the relation. Thus it was in late winter 1959, when he first wrote to Dr. Suzuki, who had been teaching and lecturing annually in the West through the 1950s, while maintaining a home on the grounds of a Zen monastery in Kamakura, near Tokyo. Merton obtained Suzuki's address from Helen Wolff, who with her husband Kurt Wolff had founded Pantheon Books, a distinguished American literary publishing house.[12]

That first letter to Suzuki, dated March 12, 1959, reads in part:

> I will not be so foolish as to pretend to you that I understand Zen. To be frank, I hardly understand Christianity. And I often feel that those who think they know all about the teachings of Christ and of His Church are not as close to the target as they think.... All I know is that when I read your books—and I have read many of them—and above all when I read English versions of the little verses in which the Zen Masters point their finger to something which flashed out at the time, I feel a profound and intimate agreement. Time after time, as I read your pages, something in me says "That's it!" Don't ask me what. I have no desire to explain it to anybody, or to justify it to anybody, or to analyze it for myself. I have my own way to walk and for some reason or other Zen is right in the middle of it wherever I go. So there it is, with all its beautiful purposelessness, and it has become very familiar to me though I do not know "what it is." Or even if it is an "it." Not to be

foolish and multiply words, I'll say simply that it seems to me that Zen is the very atmosphere of the Gospels, and the Gospels are bursting with it. It is the proper climate for any monk, no matter what kind of monk he may be. If I could not breathe Zen I would probably die of spiritual asphyxiation.[13]

Soon after this powerful letter, Merton sent to Suzuki the manuscript of what would be published a year later as *The Wisdom of the Desert: Sayings from the Desert Fathers of the Fourth Century.* Dr. Suzuki accepted Merton's invitation to contribute to the book an essay on the desert fathers, which would draw out the kinship with Zen and create in effect a dialogue with Merton. Providing a measure of the boldness for his time and community of Merton's ecumenical reach, this concept of inter-religious dialogue within the covers of one book did not please the Cistercian authorities. "[It] has been thrown out of the book by the censors," Merton archly informed a fellow priest in January 1960, "on the ground that all my readers would instantly become Buddhists. This shows what wonderful confidence we have in our faith, doesn't it?"[14] Merton recovered, no damage was done to the growing bond with Dr. Suzuki, and the paired essays were eventually published in 1961 in the literary journal, *New Directions.*[15]

In a letter to Suzuki dated April 11, 1959, Merton conveyed his wish to practice Zen in some form and demonstrated with a poet's precision that he had already assimilated a Zen attitude toward nature and its lessons. "I only wish," he wrote,

> there were some way I could come in contact with some very elementary Zen discipline, even if it were only something like archery or flower-arrangement. At the moment, I occasionally meet my own kind of Zen Master, in passing, and for a brief moment. For example, the other day a bluebird sitting on a fence post suddenly took off after a wasp, dived for it, missed, and instantly returned to the same position on the fence post as if nothing had ever happened. A brief, split second lesson in Zen.[16]

No letter survives to tell us whether and how Suzuki responded to Merton's longing for a Zen practice, but little more than a year later Merton began to explore with brush, ink, and paper the expressiveness of abstract imagery that bore an increasing resemblance to Zen calligraphy. This practice emerged as one of Merton's "elementary Zen disciplines," and in a few years reached a level of sophistication that could no longer be called elementary.

Merton was much helped in this enterprise by Suzuki's annual gift, apparently starting in 1960, of a twelve-month calendar in scroll format, featuring the pictorial art and calligraphy of the celebrated eighteenth-century Zen priest and artist, Sengai. One of Merton's most beautiful photographs of his hermitage, where he spent increasing time in the early 1960s and in 1965 took up residence, pays homage to a Sengai calendar (fig. 1). Produced by Suzuki in cooperation with a Japanese industrialist and art collector, the calendars included marvelously instructive texts by Suzuki, which he was eventually to gather into a book that remains to this day the best on Sengai.[17]

Merton cared enormously for Sengai's art. In February 1961, he wrote to his lifelong friend Robert Lax a characteristically funny, burlesque letter—this was their way with each other—in which one easily detects how much Merton needed Sengai in his world:

> I thought Suzuki had crossed me off his list (never had a list, what list? Hang by the teeth on a tree, one arm have a hibachi other arm have a statue of Our Lady of Lourdes: koan question, what list?). I thought they had forgotten forever but it is the best Sengai calendar in the world delay only make better. Now I also had you put on Suzuki's Sengai calendar list maybe you got one.[18]

Several years later, Merton would refer in one of his most memorable writings, *Day of a Stranger*, to the "reassuring companionship" of the Sengai calendar in the hermitage.[19] And in the year when he wrote the first draft of that evocative essay, he thanked Suzuki in particularly rich terms for the gift, yet again, of a calendar—and of something more:

> This year's Sengai calendar reached me somewhat late with its intimations of the treasure ship heaped high with treasures from abroad. A few days later came a treasure indeed: your calligraphy, a presence of great beauty and strength which I have given a place of honor in the hermitage. It transforms all around it. Everything about the gift

Fig. 1 Interior of Thomas Merton's hermitage in the 1960s with Sengai calendar. Photograph by Thomas Merton. Collection: Thomas Merton Center (D102).

was admirable, and I am most honored and delighted to receive such a thing from Japan and from you. It is to me a deep bond with a world and tradition which I greatly love and admire. It is above all a special reminder of you whom I venerate.[20]

Merton never learned what words and meanings Suzuki had brushed onto that handsomely mounted calligraphic scroll. "No clue as to what the characters say!!" he recorded.[21] His courteous request for a reading, by letter, either never reached Dr. Suzuki or sank to the bottom of a stack of unanswered correspondence.[22] After Merton's passing, the scroll is assumed to have been destroyed in a house fire, and were it not for a casual, documentary photograph of the scroll probably taken by Merton, which recently showed up among uncatalogued items at the Thomas Merton Center, we would have no means now of knowing what Suzuki chose to write to his friend.[23] But the photograph makes clear that Suzuki wrote the characters for *wa, kei, sei, jaku*, the cardinal values of the Way of Tea: harmony, respect, purity, tranquility. A hint as to why he may have chosen those characters was pointed out to me by Dr. Suzuki's secretary in those years, Mrs. Mihoko Okamura-Bekku, who continues to publish on the Suzuki legacy in both Japanese and English. In Suzuki's enduring book first published in 1959, *Zen and Japanese Culture*, he describes these four values as the basis not only of Tea but of the order of life in the Zen monastery.[24] And so Dr. Suzuki must have looked across the waters and seen, as Merton saw, the kinship between Japanese spirituality—Tea owed much to Zen—and the way of the Christian monk for whom contemplative prayer is the center.

The Sengai calendars, and later Dr. Suzuki's scroll and a small number of excellent books, provided fully half of the curriculum of Merton's schooling as a visual artist in the 1960s. We shall return to them.

MEETING THE TRUE MAN OF NO TITLE

Merton was authorized by his Father Abbot, Dom James Fox, to meet Dr. Suzuki in New York City for several days in June 1964. Although Merton's entire experience is vividly reported in his journals, in a published memoir, and in correspondence with friends, we should focus here on his encounter with Suzuki, which did not lack its own bright colors. A photograph of the occasion (fig. 2) renders unforgettably the warmth and mobility of both men as they made acquaintance with one another. Merton's most closely observed account of their meetings is in the memorial essay he published in 1967, the year after Suzuki's death at the age of 96; it appeared in *The Eastern Buddhist*, founded by Suzuki and his late wife many years earlier. "It was my good fortune," he wrote there,

> to meet Dr. Suzuki and to have a couple of all too short conversations with him. The experience was not only rewarding, but I would say it was unforgettable. It was, in my own life, a quite extraordinary event since, because of the circumstances in which I live, I do not get to meet all those I would meet professionally if I were, say, teaching in a university. I had known his work for a long time, had corresponded with him, and we had had a short dialogue published.... On his last trip to the United States I had the great privilege and pleasure of meeting him. One had to meet this man in order to fully appreciate him. He seemed to me to embody all the indefinable qualities of the "Superior Man" of the ancient Asian, Taoist, Confucian, and Buddhist traditions. Or rather in meeting him one seemed to meet that "True Man of No Title" that Chuang Tzu and the Zen Masters speak of. And of course this is the man one really wants to meet. Who else is there? In meeting Dr. Suzuki and drinking a cup of tea with him I felt I had met this one man. It was like finally arriving at one's own home. A very happy experience, to say the least.[25]

Later in the memoir, every word of which counts, Merton offered an observation that should find its place here:

> I did feel that I was speaking to someone who, in a tradition completely different from my own, had matured, had become complete, and had found his way. One cannot understand Buddhism until one meets it in this existential manner, in a person to whom it is alive. Then there is no longer a problem of understanding doctrines which cannot help being a bit exotic for a Westerner, but only a question of appreciating a value which is self-evident.[26]

Fig. 2 Thomas Merton with D.T. Suzuki, New York, June 16-17, 1964.

There are still more sources, including a wild letter to Lax that should not be missed ("'Who is the Western writer who understand best the Zen IT IS YOU' they declare..."[27]), but we have seen enough now to grasp the importance of the meeting. Merton derived from it what he called "a sense of being 'situated' in this world."[28] One reads this with surprise; though compressed, it could hardly be a richer statement.

The Ecumenical Imperative

By the time of this meeting in New York, Merton had been aware for some years of his ecumenical mission or imperative. It had not been assigned him by the Church and, as we have seen, it could be something of a burden for his Order. It had emerged from the private substance of his life and search, but he understood it as an author's task, a task to understand and experience and then pass on to others what he had clarified for himself. Merton's ecumenical imperative was not in the least sentimental. It had to do with recovering and sharing knowledge. The core of that knowledge was practical in the sense that it concerned religious practice, particularly in its contemplative and meditative dimensions, but it also encompassed metaphysical concepts, working attitudes, inspiring tales, and puzzles to awaken the truth-seeking mind from sleep.

Merton put some of this rather formally in mid-1961, in a letter of thanks to the president of his alma mater, Columbia University, which had conferred an award on him:

> I am presently engaged in studies that work toward a broad integration of Oriental and Occidental philosophy and spirituality (not, I hope, purely eclectic). I feel it is necessary for Christians to recognize the profound meaning of the natural wisdoms that have remained alive in the Orient, and that this recognition can help us to appreciate forgotten elements in our own spiritual tradition. I am very interested in keeping in touch with those who might be working along these lines at Columbia.[29]

The letter reveals the slight reserve discussed earlier: its reference to "natural" wisdoms implies that the supernatural wisdom of Christian revelation is intrinsically superior. However, Merton's movement was steadily toward a broader vision. Several months later he recorded in his journal something of that broader vision. He wrote of a task worthy of the rest of his life, however many years might remain to him:

> I have a clear obligation to participate, as long as I can, and to the extent of my abilities, in every effort to help a spiritual and cultural renewal of our time. This is the task that has been given me, and hitherto I have not been clear about it, in all its aspects and dimensions.
>
> To emphasize, clarify the living content of spiritual traditions, especially Christian, but also the Oriental, by entering myself deeply into their disciplines and experience, not for myself only but for all my contemporaries who may be interested and inclined to listen. This for the restoration of man's sanity and balance, that he may return to the ways of freedom and of peace, if not in my time, at least some day soon.[30]

In a further six months, February 1962, Merton was thinking about tactics. "This is what I think my real mission is," he wrote, "an ecumenical underground that reaches out everywhere to Buddhists and the Lord knows where."[31]   He seems at this point to place more trust in underground currents of relationship and shared inquiry than in institutionally validated connections. He has learned the lesson of trying openly to publish a dialogue of equals with Dr. Suzuki—and learned the identical lesson where his anti-war writings were concerned. They too had been refused normal publication by the Order and would circulate for some years as mimeographed *Cold War Letters*, an American exercise in *samizdat* or underground publication. Even in 1967, Merton would continue to feel that his deep interest in Asian meditative practice distanced him from many of his fellow Catholics. "Only the Catholics who are still convinced of the importance of Christian mysticism," he wrote at that time, "are also aware that much is to be learned from a study of the techniques and experience of Oriental religions. But these Catholics are regarded at times with suspicion, if not derision, by progressives and conservatives alike."[32]

As almost always with Merton, there is much more to notice in his writings. His returns to topics are not just returns but enrichments. But we have encountered enough to be certain that his contact with Zen, and with the Taoist wisdom of Chuang Tzu to whom Suzuki's writings led him, gave birth to a powerful recognition of the need for East-West integration at the levels of spiritual concept and religious practice. Was he in any sense compromising his Christian faith through his encounter with Zen Buddhism? In the winter of 1966, he considered that issue in the privacy of his journal and recorded a sensibly nuanced view:

> …Critically important…is the question of the purity of my own faith—my willingness to risk compromises perhaps with other doctrines? This must be faced. But I can say here I have no hesitation in firmly desiring and intending to *be a Catholic* and to hold with all my heart to the true faith of the living God manifested in Christ and in his church. And no monkeying! Amen. Whatever I seek in other traditions is only the truth of Christ expressed in other terms, rejecting all that is *really* contrary to His Truth. (Not what is irresponsibly and hastily *said to be* contrary to it.)[33]

Morning Zen, Midnight Zen

The title of this section joins two titles Merton gave to calligraphic drawings exhibited late in 1964 in Louisville at Catherine Spalding College (now a university). That first exhibition of 26 drawings would travel to other venues across the United States, primarily but not only Catholic institutions, for the next three years. Zen in the morning and at midnight obliquely tells us that Merton was practicing—that Zen practice in some form and the mind of Zen, in some form, had become part of his life. In what ways? He received no formal training; he was a reader. However, he was a devoted and experienced practitioner of the "skillful means" of his Catholic monastic tradition, offered to his own readers in books such as *New Seeds of Contemplation* (1961) and innumerable essays. What he discovered of Zen practice and the mind of Zen through reading fell on exceptionally well prepared inner terrain.

There are signs throughout the 1960s that he included in his approach to the inner life some form of silent sitting meditation. Two letters dating to 1966 make that clear without excitement or emphasis—it was simply part of his life. To the psychiatrist and author Erich Fromm, he wrote from the hermitage, "As to the solitary life, it is to my mind a very valid experiment. It seems to me at any rate much more serious and in some ways more exacting than the life in community, where relationships are to some extent stereotyped anyway. I use a bit of Zen out here too, though I am not cracking my head with it. It is a good life, a bit chilly at the moment."[34] Writing later that year to a friend in religion, he employed the same plain words in the course of explaining that, despite Vatican II and the turn away from Latin, he would continue to read psalms and prayers in Latin. Otherwise, he said, "I am using some Zen Buddhism, etc."[35] A few months later, he described his life at the hermitage to yet another correspondent in terms consistent with what we have just read: "Right now I live alone in the woods. I am a hermit, by desire and by fact. It is very good. I do my work. I pray. I meditate. I study Zen. I write quite a few articles on Buddhism. And I am 'present' to my friends in all parts of the world. My life as a hermit is much more 'open' than that which I was living in the monastery."[36] The choppy rhythm of his account of works and days brings to mind that remarkable flash of contentment and certainty in his *Day of a Stranger*: "How I pray is breathe."[37] This memorable phrase matches other passages from the hermitage years, when he preferred simple living and distrusted religious display. But it may carry an additional meaning.

I have no wish to intrude on Merton's privacy, and in this much-chronicled and self-chronicled life there remain vast zones of privacy, safely out of reach. But it does seem likely that Merton knew of the Zen sitting practice of counting breaths or staying with the breath as an object of mindfulness. Perhaps that was part of his silence in meditation. To a young theologian he wrote in 1967 lines that imply as much:

> Zen: not abstract at all the way I see it. I use it for idol cracking and things like that. Healthy way of keeping one's house clean. Gets the dust out quicker than anything I know. I am not talking about purity, just breathing, and not piling up the mental junk.[38]

As these lines make clear, Merton experienced Zen teachings and attitudes as a source of simplification and discernment. In 1962 he wrote to a Chinese friend, "There are times when one has to cut right through all the knots, and the Zen view of things is a good clean blade."[39] In the following year, much the same perspective appears in an exceptional journal entry:

> Fidelity to grace in my life is fidelity to simplicity, reject-ing ambition and analysis and elaborate thought, or even elaborate concern.
> A breath of Zen blows all these cobwebs out the window.
> It is certainly true that what is needed is to get back to the "original face" and drop off all the piled-up garments of thought that do not fit me and are not "mine"—but to take only what is nameless.[40]

Zen accompanied him in his hermit ramblings through woods and fields belonging to the monastery and friendly neighbors. His ca-pacity for appreciation, for being in Nature as a rapt witness, seems to have been magnified by his encounters with Zen sources. In the depths of the winter of 1967, as it happens on the day dedicated to St. Paul the Hermit, he recorded in his journal: "Haven't been able to do anything, think anything. Yet in the evening—the bare trees against the metallic blue of the evening were incredibly beautiful: as suspended in a kind of Buddhist emptiness. Does it occur to anyone that Sunyata is the very ground of life?"[41] This is direct observation, shined and enhanced by recollection of the fundamental Mahayana Buddhist insight into *sunyata*, the infinitely fertile emptiness at the core of things.

At times Merton would explore his direct perceptions and Zen teachings in complex, existentialist terms. The words that follow are intricate, but the experience that gave rise to them is wordlessly direct: the "rehabilitation of the sensible," presence to oneself and to the world.

> Importance of that solitude which is a solitary, spiritual, material, rehabilitation of the sensible. The sensible around me becoming conscious of itself in and through me. A solitude in which one allows nature this virginal silence, this secret, pure, unrelatable consciousness in oneself. The reality "before all thesis," before the beginning of dialectic and En-Soi. The singular and timeless (not part of any series) mutual exploration of silences and meaning with which my consciousness never manages to be quite simultaneous but in which my body is present. The self-awareness of the great present in which my body is fully and uniquely situated. "My" body? Not as "had" by me![42]

As if in critique of the complexity of this statement, which nonetheless has qualities of discovery and illumination, Merton would write to a friend in religion in the last year of his life, "What is really meant of course is continual openness to God, attentiveness, listening, disposability, etc. In the terms of Zen, it is not awareness *of* but simple awareness."[43]

Merton did not miss the spirited, confrontational literature and practice of the Zen koan, and in time contributed an essay of his own on the topic.[44] He found guidance to explore the traditional koan collections not only in Suzuki's writings but also in works published in the mid-1960s by Philip Kapleau and the authorial team Isshu Miura and Ruth Fuller Sasaki. In Miura and Sasaki's *The Zen Koan: Its History and Use in Rinzai Zen* (1965), Merton discovered the pictorial and calligraphic art of Hakuin, who like Sengai was a Zen priest of the eighteenth century and a remarkable artist. Sengai and Hakuin together were the Asian archetypes for Merton's own practice of calligraphic drawings, to which we will soon be turning.

There is a charming, thoroughly funny anecdote, recorded after Merton's death, about his singular practice of koan Zen. The speaker is John Howard Griffin, author, photographer, and first official biographer of Thomas Merton, who accompanied Merton to a discussion with a group of nuns on a humid afternoon in July 1966:

> Fr. Louis touched on Zen practices.... Merton confided the problem he was attempting to resolve. You have a young goose in a bottle. The goose grows too large for the bottle. How do you remove the goose without killing it or breaking the bottle? The idea, he explained, was to concentrate so intensely on this problem that everything else fades to insignificance.... [Merton] said he was seated in choir one day during a solemn profession when he suddenly thought, "Of course, the goose swallowed the bottle." He had seen finally that it was stupid to try to find a reasonable solution to the problem because the problem did not have to be solved: any solution would do.[45]

Perhaps one other anecdote will help to settle the notion that Merton pursued koan study, though without the benefit of a lineage teacher to coach and scold, ring a dismissive bell, and validate insights. Hermits are not without resources. Ron Seitz, poet and friend to Merton, has recorded an incident that occurred in 1966. The two men were just outside the hermitage: "...Slapping his palms together in a loud *plaapp!* and, 'That's the sound of two hands clapping.' Tom was walking towards me."[46] Merton was having fun with, but also remembering the most famous koan of all: What is the sound of one hand clapping?

Although we could explore at much greater length the experiential record of Merton's approach to Zen practice, the time has come to ask: Did it help? Did it provide the skillful means and liberating perspective he had hoped to find? Did he learn in depth something of what he once called "the Zen way of seeing—the 'knack of full awareness.'"?[47]

In response to these questions, we must look for signs rather than proof, and there are unmistakable signs in the late journals and poetry that Merton knew moments, hours of heightened and most grateful awareness. In this regard, one of the most beautiful and commanding passages in the journals is dated March 6, 1966:

> Beauty and *necessity* (for me) of solitary life—apparent in the sparks of truth, small, recurring flashes of a reality that is beyond doubt, momentarily appearing, leading me further on my way. Things that need no explanation and perhaps have none, but which say: "Here! This way!" And with final authority!
>
> It is for them that I will be held responsible. Nothing but immense gratitude! They cancel out all my mistakes, weaknesses, evasions, falsifications.
>
> They lead further and further in that direction that has been shown me, and to which I am called.[48]

The movement from discoveries that require exclamation to the spare solemnity of the final sentence is a lesson in sensibility.

We can also find signs in the late poetry, nowhere more so than in a passage of prose poetry in *Cables to the Ace*—a difficult and sometimes off-putting work in which there are nonetheless glowing treasures. In the following lines on the theme of *Gelassenheit* (inner calm), probably derived from Meister Eckhart, Merton unites into a single current of expression the perspectives and image worlds of Eckhart, St. John of the Cross, and Zen. The passage recalls the pair of essays written in partnership with Dr. Suzuki years earlier, which Merton had such difficulty publishing.

> *Gelassenheit:*
>
> Desert and void. The Uncreated is waste and emptiness to the creature. Not even sand. Not even stone. Not even darkness and night. A burning wilderness would at least be "something." It burns and is wild. But the Uncreated is no something. Waste. Emptiness. Total poverty of the Creator: yet from this poverty springs *everything*. The waste is inexhaustible. Infinite Zero. Everything comes from this desert Nothing. Everything wants to return to it and cannot. For who can return "nowhere"? But for each of us there is a point of nowhereness in the middle of movement, a point of nothingness in the midst of being: the incomparable point, not to be discovered by insight. If you seek it, you do not find it. If you stop

seeking, it is there. But you must not turn to it. Once you
become aware of yourself as seeker, you are lost. But if
you are content to be lost you will be found without knowing it, precisely because you are lost, for you are, at last,
nowhere.[49]

This passage is surely not a flight of imagination. It is a seeker's
report.

"CENTRAL IS THE EXPERIENCE OF SEEING": THOMAS MERTON'S CALLIGRAPHIC DRAWINGS

Merton's photograph of the Sengai calendar against a wall in his
hermitage (fig. 1) transposes that modest cement-block dwelling
to another time and place. The calligraphic scroll, crafted hearth
broom, and half-seen basket, stitched into a whole by a lattice of
sunlight, sum to a miniature or emblem of the new way of life to
which Merton had dedicated the hermitage. The moment is probably March 1964; the nearly illegible calendar can just be coaxed
into yielding its date. The brushed characters read "Far and Clear,"
as Merton would have known from Suzuki's commentaries accompanying this and every image.

   Earlier in this essay we noticed that Sengai's calligraphy served
as an inspiration and model—though not an exclusive model, as
we shall see—for Merton's own explorations with brush, ink, and
paper. The images in the calendars were by no means all pure
calligraphy nor all gravely serious. Sengai was both a formidable
Zen priest and a superb entertainer, who must have delighted his
parishioners with his humorous "take" on traditional Zen patri-
archs, gods and goddesses, and all manner of common things that
could be seen anew. Merton himself was delighted by the image
for October 1963, a squat turnip with lofty greens, beside which
Sengai added the inscription: "Turnips and Zen monks are best
when they sit well." Merton found this so appealing that he re-
layed it by letter to Dom Jean Leclercq, an eminent Benedictine
with whom he had cordial relations.[50] Sengai's exclusively calligraphic works, on the other hand, tended toward the severity that is
also very much a part of Zen practice. The inscription "Far and
Clear" conveys that austere intensity: it gives one almost nothing,
just enough to kindle the longing to see more and see well—the

longing for awareness that Merton had recognized as the center of Zen thought and practice.

As brief as "Far and Clear," and no less compelling, is the image for December 1961, showing two characters that read *buji*, in Suzuki's spelling. Some years later—he must have saved the calendars—Merton wrote a commentary on *buji*:

> The Japanese Zen artist and poet Sengai has left us two Japanese characters, *Bu Ji*, which are a work of art in themselves and eloquent of the spirit of *Tao*. *Bu Ji* means "nothing doing." I can say that there is more energy, more creativity, more productiveness in these two powerful signs created by Sengai than in all the skyscrapers of New York, and yet he dashed them onto paper with four strokes of his brush.[51]

Suzuki's commentary, on which Merton based his own, was more learned and reticent: "A tentative modern rendering [of the characters] is, free from anxiety or fear. Literally, they mean no business, no work, no event, or, all is well. Zen master Rinzai...has this to say: 'The true aristocrat is the one who is *buji* (free from anxiety).' Aristocracy here refers to spiritual aristocracy, and not to any social distinction."[52] In the difference between Suzuki's and Merton's glosses, we can measure the strength of Merton's impulse to naturalize Zen, to re-express it in the language of his day for people of his day.

How and why did Merton move from unreserved appreciation of Sengai's calligraphy to explorations of his own that would gradually develop into a sophisticated art—an art that no one had expected of him, least of all himself? The interpretive narrative that could accompany him from his first experiments with abstract calligraphy in the fall of 1960 through the development of his art in the years to come far exceeds the scope of this essay. Readers will find that narrative, I hope worked out to their satisfaction, in my book *Angelic Mistakes: The Art of Thomas Merton* (Boston and London: New Seeds/Shambhala, April 2006). Here we can touch on points of significance and grasp something of the whole through telling moments and examples.

The son of artists, young Tom was familiar from his earliest years with the tools, concerns, and attitudes of the studio. He made drawings as a child, it seems more intently than most children. In college he was celebrated, among other things, for his sexy and modish cartoons, published in the Columbia College humor magazine. As he recoiled from the life of the world and moved toward the monastery, his pen-and-ink and brush drawings faithfully reflected that change of heart and mind. While Merton's writings from his years in New York and later in Olean show his great promise as an author, the drawings—cooling from witty to pious, from earthy to heaven-bound—show no such thing in their own domain. He had a pleasant, serviceable talent as an artist in those years, but the *daimon* that ruthlessly urged him forward as a writer took little interest in his art.

Through his first fifteen years or so at Gethsemani, Merton made and preserved literally hundreds of brush drawings on a narrow round of themes: the Blessed Virgin, a tonsured and bearded monk sometimes explicitly identified as St. John of the Cross, the Crucifixion, little else.[53] His journals, richly informative and coursing with ideas, record scarcely anything about this phase of his explorations in art. This was his hibernation: a slow pulse of interest in creating brush-drawn images persisted, though with too little energy to invent, to try and fail, to go down new paths with curiosity and verve. If these early drawings were all that he had left, we would justly consider Merton the visual artist as a footnote of biographical interest only to Merton the writer. Further, he seems to have set aside making images of this or any kind in the later 1950s.

Something quickened late in 1960. For the five previous years he had enjoyed a sporadic but provocative correspondence with his college friend, Ad Reinhardt, and in 1957—after much comic begging—received from Reinhardt a small Black Painting of the kind that would, in time, confirm Reinhardt's reputation as a truly great and fiercely original American painter.[54] Thus Merton had in his monastic sleeping quarters, and later in the hermitage, a masterpiece of contemporary art. One can still almost hear the implicit conversation between Sengai's spare calligraphic art and Reinhardt's even sparer minimalist canvas. Although Merton in these years doubted the seriousness of much contemporary art, he knew beyond question that his comrade Ad Reinhardt was a servant of art in the highest sense. In Merton's estimation at this time, Reinhardt, Klee, and few others stood apart from the dubious mainstream of twentieth-century art. However, the imagery of contemporary art, Jackson Pollock's canvases and surely much else, dwelt in Merton's mind willy-nilly. He would debate with it, reject it, belittle it, banish it, but it had a capacity to hide out when times were tough and reappear as a topic for reflection, as unacceptable and tenacious as ever. The generation that created Abstract Expressionism was precisely his generation. All this was not without consequence. "The work of art is to be *seen*–not imagined, worked over intellectually by the viewer. Central is the experience of seeing,"[55] Merton wrote at an early point in his exploration of brush-drawn calligraphy. The values are those of Zen— and yet provocatively close to those of American artists of his time, who also wished to defend their art against deformation. The other half of Merton's study curriculum as a visual artist was the art of his own time and place, which he would slowly, even reluctantly recognize as speaking his native language.

Since the mid-1950s, Merton had been preparing a book under the working title *Art and Worship*.[56] Perhaps originally intended as a book for general audiences, it soon narrowed in purpose to the idea of providing Catholic readers with a sound basis for appreciating sacred art and more wisely commissioning or purchasing art for Catholic institutions. The project became mired in difficulty in that year of quickening, 1960, among other reasons because Merton could not identify contemporary sacred art that seemed to him fully valid. This stalled project with its unanswered question—is sacred art possible in our time?—entered into the overlapping, mostly silent conversations of this moment in Merton's creative life.

There was a further current in Merton's experience at this time, a restless dissatisfaction with his monastic life in community at Gethsemani. Correspondence with Dom James Fox and many others, as well as passages of self-examination in the journals, chart his formidably uncomfortable search for a new setting: might he transfer to an Order in which the contemplative life had a greater place, could he perhaps found a new experimental monastery in South America, would it be permissible to adopt the hermit's way of life within the Cistercian Order? To all of which Father Abbot's implicit response was the construction of a small cement-block house in the woods and fields at some distance from the monastery, ostensibly for ecumenical meetings with non-Catholic religious leaders (so it was used for a time) but more pointedly to offer Father Louis a place apart.

The renewal of Merton's practice of visual art at the end of 1960, tentative at first but quickly gaining energy, took shape in these conditions. He was certainly not setting out to make a "sacred art," as if such a thing were possible if one only tried hard. He was responding with curiosity, with an inchoate sense of possibility, to the model of Sengai's art, to the art of Reinhardt and Klee which he trusted, to the peculiar stagnation of his work on *Art and Worship*, to the need for something new that could enrich his days within the monastic community that was holding him to his vow of stability. He was responding as the son of artists, in whom the capacity for image-making had scarcely been tapped in recent decades but remained intact. He was responding as a student of Zen who knew that the practice of brush-drawn calligraphy among Zen priests was an utterly serious exercise in mindfulness. And he was responding to the ill-defined promise of the hermitage. He had a sense of adventure, a willingness to take risks, and at last a private space. "The monk is a bird who flies very fast," he wrote in 1964, "without knowing where he is going. And always arrives where he went, in peace, without knowing where he came from."[57]

I must include here a paragraph on resources. The development of Merton's drawings in the 1960s can be traced through some thirty-four primary illustrations with another fifteen to twenty supporting visual documents, selected from among hundreds of drawings and related documents preserved at the Thomas Merton Center and in other university collections. A sequential overview of Merton's drawings from this period is assembled in *Angelic Mistakes* but cannot be reproduced here for practical reasons. Readers fortunate enough to visit the Thomas Merton Center will see some of the most beautiful and representative drawings on permanent exhibition in the reading room. For purposes of this essay, I have chosen three outstanding works—one previously unpublished, the others never published in the form offered here—and will refer as sparingly as possible to works published in *Angelic Mistakes* (AM).

Late in 1960, Merton's earliest abstract calligraphic drawings owe far more to the example of Ad Reinhardt than to Sengai. AM Portfolio 1 and a number of works much like it in the Thomas Merton Center and several university libraries recall in their densely brushed, angular patterns a phase of Ad Reinhardt's art from some 12 years earlier, which Merton would have known through catalogues and other resources shared with him by Reinhardt, perhaps during Reinhardt's visit to Gethsemani in May, 1959. There is also a visual relation with the late canvases of Paul Klee, for whom Merton felt such reverence. Merton signed and dated AM Portfolio 1—in effect, taking responsibility for it and expressing the wish to preserve it. In retrospect, we can see that it is a tentative work, a leap into new terrain.

Soon the magnetic power of Sengai's calligraphic art drew Merton closer and prompted him to use the brush more freely and variously. By late 1963 or '64, an undated work now in the Burns Library, Boston College (fig. 3), reveals the unmistakable authority of an artist who has found his way. Merton returned on occasion in his few writings on art to the notion of emblems or what he called "equivalences," a term borrowed from Alfred Stieglitz or perhaps occurring to Merton independently as he faced the issues of abstract imagery that Stieglitz also had faced. This image, seemingly monumental as if it were a design for a fountain or public sculpture but in fact only four inches high, has very considerable emblematic power. Brush-drawn at the head of a vertical, scroll-like strip of paper, apparently torn somewhat roughly from a larger sheet, the image asks to be interpreted. What do we see here? What is in motion here?

By the end of 1963, such innocent questions proper to any inquiry seemed to Merton to miss the point. He discussed the issue of interpretation in a memorable letter to the first magazine editor to publish, at his invitation, a suite of his calligraphic drawings:

> It is stimulating to hear that you like the calligraphies. The title I gave them was "Shamanic Dictation" but now, thinking about it, I think it is rather cheap and misleading.... Such calligraphies should really have no literary trimmings at all, including titles. There should really be nothing that misleads the spectator by seeming to give him a "clue." That is the curse of the literary incrustations that have still remained on so much abstract art: the mania for satisfying the spectators' foolish question about "what is it?" Until they can be content to accept the fact that the picture is simply itself, there is no point in trying to explain it, especially if the explanation seems to indicate that it is something else.

Fig. 3 Thomas Merton, brush drawing, untitled, ca. 1964. Boston College, Burns Library Collection, gift of Mary McNiff.

These calligraphies (this word is not a title but simply an indication of the species of drawing to which they belong) should really be pure and simple as they are, and they should lay no claim to being anything but themselves. There should be no afterthoughts about them on the part of the artist or spectator. Each time one sees them is the first time. Each stroke is so to speak first and last, all goes in one breath, one brushful of ink, and the result is a statement of itself that is "right" insofar as it says nothing "about" anything else under the sun. Therefore to bring in the notion of a pseudo-mystical experience is fraudulent in the extreme, even though it is only a joke, and meant to warn the spectator to reverse it and understand the opposite. Such maneuvers are silly and, as I say, misleading. So I would prefer to drop "Shamanic Dictation" as nonsense, and just call them calligraphies. Actually they have a kind of musical character, in a derivative sort of way. Though of course visually only.[58]

In later years Merton consistently took this view when the issue came up, most notably in the essay he wrote as gallery notes to accompany his first exhibition.[59] He did compromise by adding titles to the works in that exhibition, with the thought that visitors would value that small element of orientation, but when he published fifteen drawings from the exhibition in *Raids on the Unspeakable* (1966), the titles were dropped and viewers were once again on their own.

Merton's stance "against interpretation," to use Susan Sontag's powerful phrase, is almost certainly grounded in the notion of *tathata* or suchness that he had encountered in Zen—a notion of the inviolate presence of each thing, best appreciated in silence without the mind running on. Merton's stance also represents a logical consequence of his experience of art-making, which was visceral and gestural rather than calculated and plotted in advance. But ultimately the attitude is too severe. It is the artist's privilege to invoke it, and the viewer's privilege to ignore it while nonetheless taking the lesson that interpretation must not be indulgence or self-exhibition. It must be austere, as the work is austere.

One can hardly miss the groundedness of the work illustrated in fig. 3—it stands heavily and firmly. As well, one is keenly aware of its multiple planes turned toward the heavens, thick and dense at the bottom of the image, reaching, porous, and open at the top. Merton almost certainly did not set out to create an image or emblem of prayer. It's far more likely that he simply set out—"the monk is a bird who flies very fast"—and found his way unexpectedly to a sign that shares in the nature of prayer.

We are in Sengai's world here. Merton's long companionship with the calendars has proved to be fruitful. Another work, dated 1964 and titled "Sun Dance" for purposes of exhibition (fig. 4), shows us something more of Sengai's impact on Merton's imagination and brushwork. Previously unpublished and for the moment known only through a photograph, this drawing is both dazzlingly brilliant and slightly awkward. It is one of several leaping figures to be found among the drawings; Merton's own exuberant energy is of that kind, a leap. As North American readers well know, the Sun Dance is a Native American ritual, initiatory and extreme in its demands. Merton comments on photographs of the Sun Dance in one of his few articles on Native Americans.[60]

The magic of the drawing lies in the difference between the upper and lower parts of the dancing figure. Feet, legs, hips belong to the Earth—the dancer stamps the Earth and leaps in the pattern of the dance—while the upper portions of the figure belong to another world, call it the world of spirit. And yet the figure is one. In the few marks that make up this image, Merton found his way to an emblem of the essential human: body and yet not only, spirit and yet not only, a possible unity. And all in motion. His words at the end of *New Seeds of Contemplation* come to mind:

> The world and time are the dance of the Lord in emptiness.... No despair of ours can alter the reality of things, or stain the joy of the cosmic dance which is always there. Indeed, we are in the midst of it, and it is in the midst of us, for it beats in our very blood, whether we want it to or not.... We are invited to forget ourselves on purpose, cast our awful solemnity to the winds and join in the general dance.[61]

If we take our distance for a moment from these two drawings, figs. 3 and 4, we might agree that Merton's art evokes the values and strivings for which he most cared as a religious seeker. In these years, the best of his drawings are a journal of another kind:

Fig. 4 Thomas Merton, brush drawing, "Sun Dance," 1964 (photograph in the Thomas Merton Center collection, location of original unknown).

silent, proceeding from unspoken depths in himself and addressing those depths in others. He wished this transaction to be, insofar as possible, clothed in tranquility and selflessness. "The peculiar quality of Chinese and Japanese art that is influenced by Zen,"
he once wrote,

> is that it is able to suggest what cannot be said, and, by
> using a bare minimum of form, to awaken us to the form-
> less. Zen painting tells us just enough to alert us to what is
> *not* and is nevertheless "right there." Zen calligraphy, by
> its peculiar suppleness, dynamism, abandon, contempt for
> "prettiness" and for formal "style," reveals to us some-
> thing of the freedom which is not transcendent in some
> abstract and intellectual sense, but which employs a mini-
> mum of form without being attached to it, and is therefore
> free from it.[62]

"SIGNATURES OF SOMEONE WHO IS NOT AROUND": THE TRANSITION TO PRINTMAKING

Toward the end of 1963 and throughout 1964, Merton reached
maturity as a visual artist. Though one could point to minor awkward passages in the works so far seen (figs. 3 and 4), their expressive power is beyond question. Further, twentieth-century art did
not insist on finish in works that offer other values. It learned to
appreciate improvisation, evident speed of execution, deliberate
roughness, enriching chance marks. Merton shared these values,
although he complained on occasion of losing control of his process—of "patchiness all along, and blots," as he once wrote to the
artist Ulfert Wilke.[63]

A sophisticated artist with roots in Louisville and an extensive
network of friends in the art world, Wilke entered Merton's life at
the right moment to help him make a key transition as an artist.
Alerted to Merton's interest in art by Ad Reinhardt, Wilke made
contact with Merton in the fall of 1963 and again in summer 1964,
just the period when Merton had become confident as an artist.
Dated works from that time—and works similar though undated—
give the impression of an art of the brush, reflecting something of
Zen calligraphy and something of Abstract Expressionism, which
could go from strength to strength for years to come.

Merton was now far more open to the American art of his own time. The long argument with Abstract Expressionism had subsided. In part through witnessing that his own art converged with the art of his contemporaries, more than a few of whom shared his interest in abstract calligraphic signs, he realized that the strivings and achievements of artists "in the world" were far from negligible. In the summer of 1964, he offered to the novices at Gethsemani an extraordinarily affirming talk on contemporary art, for which his notes survive. The ecumenical imperative, the movement toward solidarity with others, now touched and even ennobled his understanding of art:

> In spite of the fact that the majority of people have derided modern non-representative art, have attacked it, and have taken for granted that it was all a fraud, all complete nonsense, have been frightened, shocked, scandalized by it, this art has gone its own way and has established itself as one of the most important expressions of man's intellectual and spiritual life in the world today—it flourishes everywhere, not only in extremely sophisticated circles in Europe and North America, but also in Latin America, in former colonial countries, and in Soviet Russia, Poland, etc., where it is opposed and suppressed by the Communists.... It has thus become a *universal language of experience*, a common idiom of the spirit in which artists all over the world share in the development of new attitudes and new views of the world, even when they cannot speak each other's language....
>
> Through an understanding of art, we can enter into communion with the world of our time on a deep and significant level and can therefore come to a knowledge of its needs and its problems. We can be more in communion with our own time. We have to be men of our time....[64]

It was a man with these new convictions who met Ulfert Wilke. However he came to it—through independent experimentation, through a suggestion from Wilke or another artist, or by observing processes in the monastic print shop—Merton shifted in 1963-64 from direct brushwork to a rudimentary but effective process of printmaking. Brushwork was still the basis: Merton would create what he called an ink "negative" brushed onto textured paper or cardboard and then, simply with hand pressure, printed the negative onto a finer sheet of paper of a quality that Reinhardt and Wilke generously provided. Although Merton continued to make direct drawings from time to time after 1964, the great majority of his works, upon careful examination, prove to be prints. Figure 5 offers an outstanding example. Date, signature, and numbering document that this work was in the traveling exhibition that toured from Louisville to several other cities in 1964-67. That there was an exhibition at all Merton probably owed to Wilke, who must have dropped a hint to the gallery director at Louisville's Catherine Spalding College, a Catholic institution, about the real interest of Merton's art.

Merton's revision of his printed notes for the larger touring exhibition gives us the title "Sky Signature" for this work.[65] While he published it in *Raids on the Unspeakable*, it is reproduced here from the original, a gift by Merton to Daniel Berrigan now in the keeping of the Jesuit community in Manhattan. This is a sophisticated, knowing work, poised midway between Zen calligraphy and Abstract Expressionism on ground that had come to be Merton's own. Merton prized the porous, breathing textures and vanishingly minute elements of pattern that could result from transferring to fine paper an image brushed on textured cardboard. He also valued the interventions of chance or providence in his working process. He could not wholly predict the appearance of images printed in this rudimentary way, by hand pressure, but he welcomed whatever occurred with the sole exception of "patchiness" and "blots," which in excess could spoil images. In this image, as in a number of other impressive works such as AM Portfolio 15, Merton draws on the traditional artist's strategy of emphatic diagonals to create a dynamic image. His emblem or equivalent here, profoundly abstract, reads in terms of buoyancy, openness, and tranquility, as if it were an elaborate air-borne seed from the Tree of Life—but any such ascription of meaning is no more than a possible perspective. The image itself has a curious authority. Much that Merton valued in visual art, and much that returned him again and again to his improvised studio in the hermitage (a table, a few simple tools) is evident here.

Something more must be said about Merton's openness to chance effects. In the little he wrote about his printing process, he was matter of fact. "You never quite know what is going to come

Fig. 5 Thomas Merton, "Sky Signature," 1964, print derived from brush drawing. Private collection.

out, and often it is a big surprise."[66] But an extended discussion of chance/providence in *Angelic Mistakes* suggests that Merton—like some other artists influenced by Zen or the European art movement, Dada—welcomed the interventions of chance/providence as a means of reducing his role as an inevitably ego-concerned creator.[67] Merton addressed the issue of "who is the maker?" in notes toward the only essay he published on his art, and of course in the essay itself, which served as the printed exhibition guide often mentioned in the course of this discussion. Quite extensive, the notes include this compelling set of reflections:

> Signs therefore not of *idea* but of movement
> Footprints of the unconscious (as a child might make deliberate footprints in the snow)
> But difference—not a sign that "I" passed this way.
> Footprints *divested of ego and yet not anonymous*
> This I do not know how to explain.
> That movement of the world was thus registered on paper was due to
> my decision—it is important only in so far as my brushstrokes are not those
> of a machine. But neither are they "mine," nor are they those of a particular artist. Nor of a medium or shaman.... Neither rustic nor urbane, Eastern nor Western, perhaps can be called expressions of Zen Catholicism.... Fidelity to Zen-like experience of wholeness.[68]

In the finished essay, eventually published in *Raids on the Unspeakable* and also reprinted in *Angelic Mistakes*, Merton consolidated much of the preceding into a remarkable phrase: his art records the "signatures of someone who is not around."[69]

"THE PERFECT ACT IS EMPTY"

In an earlier section of this essay we looked at Merton's adoption of Zen practices and reached the view that his practice of art had a place among them. Once he had found his pace and approach through trial and error, he recorded very little in his journal about the direct experience of image-making; his commitment to silence and against interpretation, even of his own experience, was not in the least casual. But there is a passage in his late book-length poem, *Cables to the Ace*, which speaks to what may well have been the heart of his discoveries through art. The voice here is native to Zen. It is not the voice of an outsider, longing for admission to something other. Dr. Suzuki's friend and student had found in Zen some real fulfillment of his movement, initiated decades earlier, toward what Meister Eckhart called "the most intimate poverty."[70] Merton wrote:

> The perfect act is empty. Who can see it? He who forgets form. Out of the formed, the unformed, the empty act proceeds with its own form. Perfect form is momentary. Its perfection vanishes at once. Perfection and emptiness work together for they are the same: the coincidence of momentary form and eternal nothingness. Form: the flash of nothingness. Forget form, and it suddenly appears, ringed and reverberating with its own light, which is nothing. Well, then: stop seeking. Let it all happen. Let it come and go. What? Everything: i.e., nothing.[71]

NOTES

I wish to thank our editor and instigator, Bonnie Thurston, for her kind invitation to contribute to this volume. As always in my work and surely in the work of us all on the Merton legacy, Paul M. Pearson, director of the Thomas Merton Center, has generously helped in many ways. I am grateful to the Thomas Merton Center, the Merton Legacy Trust, the Burns Library of Boston College, Mrs. Mihoko Okamura-Bekku, and Alan Briceland, S.J., for permission to reproduce Merton drawings and other documents in their care.

1. Thomas Merton, "D.T. Suzuki: The Man and His Work," in *Zen and the Birds of Appetite*, New York: New Directions, 1968, p. 65 (first published 1967).

2. Merton letter to Father Aelred, S.S.F., 8 December 1964. *The School of Charity: The Letters of Thomas Merton on Religious Renewal and Spiritual Direction*, ed. Brother Patrick Hart, New York: Farrar Straus Giroux, 1990, p. 254.

3. The present article stays within the boundaries of the Merton-Suzuki relationship as Merton described and experienced it. It goes without saying that this is not the only possible perspective. Notably, see a prior essay by a distinguished contributor to this volume: Roger Corless, "In Search of a Context for the Merton-Suzuki Dialogue," *The Merton Annual 6*, ed. George A. Kilcourse, Collegeville (MN): Liturgical Press, 1994, pp. 76-91. Prof. Corless's article contributes to a gathering critique of Suzuki's presentation of Zen and Japanese culture, which has

been carried forward in Brian (Daizen) A. Victoria, *Zen at War*, New York and Tokyo: Weatherhill, 1997, and Brian Daizen Victoria, *Zen War Stories*, London and New York: RoutledgeCurzon, 2003. General biographical sources for Suzuki include A. Irwin Switzer III, *D.T. Suzuki: A Biography*, London: The Buddhist Society, 1985, and Masao Abe, ed., *A Zen Life: D.T. Suzuki Remembered*, New York and Tokyo: Weatherhill, 1986.

4. Thomas Merton and James Laughlin, *Selected Letters*, ed. David D. Cooper, New York and London: W.W. Norton, 1997, p. 108.

5. Ibid., p. 114.

6. Merton letter to Ad Reinhardt, 3 July 1956. See Roger Lipsey, "Do I want a small painting? The Correspondence of Thomas Merton and Ad Reinhardt," in *The Merton Annual 18*, ed. Victor A. Kramer, Louisville (KY): Fons Vitae, 2006

7. Thomas Merton, "Basic Principles of Monastic Spirituality," in *The Monastic Journey*, ed. Brother Patrick Hart, New York: Image, 1978, p. 31.

8. Merton letter to Etta Gullick, 24 March 1963. *The Hidden Ground of Love: The Letters of Thomas Merton on Religious Experience and Social Concerns*, ed. William H. Shannon, New York: Farrar Straus Giroux, 1985, p. 359.

9. Thomas Merton, *The Way of Chuang Tzu*, New York: New Directions, 1965.

10. Merton letter to Etta Gullick, 9 June 1965. *The Hidden Ground of Love*, op. cit., p. 370.

11. The Dalai Lama, *Freedom in Exile: The Autobiography of the Dalai Lama*, New York: HarperCollins, 1990, p. 189.

12. Merton letter to Helen Wolff, 14 April 1959, reporting on his initial contact with Suzuki. *The Courage for Truth: The Letters of Thomas Merton to Writers*, ed. Christine M. Bochen, New York: Farrar Straus Giroux, 1993, p. 96. "Everything he writes is to me very interesting and important. He is a great man," Merton confided to Mrs. Wolff.

13. Robert E. Daggy, ed., *Encounter: Thomas Merton and D. T. Suzuki*, Monterey (KY): Larkspur Press, 1988, pp. 5-6.

14. Merton letter to Father Kilian McDonnell, 29 January 1960. *The School of Charity*, op. cit., p. 128. See also Merton's letter to Jacques Maritain, 8 April 1960, *The Courage for Truth*, op. cit., pp. 30-31, in which he explores with this cherished older friend the possibility of a book that would include not only Merton and Suzuki on the desert fathers, but also articles by Erich Fromm and other leading thinkers. Maritain's letter of April 18 in response, preserved at the Thomas Merton Center, counsels Merton to be receptive to Dr. Suzuki and the other proposed authors, but to retain the dominant position in the book of essays by different hands, as a host serves his guests.

15. For convenience, see "Wisdom in Emptiness, A Dialogue: D. T. Suzuki and Thomas Merton," in *Zen and the Birds of Appetite*, op. cit., pp. 99 ff.

16. *Encounter*, op.cit., p. 18.

17. The Sengai calendars in their original form must be extremely rare. Booklet-style publications containing the illustrations and Suzuki texts for a given year were issued by the publisher and occasionally show up at Advanced Book Exchange and comparable Internet resources. The comprehensive text is D.T. Suzuki, *Sengai: The Zen Master*, London: Faber and Faber, 1971 (recently reprinted by Shambhala Publications).

18. Merton letter to Robert Lax, 10 February 1961. Arthur W. Biddle, ed., *When Prophecy Still Had a Voice: The Letters of Thomas Merton and Robert Lax*, Lexington (KY): University Press of Kentucky, 2001, p. 217.

19. Thomas Merton, *Day of a Stranger*, Salt Lake City (UT): Gibbs M. Smith, 1981, p. 35.

20. Merton letter to D.T. Suzuki, 4 March 1965. *The Hidden Ground of Love*, op. cit., p. 570.

21. Robert E. Daggy, ed., *Dancing in the Water of Life: The Journals of Thomas Merton, Volume Five, 1963-1965*, San Francisco: HarperSanFrancisco, 1997, p. 202.

22. *Encounter*, op. cit., p. 69.

23. This photograph is fig. 7 in Roger Lipsey, *Angelic Mistakes: The Art of Thomas Merton*, Boston and London: New Seeds / Shambhala Publications, 2006.

24. Daisetz T. Suzuki, *Zen and Japanese Culture*, Princeton: Bollingen Series 64, 1970, pp. 272-289, 304-07. The particular passage is on p. 273.

25. Thomas Merton, "D.T. Suzuki: The Man and His Work," op. cit., pp. 60-61.

26. Ibid., p. 62.

27. Merton letter to Robert Lax, 10 July 1964. *When Prophecy Still Had a Voice*, op. cit., p. 280.

28. *Dancing in the Water of Life*, op. cit., entry for 20 June 1964, p. 116.

29. Merton letter to President Grayson Kirk, Columbia University, 16 June 1961. Thomas Merton, *Witness to Freedom: Letters in Times of Crisis*, ed. William H. Shannon, San Diego: Harcourt Brace, 1994, p. 158.

30. Thomas Merton, *Turning Toward the World: The Journals of Thomas Merton, Volume Four, 1960-1963*, ed. Victor A. Kramer, San Francisco: HarperSanFrancisco, 1996, entry for 22 August 1961, p. 155.

31. Merton letter to John C. Heidbrink, 15 February 1962. *The Hidden Ground of Love*, op. cit., p. 407.

32. Thomas Merton, *Zen and the Birds of Appetite*, op. cit., p. 21.

33. Thomas Merton, *Learning to Love: The Journals of Thomas Merton, Volume Six, 1966-1967*, ed. Christine M. Bochen, San Francisco: HarperSanFrancisco, 1997, entry for 6 February 1966, pp. 358-359. Consider also the entry for 19 April 1965, p. 232, and related thoughts in Thomas Merton, *Mystics and Zen Masters*, New York: Farrar Straus Giroux, 1967, p. 65.

34. Merton letter to Erich Fromm, 15 January 1966. *The Hidden Ground of Love*, op. cit., p. 322.

35. Merton letter to Dame Marcella Van Bruyn, August, 1966. *The School of Charity*, op. cit., p. 311.

36. Merton letter to Victoria Ocampo, 20 January 1967. *The Courage for Truth*, op. cit., p. 211.

37. *Day of a Stranger*, op. cit., p. 41.

38. Merton letter to Rosemary Radford Ruether, 14 February 1967. *At Home in the World: The Letters of Thomas Merton & Rosemary Radford Ruether*, ed. Mary Tardiff, Maryknoll (NY): Orbis, 1995, p. 24. Consider also the frequently quoted passage on Merton's approach to meditation and prayer in a letter to a Muslim friend, in which Christian, Buddhist, and Sufi terms are quietly integrated: Merton letter to Abdul Aziz, 2 January 1966 (*The Hidden Ground of Love*, op. cit., pp. 63-64).

39. Merton letter to Paul Sih, 2 January 1962. *The Hidden Ground of Love*, op. cit., p. 551.

40. *Turning Toward the World*, op. cit., entry for 18 January 1963, p. 291.

41. Thomas Merton, *The Other Side of the Mountain: The Journals of Thomas Merton, Volume Seven, 1966-1967*, ed. Brother Patrick Hart, San Francisco: HarperSanFrancisco, 1998, entry for 15 January 1967, p. 44.

42. Thomas Merton, *A Vow of Conversation: Journals 1964-1965*, ed. Naomi Burton Stone, New York: Farrar Straus Giroux, 1988, entry for 20 January 1964, p. 17. Edited by Merton though published long after his death, this book offers good examples of Merton's own editorial process. For the present passage, cf. the much more complex, unedited journal entry in *Dancing in the Water of Life*, op. cit., p. 65.

43. Merton letter to a woman religious, 27 March 1968. *Witness to Freedom*, op. cit., p. 197.

44. Thomas Merton, "The Zen Koan," in *Mystics and Zen Masters*, op. cit., pp. 235-54.

45. John Howard Griffin, *Follow the Ecstasy: Thomas Merton, The Hermitage Years 1965-1968*, JHG Fort Worth: Editions/Latitude Press, 1983, pp. 112-13.

46. Ron Seitz, *Song for Nobody: A Memory Vision of Thomas Merton*, Liguori (Missouri): Triumph Books, 1993, p. 123.

47. Brother Patrick Hart, ed., *The Literary Essays of Thomas Merton*, New York: New Directions, 1981, p. 309. On Merton's sense of distance from the monastic community and the force of his self-doubt, consider his letter to the explorer of Tibetan culture, Marco Pallis, 28 May 1966, in *The Hidden Ground of Love*, op. cit., p. 476.

48. *Learning to Love*, op. cit., p. 367 (section entitled "Some Personal Notes"). Consider also Merton's letter to a college friend, Seymour Freedgood, 12 April 1967, in *The Road to Joy*, op. cit., p. 129.

49. Thomas Merton, *Cables to the Ace, or Familiar Liturgies of Misunderstanding* (1968), section 30, in *The Collected Poems of Thomas Merton*, New Directions: New York, 1977, p. 452.

50. Merton letter to Dom Jean Leclercq, 10 November 1963. *The School of Charity*, op. cit., p. 184.

51. Thomas Merton, *Mystics and Zen Masters*, op. cit., pp. 75-76.

52. Daisetz T. Suzuki, *Sengai*, op. cit., p. 114.

53. Selections from Merton's drawings prior to 1960 can be seen in Edward Rice, *The Man in the Sycamore Tree: The Good Times and Hard Life of Thomas Merton*, Garden City (NY): Doubleday, 1970; Thomas Merton, *Dialogues with Silence: Prayers & Drawings*, ed. Jonathan Montaldo, San Francisco: HarperSanFrancisco, 2001; and Roger Lipsey, *Angelic Mistakes*, op. cit.

54. See Roger Lipsey, "Do I want a small painting?" op. cit.

55. *Turning Toward the World*, op. cit., entry for 17 November 1961, p. 180.

56. On the ms. of *Art and Worship*, see David D. Cooper, *Thomas Merton's Art of Denial: The Evolution of a Radical Humanist*, Athens (GA) and London: The University of Georgia Press, 1989, chapter 4; and Roger Lipsey, *Angelic Mistakes*, op. cit.

57. Merton letter to Miguel Grinberg, 11 May 1964. *The Courage for Truth*, op. cit., p. 198.

58. Merton letter to Margaret Randall, 9 October 1963. ibid., pp. 216-17.

59. Thomas Merton, "Signatures: Notes on the Author's Drawings," in *Raids on the Unspeakable*, New York: New Directions, 1966, pp. 179-182.

60. Thomas Merton, "The Shoshoneans," in *Ishi Means Man*, Greensboro (NC): Unicorn Press, 1976, pp. 5-16.

61. Thomas Merton, *New Seeds of Contemplation*, New York: New Directions, 1961, p. 297.

62. Thomas Merton, *Zen and the Birds of Appetite*, op. cit., p. 6. Consider also a passage in Merton's introduction to John C.H. Wu, *The*

Golden Age of Zen: Zen Masters of the T'ang Dynasty (1967), conveniently available as "A Christian Looks at Zen," in *Zen and the Birds of Appetite*, op. cit., pp. 33 ff. (this passage, pp. 52-53): "The apparently mysterious and cryptic sayings of Zen become much simpler when we see them in the whole context of Buddhist 'mindfulness' or awareness, which in its most elementary form consists in that 'bare attention' which simply *sees* what is right there and does not add any comment, any interpretation, any judgment, any conclusion. It just *sees*. Learning to see in this manner is the basic and fundamental exercise of Buddhist meditation."

63. On Ulfert Wilke, see Roger Lipsey, *Angelic Mistakes*, op. cit, s.v. Ulfert Wilke. The Merton-Wilke correspondence will be found in Roger Lipsey, ed., "Thomas Merton and Ulfert Wilke: The Friendship of Artists," *The Merton Seasonal* 30:2, Summer 2005, pp. 3-12.

64. Thomas Merton, Notebook 14, 1964, Thomas Merton Center. With the permission of the Merton Legacy Trust.

65. Preserved in the Thomas Merton Center, the revision takes the form of handwritten notes added to the original printed version produced by Catherine Spalding College for its Thanksgiving 1964 exhibition.

66. Merton letter to Sr. Gabriel Mary, 28 April 1965, Collection of the Thomas Merton Center. With the permission of the Merton Legacy Trust.

67. See Lipsey, *Angelic Mistakes*, op. cit., s.v. "Chance/Providence" and "Unlikely Peers," for extended discussions of this issue in the contexts of Zen and Dada.

68. Notebook 14, op. cit.

69. Thomas Merton, "Signatures: Notes on the Author's Drawings," in *Raids on the Unspeakable*, New York: New Directions, 1966, pp. 179-182.

70. *Zen and the Birds of Appetite*, op. cit., pp. 109-10.

71. *Cables to the Ace*, op. cit., section 37, p. 421.

BEYOND THE SHADOW
AND THE DISGUISE:
THE ZEN PHOTOGRAPHY
OF THOMAS MERTON

Paul M. Pearson

Thomas Merton's stunning photographs of the statues of the Buddha at Polonnaruwa, Ceylon (now Sri Lanka), are probably the images that spring immediately to mind with the sub-title of this essay. Certainly those photographs, along with the journal entry Merton made on that visit, have entered into the realm of the classic vignettes from the Merton corpus, as well known as his revelation on the corner of Fourth and Walnut in Louisville. Stunning though they are, they are not the photographs I had in mind in contemplating Merton's Zen photography.

During Merton's travels of 1968 in New Mexico, California, Alaska, and in Asia, a considerable number of his photographs would fit into the category of travel photographs, holiday snaps, with which so many people are familiar.[1] There is no denying he had a good eye for such photographs, but they are images more of his physical journey than his interior journey. This, as he remarked in a circular letter from this time, was the real journey.[2] Other images, especially from his time in Asia do express this interior journey as Merton tried to capture visually, through the eye of the camera, certain places—and people—that had a profound effect on him. These places and people were frequently given significant entries in the personal journal that Merton was keeping, which later became one of the major sources for compiling *The Asian Journal of Thomas Merton*. It is noteworthy that photography, one of the newest of Merton's chosen forms of artistic expression, should so closely parallel through his travels his spiritual writings. Through much of the sixties, as demonstrated by Dr. Roger Lipsey, Merton's calligraphies and printed images were also a fundamental expression of Merton's spiritual vision and of his vision of the world.[3]

"LOVE AFFAIR WITH CAMERA"— THOMAS MERTON, PHOTOGRAPHER

Thomas Merton showed little interest in photography until the final years of his life. On a visit to Germany as a teenager he had bought his first camera, a Zeiss, which he subsequently pawned as his debts grew at Cambridge University[4] in the early thirties. In 1939 he visited an exhibit of Charles Sheeler's at the Museum of Modern Art, which he found "dull."[5] Then, from the late fifties onwards Merton had contact with some eminent North American photographers beginning with Shirley Burden.

Burden had provided photographs for a postulant's guide, *Monastic Peace*,[6] for the cover of Merton's *Selected Poems*[7] and had undertaken a photographic study of the monks at the Abbey of Gethsemani, *God Is My Life*,[8] for which Merton wrote the introduction. When Merton was considering a photographic study of the Shakers[9] in the early sixties, it was to Burden he turned.

In a journal entry for March 19, 1958 Merton records that on a visit to Louisville he bought "for a few pennies" *The Family of Man*, the book accompanying Edward Steichen's exhibition of photographs at the Museum of Modern Art. Merton goes on to describe it as "fabulous" writing "no refinements and no explanations are necessary! How scandalized some would be if I said that this whole book is to me a picture of Christ, and yet that is the Truth."[10] For many readers of Thomas Merton the journal entry from which this quotation is taken will be familiar for another reason—it is in the same entry in his personal journal that Merton records his famous "Louisville epiphany." Merton's experience of oneness with other people on a street corner in Louisville is mirrored in his experience of the photographs in Steichen's book, where Merton sees all the images as "a picture of Christ."

The following year Sibylle Akers, whom Merton described as "a very gifted photographer,"[11] visited Merton at Gethsemani. Akers took a number of formal photographs of Thomas Merton and also left him with some of her own photographs, including some of Indian women on the Island of Juntzio.[12]

In 1963 John Howard Griffin, with whom Merton had already had contact in relation to Civil Rights, wrote requesting permission to "begin a photographic archive of Merton's life and activities." When Griffin visited Merton to photograph him he recalls "Tom watched with interest, wanting an explanation of the cameras—a Leica and an Alpa." According to Griffin, Merton remarked on his friendship with Shirley Burden and also with Edward Rice, a friend from his days at Columbia and an extremely competent photographer, before stating "I don't know anything about photography, but it fascinates me."[13]

It is a little unclear when Merton began taking photographs himself at the Abbey of Gethsemani. On October 10th 1961 he records having taken "half a roll of Kodacolor at the hermitage" wondering "what earthly reason is there for taking color photographs?...or any photographs at all."[14] Yet, just a few months later in January 1962 Merton records taking photographs at Shakertown, the Shaker village close to Gethsemani, finding there "some marvelous subjects."[15]

> Marvelous, silent, vast spaces around the old buildings. Cold, pure light, and some grand trees.... How the blank side of a frame house can be so completely beautiful I cannot imagine. A completely miraculous achievement of forms.[16]

Shaker Building, Pleasant Hill, Kentucky.

Merton was obviously pleased with his results that day as in a later journal entry he says he is planning to have enlargements made of some of his photographs of Shakertown, describing it as "very satisfying."[17] Merton's description here of the objects he was photographing at Pleasant Hill provide a good starting point for understanding his concept of Zen photography—insights which go beyond the surface of the frame house and trees, and uncover within them an inner radiance of Being.

Certainly by September 22, 1964, Merton had regular access to a camera and records in his personal journal:

> Brother Ephrem has fitted me out with a camera (Kodak Instamatic) to help take pictures for a book Dom James wants done. So far I have been photographing a fascinating old cedar root I have on the porch. I am not sure what this baby can do. The lens does not look like much—but it changes the film by itself and sets the aperture, etc. Very nice.[18]

Just two days later Merton continues, in an entry where he refers to "Zen photography" for the first time:

> After dinner I was distracted by the dream camera, and instead of seriously reading the Zen anthology I got from the Louisville Library, kept seeing curious things to shoot, especially a mad window in the old tool room of the woodshed. The whole place is full of fantastic and strange subjects—a mine of Zen photography. After that the dream camera suddenly misbehaved.[19]

And Merton records that the back of the camera would not lock shut. Two days later he writes again:

> Camera back. Love affair with camera. Darling camera, so glad to have you back! Monarch! XXX. It will I think be a bright day again today.[20]

In his journals Merton records occasional access to a variety of cameras belonging to his visitors—Naomi Burton Stone's Nikon,[21] John Howard Griffin's Alpa,[22] even on one occasion a "Japanese movie camera" which he described as "a beautiful thing."[23] In August 1967 Merton refers in passing to taking some pictures of roots, this time with a Rolleiflex. However in January 1968 Merton fell

Naomi Burton Stone and Thomas Merton.

Naomi Burton Stone's photograph of Thomas Merton.

and thought he might have broken the Rolleiflex so that the back
was letting in light. He immediately wrote to John Howard Griffin
to take up an offer he had made to loan Merton a camera. In his
letter Merton describes the kind of camera he would need—the
specifications he outlines point to Merton's own vision of photography. He writes:

> Obviously I am not covering the Kentucky Derby etc. But
> I do like a chance at fast funny out of the way stuff too.
> The possibility of it in case. But as I see it I am going to be
> on roots, sides of barns, tall weeds, mudpuddles, and
> junkpiles until Kingdom come. A built-in exposure meter
> might be a help.[24]

In response Griffin loaned Merton a Canon F-X which he described
as "fabulous" and "a joy to work with." Merton once again applies
the term Zen to the camera writing:

> The camera is the most eager and helpful of beings, all full
> of happy suggestions: 'Try this! Do it that way!' Remind-
> ing me of things I have overlooked, and cooperating in the
> creation of new worlds. So simply. This is a Zen camera.[25]

Generally Merton's preferred photographic medium was black and
white, though a number of photographs in the collections at the
Thomas Merton Center at Bellarmine University are in color.[26]
Merton never did his own developing or printing; this was generally done for him either by Griffin, Griffin's son Gregory, or by
other friends. John Howard Griffin recalls that he and his son were
frequently bewildered by the pictures Merton selected from contact sheets to be enlarged. "He ignored many superlative photographs while marking others," wrote Griffin:

> We thought he had not yet learned to judge photographs
> well enough to select consistently the best frames. We wrote
> and offered advice about the quality of some of the ig-
> nored frames. He went right on marking what he wanted
> rather than what we thought he should want. Then, more
> and more often, he would send a contact sheet with a cer-
> tain frame marked and his excited notation: 'At last—this
> is what I have been aiming for.'[27]

Sadly, none of those original contact sheets have survived. They would have provided a fascinating insight into Merton's Zen photography.

In January 1967 Thomas Merton began to develop a friendship with another local photographer, Ralph Eugene Meatyard, who, through his photographs, has left us an intriguing photographic record of Merton. In his personal journal Merton recorded the visit of Jonathan Williams, Guy Davenport and Meatyard—"three kings all from Lexington"[28]—and in particular his excitement at Meatyard's work:

> The one who made the greatest impression on me as artist was Gene Meatyard, the photographer—does marvelous arresting visionary things, most haunting and suggestive, mythical, photography I ever saw. I felt that here was someone really going somewhere.[29]

Later writing about Merton and Meatyard, Davenport described Meatyard as "one of the most distinguished of American photographers,"[30] part of the Lexington Camera Club with members such as Van Deren Coke, Guy Mendes, James Baker Hall and Robert C. May. Meatyard, was a professional optician, who bought his first camera to photograph his young son in 1950. In 1956 his photographs were exhibited with those of Ansel Adams, Aaron Siskind, Henry Callaghan and other modern masters. That same year he attended a photography workshop where, working with Henry Holmes Smith and Minor White, he became interested in Zen. Davenport describes Meatyard's work as "primarily an intricate symmetry of light and shadow. He liked deep shadows of considerable weight, and he liked light that was decisive and clean"[31]— words, I would suggest, equally applicable to many of Merton's photographs.

From their meeting in January 1967 until Merton's death the following year Merton met Gene Meatyard numerous times and exchanged a brief but steady correspondence of over sixteen letters. During this time Meatyard took over one hundred photographs of Merton, some of the most enigmatic taken. These photographs capture both the paradox of Merton and Meatyard's surrealistic vision—Meatyard realized with Merton that he was:

> ...photographing a Kierkegaard who was a fan of *Mad*; a Zen adept and hermit who drooled over hospital nurses

with a cute behind…a man of accomplished self-discipline who sometimes acted like a ten-year-old with an unlimited charge account at a candy store.[32]

Thomas Merton. Photograph by Ralph Eugene Meatyard.

In *A Hidden Wholeness* Griffin describes a little of Merton's vision of photography, getting right to the heart of Merton's photographic genius, to its simplicity, like the Zen masters and desert mothers and fathers Merton so admired:

> His vision was more often attracted to the movement of wheat in the wind, the textures of snow, paint-spattered cans, stone, crocuses blossoming through weeds—or again, the woods in all their hours, from the first fog of morning, though noonday stillness, to evening quiet.
>
> In his photography, he focused on the images of his contemplation, as they were and not as he wanted them to be. He took his camera on his walks and, with his special way of seeing, photographed what moved or excited him— whatsoever responded to that inner orientation.
>
> His concept of aesthetic beauty differed from that of most men. Most would pass by dead tree roots in search of a rose. Merton photographed the dead tree root or the tex-

ture of wood or whatever crossed his path. In these works, he photographed the natural, unarranged, unpossessed objects of his contemplation, seeking not to alter their life but to preserve it in his emulsions.

In a certain sense, then, these photographs do not need to be studied, they need to be contemplated if they are to carry their full impact.[33]

From these comments by Griffin, and through looking at Merton's photographs, it is clear that Thomas Merton used his camera as a contemplative instrument, and he photographed the things he contemplated, breaking through the detritus which obscures our vision of the things around us.

Tree Root on Hermitage Porch, Abbey of Gethsemani.

THOMAS MERTON IN ASIA—TOURIST AND ZEN PHOTOGRAPHER

For Thomas Merton his photography, as his writing, became a way for him to explore and express his relationship with the world. In a journal entry from December 1963 Merton reflects on a saying of Merleau-Ponty: "I am myself as I exist in the world."[34] This led him to question the position he had been taking, of being himself

by withdrawing from the world, and stating that he agrees profoundly with Merleau-Ponty providing that the world he is referring to is not one of "delusions and clichés." He writes that "to
withdraw from where I am in order to be totally outside all that
situates me—this is real delusion."[35] Merton's description of his
camera as a "Zen camera" fits very well with the Zen koan-like
nature of this insight.

In the months prior to his departure for Asia Merton struggled
with his understanding of place—assisting with the development
of the Merton Room at Bellarmine College, reading Bachelard's
La Poetique de l'espace, and writing his own geography, *The Geography of Lograire*. As Michael Mott points out for "Ruth Merton's
son, immediate surroundings had always been of near-obsessive
importance."[36] In Thomas Merton's *Asian Journal* place, geography and journey are central motifs for Merton, and a number of
times his spiritual journey and his physical journey come together
in an important way for him which he describes in considerable
detail. This integration of the inner and outer journeys happens, I
would suggest, at least four times and each time it is related to a
specific place Merton is visiting. Each of these places Merton captured in photographs as he went beyond the surface to the inner
meaning of his experience.[37]

Firstly, at Dharamsala, where many Tibetans were living in
exile around the mountain on which the Dalai Lama had made his
home, Merton "instinctively [saw] the mountain as a mandala.
Slightly askew no doubt, with a central presence and surrounding
presences more or less amiable" describing it as a spiritual mountain and as "the 'mandala awareness' of space."[38] Up until Merton's
visit to Dharamsala in November, 1968, he had been pondering
over the meaning of the mandala concept, reading what others had
to say about it and contemplating the idea in relation to "the drama
of disintegration and reintegration," "the axis mundi," yet feeling
"all this mandala business is, for me, at least, useless."[39] By the
end of October Merton's understanding of the mandala is changing. He sees everything he thinks or does as entering "into the construction of a mandala"[40] and records advice given to him by Sonam
Kazi that "one meditates on the mandala in order to be in control
of what goes on within one instead of 'being controlled by it.'"[41]
Gradually Merton had moved from an approach to the mandala
which was theoretical, to one which touched on his own personal

development until, with his experience of the Tibetans at Dharamsala he came to an experiential understanding of the mandala through the geography of the mountain on which the Tibetans were living "clinging precariously to a world in which they have no place."[42]

Secondly, there is Merton's fascination when he was in Darjeeling with the mountain Kanchenjunga. Merton had come across pictures of Kanchenjunga before he had left for Asia and he saw it for the first time from a plane in October 1968. In mid-November, when Merton was at Darjeeling, Kanchenjunga was also visible, or not visible depending on cloud. He found the sight "incomparable" saying he needed "to go back for more,"[43] and for the following ten days he made frequent references to the mountain in his journal. He found himself tired of it, "tired of icebergs 30,000 feet high"[44] and of a "28,000-foot post card," similar to the way in which he felt tired of traveling. For a few days at the Mim Tea Estate, within sight of Kanchenjunga, Merton had the use of a bungalow for a time of quiet. As he argued with Kanchenjunga he also had time to reflect on his Asian trip up to this point and felt he was not called to settle in Asia but in either Alaska or near the Redwoods; he wrote of his desire to remain a part of the Gethsemani community. In this time of quiet Merton could reassess his Indian experience as "too much movement. Too much 'looking for' something: an answer, a vision, 'something other.' And this breeds illusion." In his bungalow at the tea estate Merton realized he could be anywhere, everything he had found in Asia, so far, he could have found anywhere except for one thing, his own "illusion of Asia" which, he questions, "needed to be dissolved by experience? Here?"[45] After having made this entry in his journal Merton dreamed that night of Kanchenjunga realizing "there is another side of Kanchenjunga and of every mountain."[46] In Kanchenjunga Merton sees an answer to his questions, the mountain holds paradoxes together, a theme central in Merton's own work. It has a side that is seen and a side that is not seen, it is a "palace of opposites in unity," "impermanence and patience, solidity and nonbeing, existence and wisdom." Developing his reflection on the mountain Merton added:

> The full beauty of the mountain is not seen until you too consent to the impossible paradox: it is and is not. When

nothing more needs to be said, the smoke of ideas clears, the mountain is SEEN.[47]

Mount Kanchenjunga

After this passage Merton appears to have resolved his argument with Kanchenjunga and only makes a couple of minor references to it.

This is similar to Merton's vision of photography and, as he tries to capture images of Kanchenjunga with his camera, Merton writes:

> The camera does not know what it takes: it captures materials with which you reconstruct not so much what you saw as what you thought you saw. Hence the best photography is aware, mindful, of illusion and uses illusion, permitting and encouraging it—especially unconscious and powerful illusions that are not normally admitted on the scene.[48]

This is reminiscent of Meatyard's understanding of Zen and his way of dealing with illusion by his frequent use of masks in his photographs, most noticeably in his collection *The Family Album of Lucybelle Crater.*[49]

Thirdly, Merton is impressed with a visit to Mahabalipuram near Madras and he found there "a sense of silence and space"[50] saying:

> Mahabalipuram is the remains of a culture such as I have not seen before. A complex of shrines carved out of, or built into, a great ancient rock formation—not cliffs but low rambling outcrops and boulders, smoothed and shaped by millions of years. Caves, porches, figures, steps, markings, lines of holes, gods and goddesses—but spread around without too much profusion.[51]

In *The Asian Journal* Merton recalled in particular the sea temples at Mahabalipuram and the Shiva lingam writing:

> I'm curious to read again after so many years Lawrence's "Virgin Youth" when today I have seen the Shiva lingam at Mahabalipuram, standing black and alone at the edge of the ocean, washed by spray of great waves breaking on the rocks.
>
> > He stands like a lighthouse, night churns
> > Round his base, his dark light rolls
> > Into darkness, and darkly returns.
>
> > Is he calling, the lone one? Is his deep
> > Silence full of summons?
>
> There is no "problem," however, in the black lingam. It is washed by the sea, and the sea is woman: it is no void, no question. No English anguish about Mahabalipuram. How right the "Lighthouse" stanza of Lawrence is, though, for this lingam on the rocky point! Night and sea are the same: so they are transferable.[52]

A few days later Merton refers back to Mahabalipuram after his visit to the fourth important place for him, Polonnaruwa, and says of them both "surely, with Mahabalipuram and Polonnaruwa my Asian pilgrimage has come clear and purified itself. I mean, I know and have seen what I was obscurely looking for."[53] For some reason the significance that Merton clearly attributed to his visit to

...a sense of silence and space.... Surely, with Mahabalipuram and Polonnaruwa my Asian pilgrimmage has come clear and purified itself.

Thomas Merton, *The Asian Journal of Thomas Merton*

Then the silence of the extraordinary faces. The great smiles. Huge and yet subtle. Filled with every possibility, questioning nothing, knowing everything, rejecting nothing, the peace not of emotional resignation but of Madhyamika, of sunyata, that has seen through every question without trying to discredit anyone or any-thing—*without refutation*—without establishing some other argument.

Thomas Merton, *The Asian Journal of Thomas Merton*

Mahabalipuram has been overshadowed in both Merton scholarship and folklore by the latter account of his experience in front of the Buddhas at Polonnaruwa. Partly I think this is due to the much more approachable nature of Merton's account of Polonnaruwa and his photographs of the giant carved statues there which segues well with his writings on Buddhism and the more popular nature of Buddhism in the West as opposed to Hinduism. However this does a disservice to Merton's account of his visit to Mahabalipuram in his journal, the opportunities he took in Asia to visit a number of Hindu shrines, meet teachers and practitioners and, as is clearly witnessed to by his *Asian Journal*, to continue reading extensively about Hinduism.[54]

At Polonnaruwa Merton experienced the ancient giant carved statues of the Buddha at the Gal Vihara as a "Zen garden," a place of unity in his life, where stillness and movement, geography and journey, came together. In his *Asian Journal* Merton's visit to Polonnaruwa on December 2nd, 1968 reads like a moment of illumination for him, an awesome aesthetic experience bordering on the mystical. Only a couple of days later did he feel he could write about this experience. Merton's description of this experience is worth quoting in full:

> The path dips down to Gal Vihara: a wide, quiet, hollow, surrounded with trees. A low outcrop of rock, with a cave cut into it, and beside the cave a big seated Buddha on the left, a reclining Buddha on the right, and Ananda, I guess, standing by the head of the reclining Buddha. In the cave, another seated Buddha. The vicar general, shying away from "paganism," hangs back and sits under a tree reading the guidebook. I am able to approach the Buddhas barefoot and undisturbed, my feet in wet grass, wet sand. Then the silence of the extraordinary faces. The great smiles. Huge and yet subtle. Filled with every possibility, questioning nothing, knowing everything, rejecting nothing, the peace not of emotional resignation but of Madhyamika, of sunyata, that has seen through every question without trying to discredit anyone or anything.... I was knocked over with a rush of relief and thankfulness at the *obvious* clarity of the figures, the clarity and fluidity of shape and line, the design of the monumental bodies.

Looking at these figures I was suddenly, almost forc-
ibly, jerked clean out of the habitual, half-tied vision of
things, and an inner clearness, clarity, as if exploding from
the rocks themselves, became evident and obvious.... The
thing about all this is that there is no puzzle, no problem,
and really no "mystery." All problems are resolved and
everything is clear, simply because what matters is clear.
The rock, all matter, all life, is charged with dharmakaya
...everything is emptiness and everything is compassion. I
don't know when in my life I have ever had such a sense of
beauty and spiritual validity running together in one aesthetic illumination.[55]

A week later Merton was dead.

Another aspect of Thomas Merton's journey is expressed in
some of the photographs he took of the people he encountered on

Merton's photograph of a child, Darjeeling, India.

his journey. Some of these encounters were purely on the surface—
elderly people or children in some beautifully expressive photographs—others symbolized his spiritual journey, both his journey
into Zen Buddhism and his wider interfaith journey. The wonderful picture of Merton with the Dalai Lama after one of their three
meetings in Dharamasala in November 1968 is such an example—

a photograph that symbolizes so well the dialogue that has subsequently followed between Buddhist and Christian monks. Their words about each other expressed their sense of brotherhood, a feeling of unity on the inner search—Merton felt "there is a real spiritual bond between us"[56] or, as the Dalai Lama wrote in his autobiography, *Freedom in Exile*, "he was a truly humble and deeply spiritual man. This was the first time that I had been struck by such a feeling of spirituality in anyone who professed Christianity. Since then, I have come across others with similar qualities, but it was Merton who introduced me to the real meaning of the word 'Christian.'"[57] Likewise other figures he met—Chatral Rimpoche with whom he felt as if they were both "*on the edge* of great realization and knew it and were trying, somehow or other, to go out and get lost in it—and that it was a grace for us to meet one another"[58]; Karlu Rimpoche, who said Merton had the "true Mahayana spirit" and gave Merton three pictures of deities he had colored[59]; Amiya Chakravarty, who wrote to Merton that "the absolute rootedness of your faith makes you free to understand other faiths"[60]—and, a few years earlier, D.T. Suzuki.[61]

In Zen Thomas Merton had discovered many things that he found missing in Catholicism and monasticism in the middle of the twentieth century, but which belonged to the Christian tradition. Zen offered an experiential approach to contemplation and a world-affirming spirituality which appealed to Merton and which he also discovered in the Church Fathers and the great Christian mystics. Zen provided Merton with a terminology to describe both his experience of God and of contemplation. Zen writings on enlightenment also complemented Merton's thinking on the true self. As Thomas Merton discovered in Zen a "good clean blade" to "cut right through all the knots,"[62] he also discovered that photography was also a tool to assist him in "going beyond the shadow and the disguise" to the reality that is immediately in front of us, the "cosmic dance which is always there" and "beats in our very blood."[63]

NOTES

1. Thomas Merton's images of place form a permanent exhibit at the Thomas Merton Center at Bellarmine University. A significant group of his "Zen photographs" has been exhibited in a traveling exhibit in recent years and will continue to be exhibited at various locations. Fur-

ther details of these exhibits can be found on the Thomas Merton Center website at: www.merton.org/events.htm

2. Thomas Merton. *The Road to Joy: The Letters of Thomas Merton to New and Old Friends*. (New York, Farrar, Straus, Giroux, 1989), 118.

3. Roger Lipsey. *Angelic Mistakes: The Art of Thomas Merton*. (Boston: New Seeds, 2006).

4. Michael Mott. *The Seven Mountains of Thomas Merton*, (Boston: Houghton Mifflin, 1994), 83.

5. Thomas Merton. *Run to the Mountain: The Story of a Vocation*, (San Francisco: Harper Collins, 1995), 68.

6. Thomas Merton. *Monastic Peace* (Trappist, KY: Abbey of Gethsemani, 1958).

7. Thomas Merton. *Selected Poems*. (New York: New Directions, 1959).

8. Thomas Merton. *God is My Life: The Story of Our Lady of Gethsemani*. Photographs by Shirley Burden. (New York: Reynal, 1960).

9. Merton's essays and correspondence about the Shakers, along with photographs taken at Pleasant Hill, can be found in *Seeking Paradise: The Spirit of the Shakers*. Edited with an introduction by Paul M. Pearson. (Maryknoll, NY: Orbis Books, 2003).

10. Thomas Merton. *A Search for Solitude: Pursuing the Monk's True Life*, (San Francisco: Harper Collins, 1996), 182.

11. *Ibid.*, 332.

12. *Ibid.*, 339.

13. John Howard Griffin. *A Hidden Wholeness: The Visual World of Thomas Merton*, (Boston: Houghton Mifflin, 1970), 37.

14. Thomas Merton. *Turning Toward the World: The Pivotal Years*, (San Francisco: Harper Collins, 1996), 169.

15. Merton, *Turning Toward the World*, 194.

16. *Ibid.*

17. Thomas Merton. *Dancing in the Water of Life: Seeking Peace in the Hermitage*, (San Francisco: Harper Collins, 1997), 23.

18. *Ibid.*, 147.

19. *Ibid.*

20. *Ibid.*, 149.

21. Thomas Merton. *Learning to Love: Exploring Solitude and Freedom*, (San Francisco: Harper Collins, 1997), 221.

22. Griffin, *A Hidden Wholeness*, 37.

23. Thomas Merton. *The Other Side of the Mountain: The End of the Journey*, (San Francisco: Harper Collins, 1998), 6.

24. Merton, *The Road to Joy*, 140.

25. *Ibid.*, 141.

26. The Merton Center has over 1400 of Merton's color, and black and white photographs with negatives, along with many other photographs without negatives. The photographs were taken on a variety of different cameras including a Kodak Instamatic, a Rolleiflex and the Canon loaned to him by Griffin. It has frequently been said that many famous photographers will take a thousand photographs to achieve the one they are looking for. Merton, with his limited resources at the Abbey of Gethsemani, produced many superlative photographs in the limited numbers he took.

27. Griffin, *A Hidden Wholeness*, 90.

28. Thomas Merton. *When Prophecy Still Had A Voice: The Letters of Thomas Merton and Robert Lax*. (Lexington: University Press of Kentucky, 2001), 354.

29. Merton, *Learning to Love*, 186.

30. Ralph Eugene Meatyard, *Father Louie: Photographs of Thomas Merton*. (New York: Timken, 1991), 27.

31. *Ibid.*, 34.

32. *Ibid.*, 35.

33. Griffin, *A Hidden Wholeness*, 49–50.

34. Merton, *Dancing in the Water of Life*, 48.

35. *Ibid.*

36. Mott, *The Seven Mountains of Thomas Merton*, 516.

37. Thomas Merton's photographs of Asia can be found in four sources:

•John Howard Griffin. *A Hidden Wholeness: The Visual World of Thomas Merton*, Photographs by Thomas Merton and John Howard Griffin, text by John Howard Griffin. (Boston: Houghton Mifflin, 1970).

•Thomas Merton. *The Asian Journal of Thomas Merton*. Edited by Naomi Burton, Patrick Hart and James Laughlin, (New York: New Directions, 1975).

•Deba Prasad Patnaik. *Geography of Holiness: The Photography of Thomas Merton*. Photographs by Thomas Merton. Edited, with an Introduction and Afterword by Deba Prasad Patnaik. (New York: Pilgrim Press, 1980).

•*The Paradox of Place: Thomas Merton's Photography*. Catalogue of the exhibition at the McGrath Art Gallery, Bellarmine University, Louisville, KY, 10th October 2003 to 11th November 2003. Contributions by Anthony Bannon, Paul M. Pearson, Paul Quenon, OCSO, and Marilyn Sundermann, RSM. (Louisville: Thomas Merton Center, 2003).

38. Thomas Merton. *The Asian Journal of Thomas Merton*. Edited by Naomi Burton, Patrick Hart and James Laughlin, (New York: New Directions, 1975), 105–6.

39. *Ibid.*, 57–9.

40. *Ibid.*, 68.

41. *Ibid.*, 82.

42. *Ibid.*, 93.

43. *Ibid.*, 135.

44. *Ibid.*, 146.

45. *Ibid.*, 148–50.

46. *Ibid.*, 153.

47. *Ibid.*, 156–7.

48. Merton, *The Other Side of the Mountain*, 284.

49. James Rhem, *Ralph Eugene Meatyard: The Family album of Lucybelle Crater and other Figurative Photographs.* New York: Distributed Art Publishers, 2002.

50. Merton, *The Asian Journal*, 202.

51. *Ibid.*, 198.

52. *Ibid.*, 197.

53. *Ibid.*, 235–6.

54. Though less prominent in the Merton corpus than his writings on Buddhism his interest in Hinduism dated back to his defense of Gandhi at Oakham School. At Columbia University in the late thirties he would have become aware of basic Hindu concepts through reading Huxley's *Ends and Means* and had met the Hindu monk, Brahmachari, who urged Merton to study some of the Christian Classics which were instrumental in Merton's conversion. Whilst working on his M.A. thesis on William Blake, Merton also read Ananda Coomaraswamy's book *Transformation of Nature in Art*, and Coomaraswamy was also influential in Merton's conversion, his outlook on art and civilization, and as a model for interfaith dialogue. At Gethsemani, as early as 1949, Merton was reading a manual on yoga and discovering similarities with authors such as St. Gregory of Nyssa and St. John of the Cross. Through the fifties and sixties there are many references in Merton writings and personal journals to representatives of Hinduism including Mahatma Gandhi, Abhishiktananda, Bede Griffiths and Kabir. He was familiar with the *Upanishads* and the *Bhagavad Gita*, even writing a preface to the *Bhagavad Gita* in 1968 "The Bhagavad Gita, As It Is" in 1968.

55. Merton, *The Asian Journal*, 233–236.

56. *Ibid.*, 125.

57. Dalai Lama. *Freedom in Exile: The Autobiography of the Dalai Lama.* (New York: Harper Collins, 1990), 189.

58. Merton, *The Asian Journal*, 143.

59. *Ibid.*, 165–6. These images were returned to Gethsemani, along with Merton's personal effects, and now hang in the Thomas Merton Center at Bellarmine University.

60. Thomas Merton, *The Hidden Ground of Love: The letters of Thomas Merton on Religious Experience and Social Concerns.* (New York, Farrar, Straus, Giroux, 1985), 115.

61. See Roger Lipsey's article "Merton, Suzuki, Zen, Ink: Thomas Merton's Calligraphic Drawings in Context" in this volume, pp. 137 ff.

62. Merton, *The Hidden Ground of Love,* 551.

63. Thomas Merton, *New Seeds of Contemplation.* (New York: New Directions, 1961), 297.

Watering can, Hermitage Porch, Abbey of Gethsemani.
Photograph by Thomas Merton.

Zen seeks not to *explain* but to *pay attention,* to *become aware,* to be *mindful.*

Thomas Merton, *Zen and the Birds of Appetite*

Photograph of Thomas Merton by John Howard Griffin.

THE LIGHT STRIKES HOME: NOTES ON THE ZEN INFLUENCE IN MERTON'S POETRY

Bonnie B. Thurston

INTRODUCTION

As a young man, Thomas Merton's aspirations were literary. He wrote fiction, poetry, and criticism as well as personal letters and journals.[1] While it could be argued that when he entered the monastery at the age of 26 he left the mainstream of literary life in the United States, in fact he kept writing, maintained contact with many contemporary writers, and his own poetry bears resemblances to that of other American poets of the mid-twentieth century. In the 1960s and 1970s Ionesco, Beckett, and Vonnegut attacked what they understood to be the characteristic features of the "Western consciousness." Merton studies of Eastern spiritualities had preceded them by at least a decade. Between 1963 and 1968 he published three books (*Mystics and Zen Masters*, *The Way of Chuang Tzu*, and *Zen and the Birds of Appetite*) and numerous articles and reviews on the subject. As does that of Gary Snyder, Merton's poetry clearly demonstrates the influence of these studies, particularly Zen.

Merton's poetic output is immense. *The Collected Poems of Thomas Merton* runs to over a thousand pages.[2] There are two distinct "periods" of Merton's poetry.[3] From 1944-1949, as he was moving through the stages of monastic commitment, he published four volumes of verse which, in my view, are largely conventionally devotional and religious in style (which tends to be lyric and metaphysical) and content. From 1948 to 1962 there was but one published volume of poetry, *The Strange Islands* (1957) which is arguably "transitional" in that it contains poems characteristic of the earlier and later "periods" of his writing. Then between 1962 and 1968 Merton prepared four more volumes for publication. The subject matter of these poems is both Christian and monastic, but also includes material expressing Merton's social and political concerns and "Zen poems." Many of these later poems, including the two long poems *Cables to the Ace* and *The Geography of Lograire*, are experimental; they push the limits of language. The impetus for this "pushing" was at least in part Merton's appropriation of Buddhism, especially Zen.

William Healy, whose study *The Thought of Thomas Merton Concerning the Relationship of Christianity and Zen* is one of the earliest on the subject, dates Merton's first interest in Zen to his university era reading of Huxley's *Ends and Means*.[4] At the same time Merton encountered Wieger's French translations of oriental texts and the Hindu monk, Bramachari, through whom Br. David Steindl-Rast, OSB believes Merton first began a serious exploration of not only Eastern, but Western spirituality. (For more on the evolution of Merton's interest in Zen see my essay at the outset of this volume.) While in his early monastic years Merton's focus was on Christianity, by 1949 his fascination with Zen was re-awakened, and it became one of his major intellectual, spiritual and artistic interests and sources of inspiration. As he wrote to D.T. Suzuki on March 12, 1959 "I have my own way to walk, and for some reason or other Zen is right in the middle of it wherever I go."[5]

Several contributors to this volume have raised the question of whether D.T. Suzuki's work accurately represents the Zen tradition of Buddhism. (See Corless, Habito, Keenan, and Lipsey.) However, the fact is that Suzuki's thought was Merton's primary source of information about Zen, and Merton's thought often echoes it. Merton observes that Zen "insists on concrete practice rather than on study or intellectual meditation as a way of enlightenment."[6] It is "nondoctrinal, concrete, direct, existential, and seeks above all to come to grips with life itself, not with ideas about life."[7] By "Zen" Merton meant "the quest for direct and pure experience on a metaphysical level, liberated from verbal formulas and linguistic preconceptions" (ZBA 44); "the ontological *awareness of pure being beyond subject and object*, an immediate grasp of being in its 'suchness' and 'thusness.'" (MZM 14. Italics Merton's)

Merton's "definition" highlights the primary aspects of Zen which appear in his poetry: its direct, experiential nature; its preference for the concrete and tangible; and the fact that it locates meaning "in the ordinary humble tasks and human problems of everyday." (ZBA 30). Those who have known Merton and studied his work might agree that the high-spiritedness, good humor, and general irreverence of some aspects of Zen practice also attracted him. What I propose to do here is to suggest how some of these aspects of Zen appear both thematically and in the literary technique of some of Merton's poems.[8] For the sake of brevity and focus, I shall deal primarily with the experience of *satori*, sudden enlightenment or insight into reality, and merely allude to other influences, I hope in a way that will make it possible for those who are interested in the subject to pursue the wider Buddhist trajectory in Merton's work as poet.

SATORI IN MERTON'S POETRY

In the introduction to Buddhism with which this volume opens, Roger Corless characterizes Zen by saying it "concentrates on enlightenment in each and every practitioner. Any other practices ... are regarded as merely tools for the awakening of the disciple." (pp. 6–7) In Zen training, one method by which the Zen master facilitates satori (one cannot "teach" or "cause" it) is the koan, a sort of conundrum, a statement, question or action of the Master, which, when penetrated ("understood") by the disciple, reveals the master's mind and/or the nature of reality. Merton wrote an essay on the koan in *Mystics and Zen Masters* which suggested its purpose was "to learn to respond directly to life." (MZM 249)

In Merton's selection of some of the accounts of the early (4th century) Desert Christians one finds a striking resemblance to the effect of the koan in Zen training. Interestingly, Merton had hoped Suzuki might provide the introduction to his collection from that material, *The Wisdom of the Desert* (1960).[9] While that was not to be, the exchange based on the material appears as the dialogue "Wisdom in Emptiness" in *Zen and the Birds of Appetite*.[10] This "desert material" also appears repeatedly in Merton's poetry. For example, in Part III of his poem "Macarius the Younger" Merton writes:

> One tribune saw the monks like a pair of sacks
> Lying in the stern, ragged bums, having nothing,
> Free men.

> "You" he said, "are the happy ones.
> You laugh at life. You need nothing from the world
> But a few rags, a crust of bread."

And one Macarius replied: "It is true,
We follow God. We laugh at life.
And we are sorry life laughs at you."

Then the officer saw himself as he was.
He gave away all that he had
And enlisted in the desert army. (CP 321)

The monk's response has the effect of a koan on the tribune. Its speed and incisiveness shows the officer to himself as he is and, thus engenders his satori. Other materials make clear that Merton thought the atmosphere of the Desert Christians was very like that of Zen. So it is not surprising that this poem which appeared in the 1963 collection, *Emblems of a Season of Fury*, should exemplify how Zen thought and techniques worked their way into Merton's poetry.

Merton understood Zen to be "pure experience on a metaphysical level," (ZBA 44) "awareness of pure being beyond subject and object," (MZM 14) direct experience of the Absolute. Such an experience allows one to see in the most mundane events and objects flashes of the Universal. (For more on this point see the previous articles by Lipsey and Pearson.) The poem "Stranger" from Merton's 1957 collection *The Strange Islands* describes the conditions under which such an experience might take place. Or perhaps it is a description of the experience itself.

When no one listens
To the quiet trees
When no one notices
The sun in the pool

Where no one feels
The first drop of rain
Or sees the last star

Or hails the first morning
Of a giant world
Where peace begins
And rages end:

One bird sits still
Watching the work of God:

One turning leaf,
Two falling blossoms,
Ten circles upon the pond. (CP 289-290)

There is nothing extraordinary here of which to take note save "every day" features of landscape. And no discernable person appears in the poem or is requisite to observe them. One bird watches God "work," and God's "labor" is but the ordinary falling of leaves which cause ripples on a pond.

These simple, fragile images give way to what I think of as Merton's "psychological landscape painting." Merton uses the external world of nature to reflect the internal world of the spirit. What is going on outside reflects what is going on inside. He is a master of this technique.

One cloud upon the hillside,
Two shadows in the valley
And the light strikes home.
Now dawn commands the capture
Of the tallest fortune,
The surrender
Of no less marvelous prize! (CP 290)

In the simple act of watching (but who is watching?) cloud shadows on the landscape at dawn, indeed of watching for dawn,[11] "the light strikes home"; illumination occurs. Enlightenment happens. "Dawn," the light of understanding, captures the literal prize of the world, and the "no less marvelous prize" of the consciousness of the poem's speaker (but who is that?).

Closer and clearer
Than any wordy master,
Thou inward Stranger
Whom I have never seen,

Deeper and cleaner
Than the clamorous ocean,
Seize up my silence
Hold me in Thy Hand!

Now act is waste
And suffering undone

Laws become prodigals
Limits are torn down
For envy has no property
And passion is none.

Look, the vast Light stands still
Our cleanest Light is One! (CP 290)

Suddenly the poem is not "about" dawn in the natural world, but a
dawning in the inner life of the speaker of the poem. The enlightenment of that dawning is not the result of a "wordy master," a
linguistic formulation or a systematic theology. It comes from an
"inward Stranger." Merton wrote to Suzuki on April 11, 1959: "The
Christ we seek is within us, in our inmost self, *is* our inmost self,
and yet infinitely transcends ourselves."[12] Or perhaps the "inward
Stranger" is a metaphor for the truth of experience which is "deeper
and cleaner" than the movement represented on the surface of the
"clamorous ocean." We have left the surface; we are in the depths.
The internal reality of the speaker moves in that silence and holds
him in its hand. The speaker is like Job who exclaims after God
speaks to him from the whirlwind, "I had heard of thee by the
hearing of the ear,/but now my eye sees thee." (Job 42:5) Between
"hearing" (second hand, intellectual information) and "seeing" (first
hand, experiential knowledge) is a whole day of creation!

The effect of the speaker's awakening is a whole new way of
looking at what was previously valued. The paths which he thought
might lead to the place "where peace begins/And rages end" (the
paths of action, suffering, Laws and limits) are now discarded.
Activity is useless; suffering no longer valued.[13] The laws which
ordered activity have become "prodigals," a lovely pun: they have
gone astray; they have become wildly generous. The speaker's
condition is that of pure possibility. The "limits are torn down,"
and there is no place for envy or passion. When one has everything, one envies nothing. In the "vast light" of this new awareness, the speaker experiences unity: "Our cleanest Light is One."
This revelation is not personal; it is "ours," belonging to all because it is in all (at least in potentiality). The Absolute resides in
the immediate.

The experience described in the closing lines of the poem
sounds to me like satori. Suzuki says: "Satori may be defined as an
intuitive looking into the nature of things in contradistinction to

the analytical or logical understanding of it. Practically, it means the unfolding of a new world hitherto unperceived in the confusion of a dualistically trained mind."[14] For Merton the enlightenment of Zen consists of an experiential awareness of the illusion of subject-object dualism. No object of awareness is "acquired" in satori. The Absolute is not an object to be obtained. The fundamental datum of experience is Being itself, not self-awareness.

Suzuki thought that the worst "enemy of Zen experience...is the intellect, which consists and insists in discriminating subject from object."[15] Merton, whose rejection of Cartesianism is here complete, observed that another "consciousness is still available.... It starts not from the thinking self-aware subject but from Being, ontologically seen to be prior to the subject-object division. Underlying the subjective experience of the individual self there is an immediate experience of Being." (ZBA 23) Satori is this immediate experience. When one experiences Being "the person and Being become one and thus the 'subject disappears.'"[16]

These remarks on satori suggest something of the way Merton (from Suzuki) understood the phenomenon. The effect of letting go of a strong sense of subject-object perception is clearly evident in his poetry from the late 1950s. Merton's poetic persona, or "voice," almost disappears in many poems. Buddhist teacher, Pema Chodron interprets the Third Noble Truth of the Buddha to say "that the cessation of suffering is letting go of holding on to ourselves."[17] Satori can mark this "letting go," after which the importance of the individual self as a perceiving entity no longer exists. Virginia Randall, who believes a quest for the transcendent self characterizes Merton's later poetry, notes that finding this transcendent self is equated with achieving enlightenment.[18]

For example, the first stanzas of "Stranger" describe a world in which the subject-object division has broken down. Initially, there is no one to hear the trees, to see the "sun in the pool," or "the last star," or to feel "The first drop of rain." (CP 389) No person hails the beginning of a new day. This literal "new day" is figuratively the "first morning" of a new awareness. While "one bird" observes the events, no human speaker appears in the poem's narrative until the sixth stanza. The opening stanzas of the poem present an immediate, concrete "picture" without editorial comment. When the human voice does appear, his/her revelation is not "individual." The absence of subject-object perception in the poem, the inclusiveness of the conclusion, and the experience being described all suggest satori.

In "Song for Nobody" (CP 337) the interpenetration of subject and object is carried even further. The lexical field of the poem in its evocation of "emptiness," "awake," "no thought" suggests Zen Buddhist training. The first two stanzas are parallel in structure. In the first the "singer" is a plant, in the second, a "spirit" (perhaps the spirit of the plant?).

> A yellow flower
> (Light and spirit)
> Sings by itself
>
> For nobody.
>
> A golden spirit
> (Light and emptiness)
> Sings without a word
> By itself. (CP 337)

The equation of corporeal and incorporeal begins the dissolution of subject-object dualism (and evokes for me, at least, the Buddhist notion of "all sentient beings"). The singing, in Christianity a traditional metaphor for prayer and praise, is done for the sake of the act itself rather than for "someone." The suggestion of infused contemplation is strong since the plant/spirit is empty, that is egoless, and the song is without words, ideational content.

> Let no one touch this gentle sun
> In whose dark eye
> Someone is awake.
>
> (No light, no gold, no name, no color
> And no thought:
> O, wide awake!)
>
> A golden heaven
> Sings by itself
> A song to nobody. (CP 337-338)

Now we learn that the flower is a Black Eyed Susan, that common field wild flower in the daisy family which has a black or brown center encircled by yellow or golden petals. Notice now that it is the *flower* that sees, that perceives "someone." The head of the

Black Eyed Susan, the "gentle sun" with a "dark eye," is not to be disturbed. To touch would be to objectify the flower and to disturb its tranquil purity of Being. That "Someone is awake" in *its* eye suggests an equation of inanimate (for lack of a better term) and human looking, the mutually threaded eye-beams of 17th century Divine, John Donne's poems or the statement of Meister Eckhart that "the eye wherein I see God is the same eye wherein God sees me."

By the poem's close the plant has become pure consciousness. Not "of" some quality, nameless and yet without thought or intellection, the plant is conscious, "A golden heaven" which "Sings by itself/A song to nobody." (CP 338) Most awake because least self-conscious, the flower is complete in itself. It requires no one to see and objectify it; its song requires no hearer to "be." The plant's existence is prior to its perception by the speaker of the poem. In fact, the speaker in "Song for Nobody" is so much in the background that a "voice" is hardly discernable. This absence of a distinct persona mirrors the statement the poem makes: the unselfconscious are complete in themselves. The speaker merely describes, does not grasp at or seek to obtain the flower. (A *dukkha*-free response?) Even the pose of a subject looking at an object is underplayed so that the flower represents pure "is-ness" which satori reflects/summons. Writing about what she calls Merton's "Zen-mystical poetry" Sr. Therese Lentfoehr refers to this as the "onto-logical approach," the attempt to deal with the formal *esse*, the "is-ness" of things.[19]

Combining speaker and spoken in this way causes a drastic reorientation of perspective. Language is wrenched from its expected patterns. When "things" like a Black Eyed Susan are no longer understood as objects to be perceived, but themselves perceive, when they are no longer objects to be acquired, the new pattern of relationships which evolves requires new linguistic structures to reflect them. This, I think, is why literary critics have termed some of Merton's later poetry "anti-poems" in their departure from expected or traditional poetic conventions. Merton the poet is trying to suggest in his poems experiences that are not fundamentally "language events." As he writes in "News from the School at Chartes," "They say deep thoughts/Cannot be put into words" (CP 358) or in "A Messenger from the Horizon," "When a message has no clothes on/How can it be spoken?" (CP 351)[20]

The most striking factor in satori is the abruptness of the reordering that occurs when it is experienced. Although it can be preceded by various practices or disciplines, they do not "cause" enlightenment. One is suddenly in the midst of it. As Merton writes in "Messenger from the Horizon," it "Flies fast by/A mute comet," which comes "without warning/A friend of hurricanes,/Lightening in your bones!" (CP 350) The "unexpected flash/Beyond 'yes,' beyond 'no'" ("Song, if You seek..." CP 34) is especially startling because it arises from and points back to the events of everyday life.

Merton wrote many poems which suggest the use of the koan in satori. (In addition to the two discussed here see "Song for the Death of Averroes" (CP 326) and "Landscape" (CP 277).) Often they follow this general, narrative pattern: a young person, child or initiate questions or responds to statements made by an authority figure. In the abruptness of the exchange an "awareness" emerges which is greater than that expected by either party. The poems build a pattern of metaphor which "points to" rather than "tells," and this indirection, too, is Zen like.

I think these poems are constructed to act upon the reader as a koan. They are a brilliant linguistic mirroring. The reader is engaged in an activity which is strongly analogous to the one the poem describes. The poems might be satori engendering.

In addition to the koan, Suzuki listed six "verbal methods" which may lead one to the "idea of absolute oneness": Paradox, "going beyond opposites," contradiction, affirmation, repetition, and exclamation.[21] What I am calling Merton's "Zen poems" exhibit all of these techniques, but particularly paradox and "going beyond opposites." Readers of the poems will have no difficulty finding examples of these two techniques. Affirmation and repetition, however, afforded Merton fresh opportunities to express his deepest spiritual convictions.

Affirmation becomes increasingly important and apparent in his verse. "Elias—Variations on a Theme" affirms "For the free man's road has neither beginning nor end." (CP 245) "Early Mass" asserts that "We are makers of a risen world." (CP 282) "The Moslem's Angel of Death" closes, "See the end of trouble!" (CP 308) Merton envisages consolation for prisoners in "There Has to be a Jail for Ladies:" "Poor ladies, do not despair—/God will come to your window with skylarks/And pluck each year like a white rose." (CP 334)

Perhaps the most startling affirmation occurs in "Birdcage Walk" (CP 275-277) as the fowler releases his birds when he becomes aware of a truth beyond conventional teaching. As a young man, the fowler was impressed by a "gaitered bishop" and strove to emulate him by becoming contemplative. "I consider my own true pond,/Look for the beginning and the end./I lead the bishop down lanes and islands." During one of the walks, the "old pontifex" remarks:

> "No bridge" (He smiled
> Between the budding branches),
> "No crossing to the cage
> Of the paradise bird!"
>
> Astounded by the sermons in the leaves
> I cried, "No! No! The stars have higher houses!" (CP 276).

As in the question-response pattern of the Roshi and his or her disciple, the young man suddenly becomes aware of a truth beyond the bishop's words. To this illumination "the magic bishop leaned his blessing...." He is able only to respond in conventional terms. The fowler, however, responds to the higher call of his "King," by becoming himself a vehicle of freedom.

> That was the bold day when
> Moved by the unexpected summons
> I opened all the palace aviaries
> As by a king's representative
> I was appointed fowler. (CP 277)

Like the poem "O Sweet Irrational Worship" (CP 344) this poem closes with the image of birds rising in praise.

Repetition also appears in the poetry. Since language with the "Zen masters is a kind of exclamation or ejaculation ...directly coming out of their spiritual experience," repetition allows "the inner sense to be read in the echoing itself."[22] In Merton's poems repetition is employed not only in repeated words or phrases (which one does find in, for example, the lyric "In Silence" [CP 280-281] or in the longer poem *Cables to the Ace* [1968] subtitled "Familiar Liturgies of Misunderstanding"), but in thematic repetition. The themes of silence and the Word, of "nothing" or negation as the path to all knowledge are woven through the poetry, creating a pattern of meaning beyond that found in any individual poem. Br. David

Steindl-Rast has pointed out the importance of Merton's repetitions of fire imagery,[23] and the few poems cited here reflect Merton's repeated use of images of flower-as-sun, of birds ascending, of the eye, of the pattern of action and illumination associated with the koan.

Suzuki closes his discussion of the verbal techniques of Zen with "silence," a silence which he describes as "deafening like thunder." Silence deafens because enlightenment wells up from it. The use of sight and sound words is an attempt to describe actuality. Satori arrives when the disciple is able to hear "a tune on a stringless harp." In Christian mysticism, infused prayer or mystical contemplation arrives as a "still small voice" (I Kings 19:12) or as "the sound of sheer silence." This illumination is "one bare/Inquisitive diamond" which will open "to you/The sun door, the noble eye!" (CP 350) The "noble eye" in which the Divine and human merge opens noiselessly, and the panorama it reveals is life itself. This moment, and its Zen counterpart satori, in which one realizes with absolute, existential certainty the reality of Reality is the crux of Merton's writing. It is what he wants to say; what he wants us to understand.

CONCLUSION

I have not treated here poems which in style or content explicitly evoke Buddhism—for example "Song: In the Shadows of the Round Ox" (CP 311-313), "A Picture of Lee Ying" (CP 322-323), or sections 18, 37, 38, 62, and 84 in *Cables to the Ace*. I have tried to demonstrate how a particular Zen experience, satori, appears in several of Merton's poems, and, in the process, I hope have pointed out how other Buddhist concepts and practices inform his writing. As one deeply grounded in Christian mystical traditions, Merton already knew of moving from "knowing" to "being known." When he began to understand *himself* as spoken rather than as speaker, his poetic self-consciousness began to disappear. In the face of the mystic's affirmation of the radical mystery of the world, Merton submitted to, bowed to, the truth in his own experience. Thus the voice in Merton's later poems becomes part of rather than separate from the world. As he explained in *Contemplation in a World of Action*:

> The world as pure object is something that is not there. It
> is not a reality outside us for which we exist…. It is a liv-
> ing and self-creating mystery of which I am myself a part,
> to which I am myself, my own unique door.[24]

In the Zen tradition, the notion that the self is essentially of the world leads to a focus on the purity of perception, on the "thing" rather than analysis of experiences of it. This concept Merton appropriated, and poems like "The Reader" (CP 202) which set the speaker apart give place to poems like "Song for Nobody" (CP 337) in which the speaker disappears. In Merton's later poetry his study of Zen manifests itself in a preference for the concrete, for the truth found in experience rather than in abstraction or speculative thinking. Thus in the later poems one finds fewer "trappings" of traditional Christian expression, fewer poems explicitly about saints or Christian feasts or the Christian Sacraments.

Both Christian mysticism and Zen led Merton to see the world in terms of questions rather than of answers. In the 1960s he wrote, "I do not have clear answers to current questions. I do have questions, and, as a matter of fact, I think a man is known better by his questions than by his answers."[25] This awareness results in a more open-ended poetry, one more universal in implication and appeal than one bound by the confines of a particular doctrine and tradition.

This is simply to say that when Merton reached out to Buddhism, he did so by going to his own deepest roots. With Chang-Tzu, Merton agreed that "Great knowledge sees all in one." There are various means; there is one End. Zen provided Merton with a sympathetic "means" and another articulation of his more abstract strivings toward the "end." Zen practice was an incarnation of what he searched for poetically and spiritually. The "concretized intuition" of Zen focuses on the purity and truth of everyday experience and insists on abolishing subject-object dualism. It gives flesh to the more abstract truths of mysticism and suggests ways to "do" what the mystics "see."

Merton's Asian pilgrimage was the outward and visible sign of the spiritual pilgrimage that was his life, during which I think perhaps he experienced more than one satori. An important one, and perhaps the final one, occurred at Polonnaruwa. That event has been alluded to frequently in this volume, and with good cause.[26]

There, and on the way there, Merton the Cistercian monk, Merton the student of Buddhism (and of Islam and of so many other spiritual paths) pointed the way and was the Way. "Look," he tells us, "the vast Light stands still/Our cleanest Light is One!" (CP 290).

NOTES

1. For more see Bonnie Thurston, "The Man of Letters (Thomas Merton)," *America* 159/11 (October 22, 1988) 284-287.

2. Thomas Merton, *The Collected Poems of Thomas Merton* (New York: New Directions, 1977). Hereafter in the text as CP. An excellent selection of Merton's poems with a fine introductory essay is Lynn R. Szabo's, *In the Dark before Dawn: New Selected Poems of Thomas Merton* (New York: New Directions, 2005).

3. For more full studies of Merton the poet see Ross Labrie, *The Art of Thomas Merton* (Forth Worth, Texas Christian University Press, 1979) and Sr. Therese Lentfoehr, *Words and Silence: On the Poetry of Thomas Merton* (New York: New Directions, 1979).

4. William Francis Healy, *The Thought of Thomas Merton concerning the Relationship of Christianity and Zen* (Rome: University of St. Thomas Aquinas in Urbe, 1975) 13.

5. William H. Shannon (ed.), *Thomas Merton: The Hidden Ground of Love, Letters* (New York: Farrar, Straus, Giroux, 1985) 561.

6. Thomas Merton, *Mystics and Zen Masters* (New York: Delta, 1967) 15. Hereafter in the text as MZM.

7. Thomas Merton, *Zen and the Birds of Appetite* (New York: New Directions, 1968) 32. Hereafter in the text as ZBA.

8. A great deal of my doctoral dissertation was devoted to this matter, and an article, "Zen in the Eye of Thomas Merton's Poetry," published in *Buddhist-Christian Studies* 4 (1984) treats it in some detail. I am grateful to one of the current editors of that journal, Professor Terry Muck, for permission to use some of that material here.

9. Thomas Merton, *The Wisdom of the Desert* (New York: New Directions, 1960).

10. See also the autumn 1959 letters of Merton to Suzuki on this subject in Shannon's collection.

11. Since a Cistercian like Merton would have had intimate familiarity with the Psalms, chanting the Psalter through weekly, one wonders the degree to which that great biblical poet might have influenced this part of Merton's poem. With immense poignancy, Psalm 130: 6 declares "my soul waits for the Lord/more than watchmen for the morning,/more than watchmen for the morning."

12. Shannon 564.

13. And this is good Christian theology which teaches that all the required or necessary suffering was done once, and for all, by Jesus on the cross of Calvary.

14. D.T. Suzuki, *Zen Buddhism: Selected Writings* (New York: Doubleday Anchor, 1956) 84.

15. Suzuki 136-137.

16. Healy 26.

17. Pema Chodron, *Awakening Loving-Kindness* (Boston: Shambala, 1996) 86.

18. Virginia Randall, "The Quest for the Transcendent Self: The Buddhist-Christian Merger in Thomas Merton's Poetry," *Cithara* 17/1 (1977) 17-28.

19. Therese Lentfoehr, "The Zen-Mystical Poetry of Thomas Merton" in *Pilgrim in Process* D. Grayston and M. Higgins (eds.) (Toronto: Griffin House, 1983) 22.

20. Merton's verse drama, "Tower of Babel" which is Part II of *The Strange Islands* (1957) addresses the limitations of language.

21. Suzuki 115-129.

22. Suzuki 125.

23. David Steindl-Rast, OSB, "Destination: East; Destiny: Fire-Thomas Merton's Real Journey," in *Thomas Merton: Prophet in the Belly of a Paradox* Gerald S. Twomey (ed.) (New York: Paulist Press, 1978) 148-172.

24. Thomas Merton, *Contemplation in a World of Action* (Garden City: Doubleday, 1971) 154-155.

25. Thomas Merton, *Conjectures of a Guilty Bystander* (New York: Doubleday/Image, 1968) 5.

26. And see the interesting study listed in the bibliography by David G. Addiss and John J. Albert, "Pollonaruwa Revisited." Recall there is discussion about the identity of the figures. (See note 16, p. 27.)

Portrait of Thomas Merton by Terrell Dickey.

Thank God! Thank God! I am only another member of the human race, like all the rest of them. I have the immense joy of being a man! As if the sorrows of our condition could really matter, once we begin to realize who and what we are—as if we could ever begin to realize it on earth....

God is seen and reveals Himself as a man, that is, in us, and there is no other hope of finding wisdom than in God-manhood: our own manhood transformed in God!

Thomas Merton, *A Search for Solitude*

PART IV
FOOTNOTES TO THE ASIAN
JOURNEY OF THOMAS MERTON

FOOTNOTES TO
THE ASIAN JOURNEY
OF THOMAS MERTON

Bonnie B. Thurston

The primary source of information about Thomas Merton's Asian journey, his last encounters with Buddhism, and the final days of his life is the journal and notes he kept while on that pilgrimage. It first appeared as *The Asian Journal of Thomas Merton*, "edited from his original notebooks" by Naomi Burton, Brother Patrick Hart and James Laughlin with Amiya Chakravarty as consulting editor.[1] The journal material reappeared in slightly altered form in the last of the published journals of Merton, *The Other Side of the Mountain: The Journals of Thomas Merton 1967-1968* which was also edited by Br. Patrick Hart, O.C.S.O.[2] The differences in the published texts of those two works would make an interesting study, but it is not the one that follows here.

Instead, I have contacted some of the *dramatis personae* of the *Asian Journal* and asked them either to clarify remarks of Merton in the journal or to reflect on the time spent with him in Asia. This could not have been accomplished without the generosity of my friends Br. David Steindl-Rast, O.S.B. and Harold Talbott both of whom gave me permission to quote our private correspondence, or without the kindness of Roger Lipsey who helped me make contact with Lobsang Lhalungpa and who provided the interview with James George. To each I am most grateful.

These four persons, Br. David Steindl-Rast, James George, Lobsang Lhalungpa, and Harold Talbott represent both a range of Merton's experiences on his Asian pilgrimage and a variety of perspectives on it. Br. David met with Merton before he left for Asia and is his fellow Christian monastic, one who also has significant experience of Buddhism. James George was the High Commissioner of the Canadian Embassy in New Delhi who befriended many Tibetan leaders, hosted Merton and provided him with many contacts. His perspective is not only that of a Western diplomat, but of one deeply knowledgeable about and sympathetic to Indian and Tibetan culture and religions. Lobsang Lhalungpa is a Tibetan layman. A scholar, teacher and musicologist he was broadcasting a Tibetan program in Delhi when Merton met him and his wife. Finally, Harold Talbott, a well known Buddhist practitioner and friend of Tibet, arranged a good deal of Merton's Tibetan travel and accompanied him to Dharamsala and on his visits with His Holiness the Dalai Lama. Each has kindly provided new information which deepens our understanding of Merton's Asian journey. Finally, Gray Henry has provided a remembrance of her 1991 meeting with Chatral Rimpoche.

Presenting their reflections has proved to be a bit difficult. One wishes to provide some context but not to detract from the voice of the primary source. In what follows I try to point the reader to places in the journals where our speaker is found. When possible, I simply reproduce verbatim the material sent to me. The interview with James George is presented as it came from Roger Lipsey and was edited by Dianne Edwards.

Br. David Steindl-Rast, O.S.B.

Merton's first reference to Br. David occurs in an April 23, 1968 entry in his journal. He is at Gethsemani and reports

> After supper, went over to the Guesthouse to see Dom Damasus Winzen and Br. David Steindl-Rast from Mt. Saviour. Br. David is the one who is at Columbia and studying Zen at the N.Y. Zendo. Spoke of Panikkar, of his idea of a Study Center for various religions .... The magazine *Monastic Studies* will probably expand to include articles by Buddhists, etc. (OSM 83)

In the spring of 1968 Merton met Br. David again at a meeting of contemplatives at Our Lady of the Redwoods Abbey in Whitethorn, California. Br. David's recollections of that meeting were published in *Monastic Studies*.[3] In November, 1968 Merton was still mulling over that meeting. A journal entry on November 2 from Dharamsala in which Merton is considering communities of people from different religious traditions reads "Brother David Steindl-Rast's idea perplexed me a little—as being first of all too academic." (AJ 85) The reference is probably to a center for spiritual studies which included Buddhists, Hindus, Jews, and Christians which Br. David was interested in helping to found.

I wrote to Br. David and asked if he would like to clarify this reference to his "idea." The following paragraphs are, verbatim, Br. David's response, which I received in March, 2005.

> First of all, I did not meet Thomas Merton at Redwood's monastery but had met him about a year earlier at Gethsemane. Fr. Damasus Winzen, our then Abbot at Mt. Saviour, took me to see Merton. At that time I was studying Zen with Hakkuun Yasutani Roshi at the Zen Center Society in New York, and Merton was interested in my practical experience. I, in turn was interested in his vastly superior theoretical knowledge about Zen. When we met again at Redwood Monastery we knew one another already. At that time I came there with Sr. Anne E. Chester, IHM, from Monroe, MI. Her superior, Sr. Margaret Brenan had spearheaded the house of prayer idea; it had taken off like wild fire and Merton was interested in the phenomenon. We wanted to meet with him in order to win him for helping with this effort to introduce Sisters of Apostolic Communities to the contemplative life.
>
> The enigmatic reference refers to my "idea" of having different monastic communities live their own life in close proximity to each other so that dialogue and certain activities could be shared more easily. Chester Calson, one of the inventors of Xerox, bought some land in the Catskill's for the Center of Spiritual Studies and for a while we dreamed to realize that plan there. This was precisely to avoid a "mixing of traditions," but anyway it never got off the ground. Much later Maurice Strong and Hanne Marstrand realized something similar on their ranch, Baca Grande, in Crestone, CO.
>
> If it's important...you might want to check whether the meeting at Whitethorn really took place in "Spring" of 1968, my recollection is that it was later in the year. At any rate it was only days before Merton's departure for the Far East.

Br. David's recollection of the time of his last meeting with Merton was correct. Merton's journals reflect that he was at Redwoods on

October 8, 1968. The entry for October 11, 1968 opens "Today begins a three-day conference—on contemplative life, houses of prayer, etc. 'Organized'…at request of Mother Benedicta of the IHMs of Monroe, Michigan." (OSM 200) On October 15 Merton was on his way to Asia.

James George

Merton's journal reports that "Last night [October 30, 1968] Commissioner and Mrs. George had me to dinner at the Canadian Embassy with Lhalungpa, his wife, Harold Talbott, and Gene Smith." (AJ 70) Upon returning from Dharmsala and writing from Calcutta on November 11 of his weekend in New Delhi Merton records

> …I said Mass in Holy Family Hospital…in the room of James George, the Canadian High Commissioner, who had had a minor operation the day before. He sat cross-legged on the bed with his wife, their son and daughter on either side. Also there were the Lhalungpas, Kunga, the companion of Trungpa Rimpoche, who is staying at the High Commissioner's, and Harold Talbott, who served the Mass. Afterward we went to the Georges' and had lunch in their garden. (AJ 129)

During the weekend Merton worked on a typewriter lent to him by the Georges, and he was taken to the airport by Mrs. George and her son with whom Merton discussed reincarnation.

Roger Lipsey interviewed James George in September, 2005. The following is a transcript of that interview. (And see the material below provided by Harold Talbott.)

A KIND OF INTENSE SINCERITY:
THOMAS MERTON IN NEW DELHI AND DARJEELING, 1968
EDITED BY DIANNE EDWARDS

The following interview, an exercise in oral history, brought together Roger Lipsey with James George, High Commissioner of the Canadian Embassy in New Delhi from 1967 to 1972. During those tumultuous years in Tibetan history, George came to know many Tibetan spiritual leaders. Both a senior diplomat and a spiritual seeker who recognized an opportunity to deepen his knowledge during his successive Middle Eastern and South Asian diplomatic postings, George was more than willing to provide Thomas Merton with introductions when he reached New Delhi during the Asian tour that ended with his death. The interview was conducted in September, 2005.

***

RL: At the time Thomas Merton came to India, you were the Canadian ambassador, based in Delhi?

JG: The title was High Commissioner, which is what Commonwealth countries call their ambassadors. It's the same function.

RL: How did you learn that Thomas Merton was in New Delhi?

JG: One of his friends at the time was Harold Talbott, who had come to India a few months before Tom. Harold had contacted me to say that Thomas Merton would like to meet with significant spiritual teachers among the Tibetans. I gave him a list, starting with the Dalai Lama and then several of the main lamas from other schools, whom I knew. Merton's initial reaction was that he wasn't so interested in meeting His Holiness. He assumed that he was the political leader of the Tibetans and he wanted to meet their real spiritual leaders. I said no, I thought he was making a mistake, that he would find a great spiritual being in the Dalai Lama, and indeed when they met he agreed with me. They resonated instantly, even though the Dalai Lama at that time was only about half Tom's age. Some years ago, Harold wrote the best account I know of those packed days [Harold Talbott, "'We Don't Want the Watcher': Thomas Merton in India," *The Vajradhatu Sun*, October/November, 1984, pp. 8-9].

RL: What was your first impression of Tom Merton?

JG: He bounced up the steps of the Canadian High Commission in Delhi all by himself in a business suit, shoved out his hand, and said, "I'm Tom Merton." Just like that. We hit it off very quickly and by the time he left ten days later, I felt very close to him. As fortune would have it, before he left I had to go into hospital for minor surgery, and on the day before my wife took him to the airport for his flight to Sri Lanka, they both came to my room in the hospital with our friend Lobsang Lhalungpa, who at the time was responsible for radio broadcasts for the Tibetan community. Tom offered what he called a "Tantric Mass" for my speedy recovery— he provided the Catholic elements, Lobsang later chanted Tibetan prayers. There were very special links.

The other moment highlighted in my memory occurred a few days prior to that. Tom had spent some time with the great lama Chatral Rinpoche in Darjeeling. When Tom was saying goodbye, Chatral said he was grateful for Tom's explanation of Christianity. He hadn't appreciated before that the two traditions, Tibetan Buddhism and Christianity, had so many common elements, although one was theist and the other not. Chatral said he felt that he and Tom had used different words for what they were discovering to be basically the same deep inner experience. Tom said he felt that through prayer (or what Chatral called meditation) he was just beginning to get close to something real. Chatral smiled broadly and replied softly "It's the same with me," and they embraced with tears in their eyes. This was perhaps the most intimate contact he had with any of the Tibetans.

RL: Did you take him up to Darjeeling?

JG: I just picked him up there. I wasn't present at the interviews—I read about them later. But Lobsang was there, and I think he did the translating. After Tom died, Brother Patrick Hart wrote asking me if I would go over what was to become *The Asian Journal*. I said fine, and he sent me the manuscript with all the Indian and Tibetan names of people and places spelled wrongly. I did a little editing. I was struck by several significant passages—for example, the suggestion that it would be valuable to have a kind of spiritual summit, perhaps in the Himalayas, where those who had had a long and deep experience in Tibetan Buddhism, Catholicism, and perhaps one or two other traditions, could exchange their experiences and not get caught on doctrine and beliefs. The focus would be on what they truly knew from personal experience, expressed in their own, perhaps quite different words. That was something he really cared about, and he was careful to add—I think it was in one of our conversations, rather than in *The Asian Journal*—that such an exchange was certainly not for beginners; they would become confused.

RL: Your daughter told me that one evening in Delhi, Merton was your dinner guest and she was there. Merton actually mentions it in *The Asian Journal*. She told me that she was so impressed with his presence that for a while she wanted to become Catholic. That's how inspiring he was. How did you experience the presence of the man?

JG: I think my daughter was probably more sensitive than I was. I certainly experienced something that I would now call presence. I wouldn't have used those words then, but there was a kind of intense sincerity, so alive that one felt his humanness and at the same time his sensibility. The breadth of his view was not contained within any cloister or any one tradition. The search probing what it means to be a real human being is beyond that.

Lobsang Phuntsok Lhalungpa

According to a note in *The Asian Journal* Lobsang Phuntsok Lhalungpa is a Tibetan scholar, teacher and musicologist. "He grew up in Lhasa and was at one time an official of the Tibetan Government prior to the Communist Chinese take-over. Later he took refuge in Kalimpong...then moving to Delhi, where Merton met him and his wife." (AJ 74) In a journal entry of October 30 from New Delhi Merton records "Lobsang Phuntsok Lhalungpa, a Tibetan layman, runs a radio station which broadcasts a Tibetan program in Delhi.... He came to the Ladakh Vihara with his wife Deki. We went up to one of the cells and talked with Lama Geshe Tenpa Gyaltsan, a teacher who is a Gelugpa monk, and another Nyingmapa monk, a man with a shiny, fresh-shaven head. The latter, I learned, was...the Nechung rimpoche, formerly abbot of the great Tibetan monastery of Nechung, and a tulku." (AJ 64-65)

The following is the substance of an email I received from Lobsang Lhalungpa on July 8, 2005:

> I did not accompany Father Merton in 1968 to Dharamsala and Darjeeling where he went to meet some Tibetan lamas. At the time I was living in New Delhi and running the Tibetan language radio broadcasts for All India Radio. Father Merton was accompanied to Northern India by my friend Harold Talbott III.
>
> I met Father Merton in Delhi several times and even arranged visits for him with a senior Cambodian monk and a Sufi mullah. We did not have any serious conversations about Buddhism or his practice during our meetings.
>
> However, before he left for Thailand he told me about his plan to bring some Tibetan monks to the United States and house them near Gethsemani so that he and the Trappist

monks could learn about Tibetan meditation techniques from them. He specifically asked me if I could come along as their translator. I was delighted to hear of his plan and assured him that I could come to help him because I was already getting ready to emigrate to Canada later that summer. Alas, the great tragedy of Father Merton's accident in Thailand happened soon thereafter which shocked and saddened all of us.

My personal impression of Thomas Merton was of a very special, spiritual person who showed every sign of being a great master. Not only was he a kind, humble, sensitive and humorous man but he also struck me as someone truly authentic. I greatly enjoyed the brief time I was able to spend with him in Delhi.

Harold Talbott

During his university education at Harvard, Harold Talbott had become a Roman Catholic. He reports that during the summer of 1957 while working for a newspaper in Memphis, Tennessee, he read Merton's *The Sign of Jonas* and went to Gethsemani to meet him. The meeting didn't happen, but Talbott returned the following Thanksgiving after his baptism to receive his first communion with the Cistercians at Gethsemani.[4] Talbott had gone to Asia as secretary to Dom Aelred Graham, then recently retired Prior of Portsmouth Priory in Rhode Island. Graham had written *Zen Catholicism* and had been asked to serve as *peritus*, the expert on Buddhism for the Second Vatican Council. "...Merton wrote to Aelred and asked how he could meet the lamas in India, Aelred explained that I was there studying with the Dalai Lama and that I could introduce him to the lamas."[5]

Of all the persons mentioned in Merton's *Asian Journal* it is probably Harold Talbott who spent the most time with him. On October 28 Merton records in his journal that Harold Talbott met him at the airport in New Delhi. (AJ 54) They were together for the rest of October, and until November 24 when Merton notes "Harold and I had a farewell party, sitting in my room." (AJ 167) It was Talbott who arranged and accompanied Merton on his travels in the Himalayas, he who introduced Merton to lamas and Tibetan teachers.

Students of Merton and of Tibetan Buddhism know that Harold Talbott has been very generous in giving interviews about his time with Merton (and has provided invaluable service as a translator since, especially of the works of Tulku Thondup).[6] It was my great pleasure and privilege to meet Harold in December, 2000 in con-

Harold Talbott with Mr. and Mrs. Lobsang Phuntsok Lhalungpa.

nection with a video sponsored by The Thomas Merton Center Foundation. We subsequently became friends and have exchanged many letters, only a few of which dealt with Thomas Merton. However, in July, 2004 Harold sent me a lengthy memoir which contains some new material on Merton. Unless otherwise noted, the following material is drawn from that memoir. I am immensely grateful to Harold for allowing me to share his private work in this very public format, and for his own reflections which he provided after a trip to Sikkim in April, 2006:

> That autumn [1968] I got a letter from Thomas Merton saying that he was coming to India in November. He had asked Dom Aelred Graham to advise him how to make contact with Tibetan Buddhist Lamas in India. Dom Aelred suggested that he look me up. I wrote back that I'd be happy to take him to see all the Lamas whom I knew, and we arranged to meet in New Delhi.
>
> When the time of his arrival came, I met him at the airport in New Delhi, and we began our travels together, which lasted for the next few weeks. As soon as he arrived

I introduced him to the Lhalungpas. He and Deki liked each other at once. She was very pretty, kind, and full of fun.[7] Lobsang took us to the Ladakh Bodhvihara to meet two Lamas who were good friends, Geshe Tenpa Gyaltsen and Nechung Rinpoche.(Memoir)

While I was traveling with Thomas Merton, I was observing him and was curious about his Faith in Jesus Christ inhering in him along with his intention to train with Chatral Rinpoche in order to practice the Long Chen Nying Thig lineal transmission of the practice of Dzogpachenpo of the Nyingmapa Buddhists of Tibet. (Letter, Feb. 21, 2003)

I had met the Georges when Thomas Merton was visiting New Delhi. I took to them at once. They were very interested in religion, particularly Sufism and Buddhism. They had been posted in Sri Lanka and had been able to study Buddhism there at first hand. I learned that both Mr. and Mrs. George were teachers in the Gurdjieffian movement. I think it was their spiritual gifts, convincing Lama Gyurda-La that they were qualified to receive training in Dzog Chen, that made him include the rest of us on their coattails. I am deeply grateful to them. (Memoir)

From New Delhi Tom and I traveled to Dharmsala where he had three audiences with the Dalai Lama lasting three hours each. Tom was so kind that he insisted on my accompanying him to his meetings. I will never forget his many kindnesses including that one, which allowed me to be present at the discussions between these two great men.
    ... It was as if things had been arranged so that I was meant to be with the Dalai Lama for a short while, then to bring him and Tom together, and then, just before Tom was to die, to be cast out of Dharmsala and be separated from the Dalai Lama as well, and carry out Tom's strong recommendation to find a Dzogchen Lama. (Memoir)

... when Thomas Merton stayed with me [in Dharmsala] and it was very cold, I gave him this makeshift bed to sleep on and took the small couch in the front room for myself. He suffered from a bad back and had a terrible cold, and we both froze....

Next to the bedroom was a little study.... Merton also liked sitting and reading and writing at the desk in this room. I think when I saw his light go on at two in the morning—I was too cold to sleep much—he would go into the study and say his breviary—anything to get off that bed— and I was delighted when I read his *Asian Journal* to find that he read some of the books I had there, such as Conze's *Buddhist Thought in India*.(Memoir)

Talbott records that in India Merton "met Lamas of the four major lineages of Tibetan Buddhism, and he became enthralled with the Dzogchen yogi, Chatral Rinpoche."[8] (Memoir) As Merton's journals make clear, a primary interest in these meetings was meditation practice. He was unaware of the secrecy that can surround such practices. "For example, when Merton asked the Abbot of Namgyal Tratsang, in exile from Lhasa in Dharmsala, to explain the Tantric Buddhist uses of the Mandala for meditative purposes, the Abbot replied that in Tibet, during the thirteen hundred years of Buddhist civilization there, no Lama would consider uttering the *word* [italics Talbott's] Mandala to anyone except to a person under his or her training as a Tantric practitioner. Secrecy is the *ne plus ultra* or *the* [italics Talbott's] requirement for the successful practice of the esoteric dimension of Buddhism, the Tantra or the Vajrayana." (Letter of May 27, 2002)

> I like it that [Merton] said that his meditative practice was "walking in the woods." I am just convinced that the 'naked,' natural, utmost simple practice of Dzogchen on the true nature of the mind was his dish. And I think he was thrilled to discover the vast and complex treasury of forms and practices that confront the observer of the Tantric Tradition of Tibet was all an expression of an awakening that is in itself so utterly simple." (E-mail message of October 16, 2003)

It seems to me particularly apt to end these notes on Merton's Asian journey with Harold Talbott's extremely intriguing reflection on

Darjeeling and mount Kangchenjunga which also so affected
Merton. (See his journal entries from November 12 to 24.)

> Darjeeling looks out upon Kangchenjunga, which stops
> the mind with its white majesty. The whole mountain range
> moves in stillness like music. The mountain and the deo-
> dars make Darjeeling a noble place, just as the presence of
> the great Lamas make it a holy one. Even its name evokes
> Nyingmapa Dharma, for it is the Anglicization of the name
> of a major Terton, Dorje Lingpa. There was also a Catho-
> lic presence, the Canadian Jesuits ... and The Convent of
> Loretto, where Mother Teresa taught History and coached
> basketball. Mountains, deodars, and then of course another
> emblem of Darjeeling, the glorious, eponymous tea....
>
> ...Lamas and tea planters were each an integral aspect
> of that celestial town. I once met a Darjeeling tea planter
> .... He was an English Catholic who owned Mim Tea Es-
> tate, and he loaned Merton a house on the property so that
> he could make a retreat. This planter also allowed Thugsey
> Rinpoche to build a hermitage monastery in a forest on the
> estate. I went there with Merton and he loved the place....
>
> Thomas Merton died shortly after that visit, and some
> time after his death I had a conversation with Thugsey
> Rinpoche. He asked me for a photograph of Merton. I asked
> him why he wanted it and he replied that Merton had liked
> his hermitage at Mim and he was going to put the photo-
> graph on his shrine and say prayers and see if perhaps
> Merton would take rebirth and become a monk in his mon-
> astery. [W]hen I saw Thugsey Rinpoche again I asked him
> about Merton. "He is here," he answered, meaning that he
> had taken rebirth and was on earth, "but I can't say any
> more."

Harold Talbott

RETURN FROM SIKKIM, APRIL 2006
THOMAS MERTON, CHATRAL RINPOCHE AND DZOGCHEN

Some of the following reflections on Thomas Merton and Dzogchen might seem too technical to be of interest to those who are devoted to him and his writings. But they show the instant affinity he demonstrated with such joy and delight when he was presented with the Dzogchen tradition of Nyingmapa Buddhism. The two points I want to put across are that he connected with a Dzogchen guru, and he asked him to teach him; and he got the sense of Dzogchen and its meditation. If Tom hadn't died and the Lama, Chatral Rinpoche, had been able to teach him, what follows is the general context in which he would have received his training.

***

First let me say what Tom has meant to my life. When I was seventeen and had just entered the Church—having become a Catholic in the Roman Communion after having gone to an Episcopal school, Tom said to me, "The Church is a very big place; always go your own way in it." Eleven years later when he was staying in a bungalow with me in Dharmsala, I reminded him of the advice he'd given me. "Did I say that?" he asked with amusement; "that's pretty good! And look where we both have gone!"—meaning the Tibetan tradition of Buddhism. Very shortly after that conversation, Tom did me a tremendous service. He advised me with urgency and certitude, so that I would not miss the opportunity to "Go and find a Dzogchen yogi and study with him."

During the many years that I have lived since he died, Tom has guided me and introduced me to wonderful friends. He observes some of my action and speech with his wry sense of humor and sharp critical mind. But he always encourages my study and practice under the great Nyingmapa Buddhist teachers of our time, whom he advised me to go and meet. He was so joyful and happy at being among the Indian and Tibetan people. Then the inward quality of his encounters was that he was always accepted as an accomplished spiritual master. He was completely open to the Buddha Dharma that great realized Lamas were exchanging with him.

He had tremendous *metta* or friendliness, and this accounted in part for his warm and universal acceptance in India.

In the case of the great Chatral Rinpoche, the mutual recognition was like a revelation of the absence of barriers that can exist between two people who meet. "Let's see who can get enlightened first," said Chatral Rinpoche. And Tom said, "He's the greatest man I ever met."

I have just come back from ten days in Sikkim. It was there forty years ago that I met my teacher when I accompanied Dom Aelred Graham on a visit to Dodrup Chen Rinpoche. For centuries Sikkim was a Buddhist kingdom. It is still a Hidden Land of Guru Rinpoche, the great Dzogchen Master who brought Buddhism from India to Tibet in the 9th century. Sikkim, and Darjeeling where Tom and Chatral Rinpoche had their meeting, are connected by a mountain road. They both look out upon Kanchenjungna, the thought-stopping snow peaks.

Dzogchen practice starts with an introduction to the nature of the mind from an enlightened Lama. Then you practice meditation to maintain, strengthen, and extend that awareness. The introduction to the View of the absolute nature produces an abrupt empty openness, which afterward registers as amazement, then a subtle vast luminous experienceless dwelling of the mind in emptiness. The Dzogchen introduction and the subsequent meditation practice are utmost simplicity, the freedom of the mind from concepts, habituations, thoughts, and emotions. But it cannot be entered into without a grounding in extensive devotional practice. Devotional practice is all. Even enlightened Lamas are perpetually leading others in devotional practice and thus conveying their blessings.

Again, Dzogchen, the highest of the nine *yanas* or vehicles of the Nyingma system, is the View and practice that instills awareness of the true nature of the mind. The View, empty or open, is the Dharmakaya, the formless absolute nature, called in Tibetan Kuntuzangpo-All Good. Manifesting from absolute nature for the sake of highly attained Bodhisattvas is Dorje Sempa, the Blissful Form aspect, and the third of this Ku Sum or three Bodies of Buddhahood is the Tulku aspect, that is, the illusory nature embodied in the infinite forms manifesting compassionately in order to awaken the varied minds of beings. The first human Tulku in the Dzogchen lineage is Garab Dorje.

There is a stanza he uttered to his disciple Manjusrimitra that portrays the Dzogchen view and practice: Here it is translated by Tulku Thondup Rinpoche:

The nature of the mind is Buddha from the beginning.
Mind has no birth or cessation: It is like the sky.
If the pure meaning of the equality of all phenomena is realized,
And if that understanding is maintained without any seeking,
That is the meditation.

Tom, by his nature, understood something of what these lines are saying about the nature of the mind and the way to practice to attain full awareness. This is what attracted him to Dzogchen.

Sikkim and Darjeeling both face Kanchenjungna, and they are both places sacred to Guru Rinpoche's Terma tradition. Guru Rinpoche taught "the twenty five" and other disciples in Tibet. Then he and his consort, Khadro Yeshe Tshogyal, concealed those Tantric teachings throughout Tibet and the Himalayas, in rocks, lakes, the sky, etc.; or in the mind-streams of the disciples who'd received them – his circle of esoteric initiates.

Thus in future times according to the needs of the people of successive generations a Terton, or hidden treasure discoverer, would unearth the object or the text, extricate it from a rocky mountain side, dive for it into a mountain lake, or in the case of *Gong-Ter* or mind treasure, recall it from his or her own awakened mind. The female and male Tertons who discover the teaching to this day are the rebirths of the recipients of the Termas from Guru Rinpoche. They become aware of the Terma from within their minds or draw it from the land water or sky, and teach the people of their time how to practice it.

The Nyingma tradition also has a lineal transmission of the teachings of Shakyamuni Buddha and commentaries by Indian and Tibetan panditas, and Nyingma tantras.

In each Terma there are Dzogchen teachings. Chatral Rinpoche (he's more than a hundred years old now) gives teachings from various Termas. My own teacher does so as well. But he presides over the Longchen Nyingthig Terma (Heart Essence of the Vast Expanse). Perhaps it is the preliminary practice from the Longchen Nyingthig that Chatral Rinpoche would have asked Tom to perform in his Bhutanese retreat cabin that he had promised him.

I think what attracted Tom to this great teacher was partly Chatral Rinpoche's free yogi nature, oblivious to harsh conditions, weather-beaten by a life of vagabondage in Tibet, his great strength, manifest compassion, his witty and combative and penetrating mind, and his openness and respect for Tom's Catholicism. In other words it was a mirror encounter. Tom found Dzogchen utterly enthralling, to be sought after with his engaged and energetic mind and body. Chatral Rinpoche reflected what Tom wanted.

In order to receive the Dzogchen teachings you have to complete four "ponderings" on aspects of Buddhism that "turn the mind from *samsara*." Then you have to complete five demanding devotional practices which could take six months to a year in retreat. After that you have to recite a million mantras of Guru Rinpoche. Practical gurus who are mindful that this is the "end age," "the dregs of time," may start you on Dzogchen training without your having completed the million mantras of Guru Rinpoche. I wonder if Tom knew what he was getting into.

Tom was an enthusiast—and how great that is! He loved Chinese and Japanese Zen. Maybe he'd have chosen to study Zen and practice Zazen once he got to Japan. He might have resumed his participation in the anti-Vietnam war and Civil Rights movement in America. But writing you, Bonnie, just now I had a thought about Tom's Asian journey and how he might have lived and acted thereafter.

In his *Asian Journal*, at Polonnarua in Ceylon, before the monumental stone statues of the Lord Buddha reclining at the time of his Mahaparinirvana with Ananda standing next to him, Tom has this experience of emptiness, clarity and compassion. "I know and I have seen what I was obscurely looking for." So he was henceforth free to devote the rest of his life as he saw fit.

But one thing I know is that Tom absorbed the flavor of the Dzogchen teachings of the Nyingma tradition of Tibetan Buddhism the moment he encountered them. It was amazing to witness his affinity for this approach to absolute reality. He was an awakened man through his thirty years of Cistercian practice and from several years of living in a hermitage. I think that during his exchange with Chatral Rinpoche, the two of them sitting on benches hastily put together at the site of a nunnery Chatral Rinpoche was building on a tiny piece of land on the terraced mountain side planted with tea bushes in Darjeeling, these two men facing each other, both

laughing, Tom received a transmission of wisdom from Chatral Rinpoche, "the greatest man he'd ever met."

Virginia Gray Henry

MEETING CHATRAL AND THE BLESSING OF THE BEADS

In 1991, I was in Tibet visiting monasteries with Bob Thurman, preparing for the creation of "The Year of Tibet in Kentucky" to be held in honor of Thomas Merton at Bellarmine University and in commemoration of the forty years of exile suffered by His Holiness the Dalai Lama and his people. Before leaving for Lhasa, a few days were spent in Kathmandu, where Tom Kelly, one of the greatest photographers of the Tibetan and Himalayan cultures, lives. He has captured Tibetan life in such wonderful books as *Tibet: Reflections from the Wheel of Life* and *Hidden Himalayas,* both published by Abbeville Press. I had met Tom's twin brother, Robert, while flying out to Nepal. I then had the great fortune of being invited to Tom and Carol's wedding, which was quite something – eating off leaves sewn together which served as plates amidst painted elephants while meeting dear souls of all sorts.

One morning, Tom suggested that I might like to come along while he made a last attempt at photographing one of the great Tibetan spiritual masters of all times who had previously refused every approach. I asked, "To what do I owe such an invitation?" Tom answered, "Aren't you here for Merton? This is Chatral Senghe Dorje Rinpoche—the one Merton wrote of in his Asian journals." Merton described Chatral as "the greatest rinpoche I have met so far and a very impressive person...if I were going to settle down with a Tibetan guru, I think Chatral is the one I would choose. But I don't know yet if that is what I'll be able to do—or whether I need to" (*Asian Journal,* 144). The name of this great master has much to teach us. *Chatral* means "disengaged from activity." *Senghe* is "the Way". The *dorje* are the crossed thunderbolts which indicate adamantine purity and indestructible empty awareness. *Rinpoche* is an honorific term meaning "precious and revered one."

On the dawn of June 21, Robert, Ian Baker (a scholar and disciple of Chatral) and I rode in a broken-down Nepalese taxi with a lot of film equipment. Tom rode alongside on a motorcycle out through endless fields and rice paddies into the countryside. Soon we arrived at a small nunnery. Even from the road we could hear sacred chanting pulsing out from within this colorfully decorated edifice which itself seemed alive. We carried the cameras and a tiger skin for Chatral to sit on, that is, if he agreed even to come out. (There are certain special *siddis* or qualities/powers associated with the tiger skin—as with everything in creation.)

Full of hope, Ian, who spoke Tibetan, went into the nunnery. As we laid out the skin, monkeys came screeching down the cliffsides which surrounded the small area chosen for the photograph.

Suddenly, and much to our surprise, Chatral appeared gazing upward at the commotion. As he strode toward us, it was as though a lion approached. The master was very powerful looking: weather-beaten, deep creases in his skin and quite a *presence*. He was accommodating. As he sat down on the tiger skin he playfully lifted its head and, turning toward the monkeys, shook it at them with a smile. The monkeys withdrew respectfully. After the photography was accomplished, I asked, through Ian, if Chatral would agree to be photographed with me in honor of my coming on Merton's behalf. I could see that this was the limit of what he would be willing to do.

After this, I walked over and joined Robert at the spot through which the master would pass on his return to the nunnery. On the way driving out in the taxi, Robert and I had discussed the importance of using an invocatory prayer with the aid of a rosary for activating one's spiritual Heart. I had bought a rosary (*mala*) the day before which was in my pocket, but was as yet unblessed. As Chatral approached I handed Robert the rosary. At the moment this spiritual giant passed between us, Robert thrust the rosary into his hand. He did what all saints and masters universally do with rosaries—he lifted them to his lips, kissed them, and blew his breath over them having rubbed them between his two hands.

Sometime later when Robert had returned to his studio (he is an accomplished artist) in New York City, he placed these blessed beads upon his breast as he lay resting. Of that experience Robert has recounted:

> "Chatral blessed my beads by holding them and blowing into them.... Later when I was lying back in my bed in New York and praying with the beads, I presumably fell asleep with the beads over my heart or chest and that's when I had this sense of presence. And I opened my eyes and I felt this surge of energy almost like a phantom above go 'whooook'—into my core."

***

Considered by many to be the greatest living master of Dzogchen (the highest and most subtle of Tibetan Buddhist teachings based on the idea that our true nature is already enlightened), Chatral Rinpoche spent much of his life wandering in wild, uninhabited places. Guiding his close disciples in the practices of the Dzogchen Nyingtik—the innermost essence—Chatral Rinpoche resides much of the year in the "hidden land" of Yolmo Kangri. This excerpt from his "Hymn to Yolmo" evokes the qualities of this mystical sanctuary:

> Once preoccupied by disease and death, happiness and
> the pursuit of pleasure,
> I now rejoice in this hidden dwelling.
> The snowy surface of the upper slopes glow like the
>   planet Venus.
> All around nothing but rocky crags and deep forests—
>   defying all direction.
> Countless siddhas achieved realization here, subsisting
>   on wild roots and mushrooms, flowers, and nettle soup...
> Following the path of emptiness and bliss
> May you too achieve the Great Perfection!

Text by Carroll Dunham and Ian Baker
Tibet: Reflections from the Wheel of Life
Abbeville Press, 1993, p.182

Chatral gazing upward at the commotion.

Shaking the tiger head at the monkeys.

Robert Kelly and Ian Baker

Tom Kelly's photograph of the Master with Gray Henry.

The beads, just blessed.

NOTES

1. Naomi Burton, Br. Patrick Hart and James Laughlin (eds.), *The Asian Journal of Thomas Merton* (New York: New Directions, 1968/ 1973). Hereafter in the text as AJ.

2. Br. Patrick Hart, O.C.S.O. (ed.), *The Other Side of the Mountain*: *The Journals of Thomas Merton 1967-1968* (San Francisco: HarperSanFrancisco, 1999). Hereafter in the text as OSM.

3. David Steindl-Rast, O.S.B., "Recollections of Thomas Merton's Last Days in the West," *Monastic Studies* 7 (September, 1969) 1-10.

4. *Tricycle* interview 16.

5. Ibid.

6. See, in particular, "'We don't want the watcher': Thomas Merton in India," *Vajradhatu Sun* (October-November, 1984) 9; "'The Jesus Lama': Thomas Merton in the Himalayas," *Tricycle*: *The Buddhist Review* 1/4 (Summer 1992) 14-24, and the video interview with Talbott "The (Almost) Final Days of Thomas Merton" recorded by The Thomas Merton Center Foundation at the Clifton Center in Louisville, Kentucky December 7, 2000.

7. Editor's note: There are at least four references to her in the *Asian Journal*, pp. 70, 143, 150, 359.

8. Merton scholar, Donald Grayston met Rimpoche in December, 2000 and reported movingly on that meeting in a workshop on June 5, 2003 at the International Thomas Merton Society general meeting in Vancouver, B.C.

The heart Sutra, the most famous of the *Prajna-paramita* texts, closes with the mantra recitation in Sanskrit: *Gate, gate, paragate, parasamgate, bodhi, svaha*! 'gone, gone, gone beyond, gone completely beyond, awake – wow!'…the completely awake limitless and empty awareness that is our own Buddhahood.

Judith Simmer-Brown

PART V
BIBLIOGRAPHY
CONTRIBUTORS
ACKNOWLEDGMENTS

MERTON AND BUDDHISM: A BIBLIOGRAPHY

Paul M. Pearson

This bibliography of items published about Merton and Buddhism only covers items published in the English Language, except in the section on theses and dissertations. A number of items are included which deal with Merton's interest in ecumenism and inter-faith dialogue only when they include substantial comment on Merton's dialogue or interest in Buddhism. Similarly, accounts of the Bangkok conference have only been included if they include substantial comment on Merton's dialogue or interest in Buddhism. Book reviews have not been included. This bibliography covers materials published prior to December 31, 2005.

BOOKS

Addiss, David G. and John Joseph Albert. *Polonnaruwa Revisited: A Speculum on Thomas Merton, the Buddha, Lymphatic Filariasis and the "Shadow Figure" at Polonnaruwa, Sri Lanka*. Georgia: The Society of Indwellers, 2005.

Gunn, Robert Jingen. *Journeys Into Emptiness: Dôgen, Merton, Jung, and the Quest for Transformation*. New York: Paulist Press, 2000.

King, Robert. *Thomas Merton and Thich Nhat Hanh: Engaged Spirituality in an Age of Globalization*. New York: Continuum, 2003.

Lee, Cyrus. *Thomas Merton and Chinese Wisdom*. Erie, PA: Sino-American Institute, 1994.

Lipski, Alexander. *Thomas Merton and Asia: His Quest for Utopia*. Kalamazoo, Mich.: Cistercian Publications, 1983.

Tam, Ekman P. C. *Christian Contemplation and Chinese Zen-Taoism: A Study of Thomas Merton's Writings*. Shatin, Hong Kong: Tao Fong Shan Christian Center, 2002.

ARTICLES

Adams, Daniel J. "Thich Nhat Hanh Then and Now." *Merton Seasonal* 20.3 (Summer 1995): 14-15.

Albert, John OCSO. "Thomas Merton and the Dalai Lama: A Special Friendship Remembered." *Merton Seasonal* 12.4 (Autumn 1987): 19-23.

Albert, John OCSO. "Two Studies in Chuang Tzu: Thomas Merton and Oscar Wilde." *Merton Seasonal* 12.1 (Winter 1987): 5-14.

Albin, Colin. "Merton and Inter-Faith Dialogue: Exploring a Way Forward." *Thomas Merton: Poet-Monk-Prophet*. Eds., Pearson, Sullivan and Thomson. (Abergavenny: Three Peaks Press, 1998): 154-68.

Ali, Zakaria. "The Solitude of Thomas Merton: An Asian Perspective." *Merton Seasonal* 23.4 (Winter 1998): 21-25.

Altany, Alan. "The Thomas Merton Connection: What was the Christian Monk looking to find in his Dialogue with Buddhism?" (http://www.thomasmertonsociety.org/altany2.htm)

Barbour, John D. "Thomas Merton's Pilgrimage and Orientalism" in *Literature, Religion, and East/West Comparison: Essays in Honor of Anthony C. Yu* edited by Eric Ziolkowski. (Newark: University of Delaware Press, 2005): 243-259.

Beeching, John MM. "Merton's Eastward Quest." *Maryknoll* 87.11 (December 1993): 58-62.

Biallas, Leonard J. "Merton and Basho: The Narrow Road Home." *The Merton Annual* 15 (2002): 77-102.

Bludworth, Patrick. "Desert Fathers and Asian Masters: Thomas Merton's Outlaw Lineage." *The Merton Annual* 17 (2004): 166-194.

Buchanan, William. "Merton's Asian Trail: Some Travel Notes." *Merton Seasonal* 13.3 (Summer 1988): 6-9.

Burbridge, Brent. "Natural Buddha: Thomas Merton: Christian Monk, Eastern Mystic." *Ascent Magazine* 15 (Fall 2002): 10-15.

Cameron-Brown, Aldhelm OSB. "Zen Master." *Thomas Merton, Monk: A Monastic Tribute*. Ed., Patrick Hart, OCSO. (New York: Sheed and Ward, 1974): 161-171.

Carr, Anne E. "Merton's East-West Reflections." *Horizons* 21.2 (Fall 1994): 239-252.

Chu-Cong, Joseph OCSO. "Thomas Merton and the Far East." *Cistercian Studies* 14 (1979): 45-58.

Chu-Cong, Joseph OCSO. "The Far East." *The Legacy of Thomas Merton*. Ed., Patrick Hart, OCSO. (Kalamazoo, MI.: Cistercian Publications, 1986): 49-65.

Collins, Patrick W. "From Communication Toward Communion: Gustave Weigel's Ecumenism and Thomas Merton's Inter-Religious Dialogue." *U.S. Catholic Historian* 14.5 (1996): 99-124.

Commins, Gary. "Thomas Merton's Three Epiphanies." *Theology Today* 56.1 (April 1999): 59-72.

Conner, James OCSO. "The Original Face in Buddhism and the True Self in Thomas Merton." *Cistercian Studies* 22.4 (1987): 343-351.

Conner, James OCSO. "Western Monasticism Meets the East." *Catholic World* 233.1395 (May-June 1990): 137-143.

Corless, Roger. "Fire on The Seven Storey Mountain: Why are Catholics Looking East?" *Toward an Integrated Humanity: Thomas Merton's Journey*. Ed., M. Basil Pennington. (Kalamazoo, MI.: Cistercian Publications, 1988): 204-221.

Corless, Roger. "In Search of a Context for the Merton-Suzuki Dialogue." *Merton Annual* 6 (1993): 76-91.

Corless, Roger. "The Christian Exploration of Non-Christian Religions: Merton's Example and Where It Might Lead Us." *Merton Annual* 13 (2000): 105-122.

Costello, Hilary OCSO. "Thomas Merton: Pilgrim, Freedom Bound." *Cistercian Studies* 13 (1978): 340-352.

Costello, Hilary OCSO. "Pilgrim: Freedom Bound." *The Legacy of Thomas Merton*. Ed., Patrick Hart, OCSO. (Kalamazoo, MI.: Cistercian Publications, 1986): 67-82.

Cox, Craig. "Passion Play: East Meets West in the Writings of Catholic Monk Thomas Merton." *Utne* 106 (July-Aug. 2001): 98-99.

Daggy, Robert E. "Thomas Merton's Writings in Japan." *Merton Seasonal* 3.1 (Spring 1978): 4-5.

Daggy, Robert E. "Mei Teng, The Silent Lamp: Thomas Merton and China." *Merton Seasonal* 8.1 (1983): 2, 9.

Daggy, Robert E. Introduction in *Encounter: Thomas Merton and D.T. Suzuki* (Monterey, Ky.: Larkspur Press, 1988): xiii-xx.

Daggy, Robert E. "Afterword: Mo Tzu and Thomas Merton" in *Thomas Merton and Chinese Wisdom*, by Cyrus Lee (Erie, PA.: Sino-American Institute, 1994): 117-131.

Daggy, Robert E. Foreword in *Thomas Merton and Chinese Wisdom*, by Cyrus Lee (Erie, PA.: Sino-American Institute, 1994): i-vi.

Daggy, Robert E. "Asian Perspectives of Thomas Merton." *Inner Directions Journal* (Fall 1995): 9-10.

Daggy, Robert E. "Universal Love in Mo Tzu and Thomas Merton." *Inner Directions Journal* (Fall 1995): 10-11.

Dalai Lama. "Merton the Pilgrim." *Merton, By Those Who Knew Him Best.* Ed., Paul Wilkes. (San Francisco: Harper & Row, 1984): 145-148.

Dart, Ron. "Thomas Merton and Alan Watts: Contemplative Catholic and Oriental Anarchist." *The Merton Journal* 11.2 (Advent 2004): 12-15.

D'Silva, Teresita, OSB. "Bangkok Diary-December 1968." *Merton Seasonal* 23.4 (Winter 1998) 3-10.

Dunne, Nicholas. "Thomas Merton's Final Journey." *Catholic Asian News* 15. 12,13. (December 1988-January 1989): 37-40.

Eastman, Patrick W.H. "Marriage of East and West: The Contribution of Thomas Merton and Bede Griffiths to Inter-Religious Dialogue." *Thomas Merton: A Mind Awake in the Dark.* Eds., Pearson, Sullivan and Thomson. (Abergavenny: Three Peaks Press, 2002): 94-101.

Fader, Larry A. "Beyond the Birds of Appetite: Thomas Merton's Encounter with Zen." *Biography* 2 (Summer 1979): 230-254.

Faricy, Robert SJ. "Thomas Merton and Zen." *The Merton Annual* 9 (1996): 142-151.

Fields, Rick. "Merton," in *How the Swans Came to the Lake: A Narrative History of Buddhism in America*, by Rick Fields. (Boulder, Colorado: Shambhala Publications/Random House, 1981): 295-303.

Fittipaldi, Silvio E. "Preying Birds: An Examination of Thomas Merton's Zen." *Horizons* 9 (Spring 1982): 37-46.

Fitzgerald, Michael L. "The Prophets of Dialogue: Massignon, Monchanin and Merton." *The Merton Journal* 11.1 (Easter 2004): 34-40.

Fox, Ruth OSB. "Thomas Merton's Search for Wisdom As Revealed in The Asian Journal." *Cistercian Studies* 25.2 (1990): 131-141.

Goulet, Jacques. "Thomas Merton's Journey toward World Religious Ecumenism." *The Merton Annual* 4 (1991): 113-129.

Grayston, Donald. "Merton's Quarrel with Kanchenjunga." *Merton Seasonal* 11.2 (Spring 1986): 2-6.

Grayston, Donald. "Finding 'the Great Compassion, Mahakaruna': Thomas Merton as Transcultural Pioneer." *The World in My Bloodstream: Thomas Merton's Universal Embrace.* Ed., Angus Stuart. (Abergavenny: Three Peaks Press, 2004): 54-65.

Grzybowski, Wacùaw. "Passage to More than India: Merton's Discovery of Asian Spirituality." *British and American Studies in Torun* (1996): 11-26.

Hanh, Thich Nhat. "Merton the Pilgrim." *Merton, By Those Who Knew Him Best.* Ed., Paul Wilkes. (San Francisco: Harper & Row, 1984): 151-153.

Hanh, Thich Nhat. Introduction to *Contemplative Prayer* by Thomas Merton. (New York: Image Books, 1996): 1-8.

Hardcastle, Judith. "The Mysticism of World Faiths in Merton's Inner Experience." *The World in My Bloodstream: Thomas Merton's Universal Embrace.* Ed., Angus Stuart. (Abergavenny: Three Peaks Press, 2004): 134-142.

Hart, Patrick OCSO. "Thomas Merton's East-West Dialogue." *Monastic Exchange* 2 (Winter 1970): 18-20.

Hart, Patrick OCSO. "The Ecumenical Concern of Thomas Merton." *Lamp* 70 (December 1972): 20-23.

Hart, Patrick OCSO. "The Ecumenical Monk." *Thomas Merton, Monk: A Monastic Tribute.* Ed., Patrick Hart, OCSO. (New York: Sheed and Ward, 1974): 209-217.

Hart, Patrick OCSO. "Ecumenical Monk." *Ecumenical Monks Bulletin* (Pentecost 1979): 7-10.

Hart, Patrick OCSO. Editor's Note to "The Zen Insight of Shen Hui," by Thomas Merton. *Merton Annual* 1 (1988): 3-4.

Hinson, E. Glenn. "Expansive Catholicism: Merton's Ecumenical Perceptions." *Cistercian Studies* 14 (1979): 290-304.

Hinson, E. Glenn. "Expansive Catholicism: Ecumenical Percep-
tions of Thomas Merton." *The Message of Thomas Merton.*
Ed., Patrick Hart, OCSO. (Kalamazoo, MI.: Cistercian
Publications, 1981): 55-71.

Jadot, Jean. "Merton the Pilgrim." *Merton, By Those Who Knew
Him Best.* Ed., Paul Wilkes. (San Francisco: Harper & Row,
1984): 155-157.

Kang, Kun Ki. "Prayer and the Cultivation of Mind: An Examination of Thomas Merton and Chinul." *Merton Annual* 2
(1989): 221-238.

Kilcourse, George A. Jr. "'Unmasking An Illusion:' Thomas
Merton's Contemplative Ground of Dialogue." *American
Benedictine Review* 52.1 (March 2001): 35-59.

King, Peter C. "Roots and Wings: Thomas Merton and Alan Watts
as Twentieth Century Archetypes." *The Merton Journal*
8.2 (Advent 2002): 36-44.

Kinzie, Charles E. "Merton Rimpoche: A Stranger in an Iron Cage."
Contemplative Review 18 (Fall 1985): 1-13.

Kinzie, Charles E. "The One Mountain of Thomas Merton: The
Dharma of Polonnaruwa." *Living Prayer* 21.2 (March-April
1988): 18-26.

Knitter, Paul F. "Thomas Merton's Eastern Remedy for
Christianity's Anonymous Dualism." *Cross Currents* 31
(Fall 1981): 285-295.

Kramer, Victor A. "Merton's Art and Non-Western Thought." *Journal of the American Academy of Religion* 41 ([supplement]
March 1978): 27-41.

Lane, Belden C. "Merton as Zen Clown." *Theology Today* 46.3
(October 1989): 256-268.

Leclercq, Jean OSB. "Merton and the East." *Cistercian Studies* 13
(1978): 309-317.

Lee, Cyrus. "Thomas Merton and Zen Buddhism." *Chinese Culture* 13 (March 1972): 35-48.

Lee, Cyrus. "Life, Death and Reincarnation: A Comparative Study
on Hanshan Tzu and Thomas Merton." *Chinese Culture*
22 (December 1981): 111-120.

Lee, Cyrus. "Thomas Merton's Imitation of Chuang Tzu" *Merton
Seasonal* 8.1 (Winter-Spring 1983): 3-8.

Lee, Cyrus. "Thomas Merton and Chinese Wisdom." *Chinese Culture* 30.2 (June 1989): 39-50.

Lee, Cyrus. "Thomas Merton and Chinese Wisdom." *China Studies* [Institute of China, Sook-Myung Women's University, Seoul, Korea] (December 1991): 59-67.

Lentfoehr, Thérèse SDS. "The Zen-Mystical Poetry of Thomas Merton." *Thomas Merton: Pilgrim in Process*. Eds., Donald Grayston and Michael W. Higgins. (Toronto: Griffin House, 1983): 17-26.

MacCormick, Chalmers. "The Zen Catholicism of Thomas Merton." *Journal of Ecumenical Studies* 9 (Fall 1972): 802-818.

Marechal, Paul. "Transcendental Meditation and its Potential Value in the Monastic Life." *Cistercian Studies* 8 (1973): 210-237.

Marechal, Paul. "Transcendental Meditation and the Monastic Life." *Creative Intelligence* [London]. 25-32.

McInerny, Dennis Q. "Thomas Merton and Oriental Thought." *Cistercian Studies* 14 (1979): 59-72.

McMillan, Allan M. "Thomas Merton's Seven Lessons for Inter-Faith Dialogue." *The Merton Annual* 15 (2002): 194-209.

Mealy, Anne. "Thomas Merton: His Interest in Eastern Monasticism." *Bluegrass Literary Review* 2 (Spring-Summer 1981): 19-26.

Meatyard, Christopher. "Merton's 'Zen Camera' and Contemplative Photography." *Kentucky Review: Thomas Merton Symposium* 7 (1987): 122-144.

Moffitt, John. "Thomas Merton and the Anatta Doctrine." *Insight* 2 (Spring 1977): 12-14.

Moffitt, John. "Thomas Merton: the Last Three Days." *Catholic World* 209 (July 1969): 160-163.

Neuman, Matthias OSB. "Revisiting Zen and the Birds of Appetite after Twenty-five Years" *The Merton Annual* 8 (1995): 138-149.

O'Hanlon, Daniel J. SJ. "The Influence of Eastern Traditions on Thomas Merton's Personal Prayer." *Cistercian Studies Quarterly* 26.2 (1991): 152-164.

Padovano, Anthony T. "Merton's Journey to the East." *Drew Gateway* 50 (Spring 1980): 17-23.

Patnaik, Deba Prasad. "Syllables of the Great Song: Merton and Asian Religious Thought." *The Message of Thomas*

Merton. Ed., Patrick Hart, OCSO. (Kalamazoo, MI.: Cistercian Publications, 1981): 72-90.

Pearson, Paul M. "Journey to Sri Lanka and Three Poems." *Merton Seasonal* 15.3 (Summer 1990): 8-11.

Pearson, Paul M. "The Ox Mountain Parable: An Introduction." *The Merton Annual* 15 (2002): 14-19.

Pennington, M. Basil. OCSO. "Merton's Bell Still Rings Out: The Dialogue Goes On." *Regional Mailbag* [U.S. Region of Cistercians] 215 (July-August 1989): 2-3.

Pieris, Aloysius. SJ. *Love Meets Wisdom: A Christian Experience of Buddhism*. (Maryknoll, NY.: Orbis Books, 1988): Merton is discussed on pp. 9, 12, 13, 15, 16, 32, 42.

Raab, Joseph Q. "Madhyamika and Dharmakaya: Some Notes on Thomas Merton's Epiphany at Polonnaruwa." *The Merton Annual* 17 (2004): 195-205.

Randall, Virginia R. "The Quest for the Transcendent Self: The Buddhist-Christian Merger in Thomas Merton's Poetry." *Cithara* [St. Bonaventure University] 17 (November 1977): 17-28.

Randall, Virginia R. "The Mandala as Structure in Thomas Merton's The Geography of Lograire." *Notre Dame English Journal* 11 (October 1978): 1-13.

Samway, Patrick H. "John Moffitt: Poet from Gorakhpur to America." [Discussion of Moffitt and Merton at Bangkok Conference in 1968.] *America* (10 April 1993): 17-22.

Schloegel, Irmgard. Introduction to *Thomas Merton on Zen* by Thomas Merton. (London: Sheldon Press, 1976): vii-x.

Shannon, William H. *Silent Lamp: The Thomas Merton Story*. (New York: Crossroad, 1992): 264-285.

Shannon, William. "Thomas Merton in Dialogue with Eastern Religions." *The Vision of Thomas Merton*. Ed., Patrick F. O'Connell. (Notre Dame, IN: Ave Maria Press, 2003): 211-223.

Simmons, Carl. "A Vision of Community: Thomas Merton and the East." *AB Bookman's Weekly* 90.20 (November 1992): 1832, 1834. 1836, 1839-1846.

Smeyers, Sister Bernadette M. OSB. "Thomas Merton and Bangkok: A Few Reminiscences 8-15 December 1968.) *Merton Seasonal* 18. 3 & 4 (Summer-Autumn 1993): 16-17.

Sobhano, Venerable. "Thomas Merton and 'The Asian Tradition.'" *The Merton Journal* 1.1 (1994): 2-4.

Steindl-Rast, David OSB. "Exposure: Key to Thomas Merton's Asian Journal?" *Monastic Studies* 10 (Spring 1974): 181-204.

Steindl-Rast, David OSB. "Destination: East; Destiny: Fire - Thomas Merton's Real Journey." *Thomas Merton: Prophet in the Belly of a Paradox.* Ed., Gerald Sean Twomey. (New York: Paulist Press, 1978): 148-172.

Stenqvist, Catharina. "Merton, Zen and Phenomenology." *Studies in Spirituality* 4 (1994): 236-244.

St. John, Donald P. "Merton's Chuang Tzu: An Ecological Reading." *Teilhard Studies* 37 (Winter-Spring, 1999): 21- 36.

Sullivan, Danny, and Kim Wolfe-Murray. "When the Light of the East Meets the Wisdom of the West." *Thomas Merton: A Mind Awake in the Dark.* Eds., Pearson, Sullivan and Thomson. (Abergavenny: Three Peaks Press, 2002): 102-116.

Sussman, Irving. "A Meditation on The Asian Journal of Thomas Merton: Journal of a Voyage Home." *Way* [London] 30 (September 1974): 8-17.

Swearer, Donald K. "Three Modes of Zen Buddhism in America. Discussion of Alan Watts and Thomas Merton." *Journal of Ecumenical Studies* 10 (Spring 1973): 290-301.

Talbott, Harold. "'We don't want the watcher': Thomas Merton in India." *Vajradhatu Sun* (October-November 1984): 9.

Talbott, Harold. "The Jesus Lama: Thomas Merton in the Himalayas." Interview with Harold Talbott. *Tricycle: The Buddhist Review* 1.4 (Summer 1992): 14-24.

Talbott, Harold. "The Jesus Lama: Thomas Merton in the Himalayas." Interview with Harold Talbott. *The Merton Journal* 3.1 (Easter 1996): 2-8.

Tam, Ekman PC. "Message to the Wounded World: Unmask the True Self—Zen and Merton." *Journal of Religious Studies* 17.1 (1998): 71-84.

Taylor, Terry. "When East Met West." *LEO: Louisville Eccentric Observer* [Louisville, KY]. (29 November 2000): 12.

Taylor, Terry. "Merton's Buddhist Ties Were Stong, Brief." *Forsooth* 12.1 (Feb. 2001): 1, 5.

Thompson, William M. "Merton's Contribution to Transcultural Consciousness." *Thomas Merton: Pilgrim in Process*. Eds., Donald Grayston and Michael W. Higgins. (Toronto: Griffin House, 1983): 147-169.

Thurston, Bonnie B. "Zen in the Eye of Thomas Merton's Poetry." *Buddhist-Christian Studies* 3 (1983): 103-117.

Thurston, Bonnie B. "Zen Influence on Thomas Merton's View of the Self." *Japanese Religions* 14.3 (1986): 28-47.

Thurston, Bonnie B. "Why Merton Looked East." *Living Prayer* 21.6 (November- December 1988): 43-49.

Thurston, Bonnie B. "Zen Influence on Thomas Merton's View of the Self." *Merton Annual* 1 (1988): 17-31.

Thurston, Bonnie B. "Thomas Merton: Pioneer of Buddhist-Christian Dialogue." *Catholic World* 233.1395 (May-June 1990): 126-128.

Thurston, Bonnie B. "'One Aesthetic Illumination:' Thomas Merton and Buddhism." *A Hidden Wholeness: The Zen Photography of Thomas Merton*. Ed., Paul M. Pearson. (Louisville, KY: Thomas Merton Center, 2004): 16-20.

Viens, Joachim. "Thomas Merton's Final Journey: Outline for a Contemporary Adult Spirituality." *Toward an Integrated Humanity: Thomas Merton's journey*. Ed., M. Basil Pennington. (Kalamazoo, MI.: Cistercian Publications, 1988): 222-239.

Weishaus, Joel. "A Fascination with Zen." Interview with Joel Weishaus re: *Woods Shore Desert,* by Thomas Merton. Interview by Stephen W. Terrell. *Santa Fe Reporter* (20 July 1983): 2.

Werblowsky, R.J. Zwi. "Mystics and Zen Masters." *Cistercian Studies* 13 (1978): 318-321.

Woodcock, George. Thomas Merton and the Monks of Asia." Introduction to *Thoughts on the East* by Thomas Merton. (New York: New Directions Books, 1995): 9-15.

Woodhouse, Patrick. "Out of India: Towards a More Inclusive Spirituality." *Merton Journal* 6.2 (Advent 1999): 31-40.

Wolfe-Murray, Kim and Danny Sullivan. "When the Light of the East Meets the Wisdom of the West." *Thomas Merton: A Mind Awake in the Dark*. Eds., Pearson, Sullivan and Thomson. (Abergavenny: Three Peaks Press, 2002): 102-116.

Wu, John Jr. "The Zen in Thomas Merton." *Your Heart is My Hermitage*. Eds., Sullivan and Thomson. (London: Thomas Merton Society of Great Britain and Ireland,1996): 90-103. (http://www.thomasmertonsociety.org/wu.htm)

Zeik, Michael D. "Zen Catholic." *Commonweal* 78 (14 June 1963): 324-325.

Zeik, Michael D. "Merton and the Buddhists: Had He Outgrown His Catholicism?" *Commonweal* 35 (12 October 1973): 34-37.

RECORDINGS

Talbott, Harold. *The (almost) final days of Thomas Merton*: *A Conversation with Harold Talbott* [videorecording] Louisville, KY: Thomas Merton Center Foundation, 2000.

THESES AND DISSERTATIONS

Albin, Colin Leslie. "Dialogue with Asian Religions: Exploring 'A Way' with Thomas Merton." master's (University of Lancaster, Lancaster, England, 1997).

Araujo, Luiz Gonzaga Sampaio de. "Kénosis e Compaixão: Perspectivas de Diálogo Inter- Religioso Entre Cristianismo e Budismo a Partir das Contribuições de Thomas Merton e Daisetz Teitaro Suzuki." master's (Universidade Federal de Juiz de Fora, Juiz de Fora, Brazil, 1999).

Campbell, Annette. "Thomas Merton's Dilemma: The Kerygma and/or Zen Consciousness." master's (McMaster University, Hamilton, Ontario, Canada, 1983).

Collier, Trent Bryce. "A Madman Runs to the East: Thomas Merton and Zen Buddhism." senior honors paper (Ohio Wesleyan University, Delaware, Ohio, 1996).

Davies, Marguerite. "Thomas Merton's Rethinking of the Christian Monastic Life in the Light of the Bodhisattvacarya of Mahayana Buddhism." master's (University of St. Michael's College, Toronto, Canada, 1973).

Gunn, Robert Walker. "The Experience of Emptiness in the Process of Self-Transformation in Zen Buddhism, Christianity and Depth Psychology as Represented by Dogen Kigen, Thomas Merton and Carl Jung, with Donald Winnicott and Heinz Kohut." doctoral (Union Theological Seminary, New York, 1997).

Healy, William Francis. "The Thought of Thomas Merton Concerning the Relationship of Christianity and Zen." doctoral (Pontifical University of St. Thomas Aquinas, Rome, Italy, 1975).

Houchens, Gary Wayne. "A Life of Paradox: Thomas Merton's Asian Trajectory." master's (Western Kentucky University, Bowling Green, Kentucky, 2000).

Kang, Kun Ki. "Thomas Merton and Buddhism: A Comparative Study of the Spiritual Thought of Thomas Merton and that of National Teacher Bojo." doctoral (New York University, New York, 1979).

Lencioni, Joe. "Total Kenosis, True Shunyata, and the Plerotic Self of Thomas Merton and Abe Masao." bachelor's (Gustavus Adolphus College, St. Peter, Minnesota, 2004).

McKeown, Les. "Thomas Merton's Assimilation of the Writings of St. John of the Cross Leading to His Embrace of Zen Vocabulary in Relation to Contemplation." doctoral (University of Wales, Lampeter, 2004).

Maginn, Rita A. "The Spirituality of Thomas Merton Viewed from the Perspective of the Influence of the Zen Experience." master's (Jesuit School of Theology at Berkeley, California, 1983).

Miller, Samuel G. "Zen in the Christian Consciousness of Thomas Merton." bachelor's (Duke University, Durham, North Carolina, 1975).

Nguyen, Chinh Ngoc. "The Influence of Daisetz T. Sukuki's Zen on Thomas Merton's Understanding of Contemplation." masters (St. Patrick's School of Theology, Menlo Park, California, 1999).

Park, Young Mann. "Thomas Merton's Prayer: From an Asian Christian Perspective." doctoral (Graduate Theological Union Berkeley, California, 1995).

Pins, Herbert J. "Thomas Merton Valued Zen Discipline for Achievement of Transcendental Self." master's (DePaul University, Chicago, Illinois, 1972).

Raab, Joseph Quinn. "Openness and Fidelity: Thomas Merton's Dialogue with D.T. Suzuki, and Self-Transcendence." doctoral (University of St. Michael's College, Toronto, 2000).

Ruttle, Paul. "Buddhist Components in the Thought and Spirituality of Thomas Merton." master's (St. John's University, Jamaica, New York, 1980).

Steyn, Helena Christian. "Thomas Merton and Theravada Buddhism—A Comparative Study of Religious Experience." master's (University of South Africa, Pretoria, South Africa, 1988).

Tam, Ekman Pui-Chuen. "The Influence of Zen-Taoism on Thomas Merton's View of Contemplation." doctoral (St. Paul University/University of Ottawa, Ottawa, 2001.)

Velamkunnel, Joseph. "Transcendental Experience of God According to Thomas Merton: A Comparative and Theological Study of Oriental and Christian Mysticism." doctoral (Pontifical Gregorian University, Rome, Italy, 1975).

Veliyathil, Paul. "Thomas Merton's View of Contemplation and Action in the Light of the Karma-Yoga Ideal of The Bhagavad-Gita." doctoral (Toronto School of Theology, Toronto, Canada, 1985).

Zyniewicz, Matthew Charles. "The Interreligious Dialogue Between Thomas Merton and D.T. Suzuki." doctoral (University of Notre Dame, Notre Dame, Indiana, 2000).

LIST OF CONTRIBUTORS

JUDITH SIMMER-BROWN has practiced Tibetan Buddhism for 30 years, is an acharya (senior dharma teacher) of the Shambhala Buddhist Lineage and Professor of Religious Studies at Naropa University in Boulder, Colorado. Dr. Simmer-Brown has been active in international Buddhist-Christian dialogue for twenty years and in the contemporary North American discussion surrounding Buddhism in the West. Her books include *Dakini's Warm Breath: The Feminine Principle in Tibetan Buddhism* (Shambhala) and *Benedict's Dharma: Buddhists Comment on the Rule of St. Benedict* (Riverhead).

ROGER J. CORLESS is Professor of Religion, Emeritus, at Duke University. He studied at King's College, University of London (B.D., 1961) and the University of Wisconsin at Madison (Ph.D., Buddhist Studies, 1973). His special interests are Pure Land Buddhism, Christian Spirituality, and Buddhist-Christian Dialogue. He is a co-founder of the Society for Buddhist-Christian Studies and its journal *Buddhist-Christian Studies* (University of Hawaii Press).

RUBEN L.F. HABITO was born in the Philippines and served as a Jesuit in Japan from 1970 to 1989. He completed doctoral studies in Buddhism at the University of Tokyo in 1978 and taught at the Jesuit-run Sophia University in Tokyo. He practiced Zen under Yamada Koun Roshi of Kamakura, Japan. In 1988 he was designated a Zen Teacher with the name Keiun-Ken ("Grace Cloud"). He is Professor of World Religions and Spirituality at Perkins School of Theology, Southern Methodist University and spiritual director at Maria Kannon Zen Center, Dallas, Texas. He is active in academic associations and is currently president of the Society for Buddhist Christian Studies. His books include *Living Zen, Loving God* (Wisdom, 2004), *Healing Breath: Zen Spirituality for a Wounded Earth* (MKZC Publications, 2001) and *Ordinary Enlightenment: Tendai Hongaku Doctrine and Japanese Buddhism* (International Institute for Advanced Buddhist Studies, 1996).

256

JOHN P. KEENAN is Professor Emeritus of Religion at Middlebury College in Vermont where he taught Asian religions. As a Buddhologist, he has specialized in the study of and translations from the Yogacara tradition. He has written several works employing Mahayana Buddhist philosophy as a grid through which to read Christian scripture; they include *The Meaning of Christ: A Mahayana Theology*, *The Gospel of Mark: A Mahayana Reading* and *The Wisdom of James: Parallels with Mahayana Buddhism*. Keenan is an Episcopal priest now serving at St. Mark's Episcopal Church in Newport, Vermont.

ROGER LIPSEY is the author of *Angelic Mistakes: The Art of Thomas Merton* (Shambhala Publications/Need Seeds, Boston and London, 2006). His earlier publications include *The Spiritual in Twentieth Century Art* recently re-issued by Dover Books. Lipsey was editor and biographer of Ananda K. Coomaraswamy. He earned his doctorate in the history of art at the Institute of Fine Arts, New York University.

PAUL M. PEARSON is Director and Archivist of the Thomas Merton Center at Bellarmine University, Louisville, Kentucky and current President of the International Thomas Merton Society. His most recent book, *Seeking Paradise: Thomas Merton and the Shakers,* was published by Orbis. He is a regular contributor to Merton conferences in Europe and the U.S.A. In 1999 he was honored by the International Thomas Merton Society for his contribution on an international level to the promotion of Merton's life and writings.

BONNIE BOWMAN THURSTON wrote her doctoral dissertation on Thomas Merton and taught religion and scripture at university for many years before resigning a professorship in New Testament to live in solitude. She was a founding member of the International Thomas Merton Society and the Society for Buddhist Christian Studies and has lectured widely on Merton. An ordained minister in the Christian Church (Disciples of Christ), her books include *Philippians and Philemon* (Sacra Pagina, Liturgical Press), *Preaching Mark* (Fortress), *Women in the New Testament* and *To Everything a Season: A Spirituality of Time* (Crossroad/Wipf and Stock) and two collections of poetry.

JAMES WISEMAN, O.S.B. is a monk and prior of St. Anselm's Abbey in Washington, D.C. He is associate professor of theology at The Catholic University of America where he teaches courses in Christian spirituality, world religions, and issues arising from the interface between science and religion. He was for six years chairman of Monastic Interreligious Dialogue (1994-1999) and has edited the MID Bulletin since 1998. He was a participant at the Gethsemani Encounters in 1996 and 2002 and co-edited the volumes that arose from those meetings, *The Gethsemani Encounter* (Continuum, 1997) and *Transforming Suffering* (Doubleday, 2003).

PHOTOGRAPHY

Fons Vitae wishes to express gratitude to the following:

Molly Bingham
Christophe Boisvieux
Laura Lee Brown
Phil Cousineau
Terrell Dickey Family
Shems Friedlander
Fedor Gouverneur
Gray Henry
Robert Jones
Thomas Kelly
Mihoko Okamura-Bekku
Paul M. Pearson
Brother Paul Quenon
William Stoddart
Morgan and Shelley Ward

The Thomas Merton Center at
　Bellarmine University
The Merton Legacy Trust
The Abbey of Gethsemani Archives
The Ralph Eugene Meatyard Estate
Burns Library Boston College
The John Howard Griffin Estate
The Kirlin Charitable Foundation
The Louisville Courier-Journal

M. Bingham 7; C. Boisvieux cf H-I; L.L. Brown 5, 6, 7, 9, 11, 241; P. Cousineau cf P; T. Dickey 214; S. Friedlander 95; F. Gouverneur 114; G. Henry xviii, xix, xx, 8, 14, 20, 28-29, 30, 38, 52, 90, 100, 134-5, 180 (Burton Stone Photos-Gift from Gwen Davenport), 189, 190, 233-6-7-8, 239, 240, cf B (1, 3), cf C (1,3), cf F-G, cf J (1), cf K (1,4), cf L, cf N, cf O (2-4); R. Jones 5, 9, 136, 216, cf A, cf B (2,4), cf C (4), cf D-E, cf J (2,3), cf K (2-3), cf M, cf O (1); T. Kelly 238; M. Okamura-Bekku 147; P.M. Pearson 6, 20, 190, 215, 100; W. Stoddart 19; P. Quenon xvii; M. and S. Ward 242

The Merton Legacy Trust and the Thomas Merton Center at Bellarmine University 19, 36, 63, 64, 73, 101, 108, (D102) 144, 161, 164, 168, 178, 184, 192, 197; 227 The Abbey of Gethsemani Archives 19, 25; The Ralph Eugene Meatyard Estate 183; Burns Library Boston College 161; The John Howard Griffin Estate 198; The Kirlin Charitable Foundation 69-70; The Louisville Courier-Journal xvii

ILLUSTRATIONS WITHOUT CAPTIONS: **xviii** *Khmer. Cambodia*; **xix** *11ᵗʰ century. Tibet*; **xx** *Khmer. Cambodia*; **28-9** *Khmer Buddha protected by Naga Muchalinda, 11ᵗʰ-12ᵗʰ centuries. Cambodia (National Museum of Singapore)*; **30** *Bodhisattva, 18ᵗʰ century. North Vietnam*; **117** *Southeast Asian Buddha from Clay Lancaster Estate*; **95** *Lohan, part of a set of 9ᵗʰ-10ᵗʰ century ceramic sculptures—designed so that as wind would pass through holes in the supporting platform, it would make sound intended to aid the monks in meditation. China (Metropolitan Museum of Art, NYC)*; **114** *Ryoanki temple meditation garden. Kyoto, Japan*; **134-5** *Zen monks sculpted from wood. Japan (The Art Institute of Chicago)*; **136** *Datong Yungang cave. China*; **189** (top and left center) *Mahabalipuram Temple complexes near Chennai, India*, (center and bottom) *The Sea Temple on the Bay of Bengal*, (center right) *The Sacred Lingam*; **191** *The sitting and reclining Buddhas at Gal Vihara, 12ᵗʰ century C.E. Polonnaruwa, Sri Lanka*; **214** *Portrait of Merton painted by his friend, Louisville artist Terrell Dickey*; **215** *Feet of reclining Buddha at Polonnaruwa, Sri Lanka*; **216** *The Shwedagong Pagoda containing relics of the Buddha—a pilgrimage site in central Yangong, Myanmar*; **239** *Dambulla Rock Temple. Sri Lanka*; **240** *The Touching of the Earth pose. India*; **241** *Cambodian bas-relief*; **242** *Tibetan wall fresco along a trail at about 10,000 feet between Upper Pisang and Gyaru, two villages in Nepal along the Annapurna Circuit.*

COLOR CENTERFOLD, pages A-P, upper left (clockwise): A. *Bayon Angkor Thom. Cambodia*; B. 1) *India*, 2) *Dazu Puxian cave. China*, 3) *Cambodia (Singapore National Museum)*, 4) *Binglingsi cave. China*; C. 1) *India*, 2) *Japan*, 3) *Japan*, 4) *Binglingsi cave. China*; D-E. *Binglingsi cave. China*; F. *Dambulla Rock Temple. Sri Lanka*; G. *Southeast Asia (Singapore National Museum)*; H-I. *Kamakura Buddha. Honshu, Japan*; J. 1) *India*, 2) *Magao cave. China*, 3) *The Datong Yungang cave. China*; K. 1) *China (Metropolitan Museum of Art, NYC)*, 2) *Datong Yungang cave. China*, 3) *Magao cave. China*, 4) *Japan*; L. *Khmer. Cambodia*; M. *Qi Dynasty, 6ᵗʰ century C.E. China*; N. *National Museum. Colombo, Sri Lanka*; O. 1) *Magao cave. China*, 2) *figure of a buddha, 8ᵗʰ-9ᵗʰ centuries (National Museum, Colombo, Sri Lanka)*, 3) *boddhisatva, 18ᵗʰ century. North Vietnam (Singapore National Museum)*, 4) *Pagan, Myanmar*; P. *Temple at Borobodur, 778–856 C.E. Java, Indonesia.*

PERMISSIONS

INDEX